Rebuilding America's Cities

Rebuilding America's Cities

Roads to Recovery

Edited by
Paul R. Porter
David C. Sweet

CENTER
FOR URBAN
POLICY   RESEARCH

Cover design by Leslie Mullen
Photograph by NEW JERSEY NEWSPHOTOS
Copyright 1984, Rutgers, The State University of New Jersey

Published in the United States of America
by The Center for Urban Policy Research
Building 4051 - Kilmer Campus
New Brunswick, New Jersey 08903

Library of Congress Cataloging in Publication Data
Main entry under title:

Rebuilding America's cities.

    Proceedings of the Cities' Congress on Roads to Recovery,
held June 1982 in Cleveland, Ohio.
    Includes index.
    1. City planning—United States—Congresses. 2. Urban
policy—United States—Congresses. I. Porter, Paul R.
(Paul Robert), 1908–   . II. Sweet, David C.
III. Cities' Congress on Roads to Recovery (1982:
Cleveland, Ohio)
HT167.R39 1984   307.7'6'0973   84–4299
ISBN 0–88285–099–7

Contents

v

Acknowledgments

We gratefully thank our fellow authors for their agreeable cooperation in making this an edited rather than an assembled book. So that their contributions might support those of others, they patiently made suggested revisions and generously yielded to other authors opportunities to say what they themselves would have liked to say. We acknowledge a debt to Virginia Benson, associate professor at the Cleveland State University College of Urban Affairs, for allowing access to her research-in-progress and to Danica Houle, Beatriz Rodriguez, and Lois Cochran who conscientiously and capably converted the authors' texts into publishable copy.

The Cities' Congress on Roads to Recovery, initiated and organized by the CSU College of Urban Affairs, provided the occasion for the book. We are indebted to the 300 people from 49 cities who participated in the Congress and especially to the 52 persons from 18 cities whose presentations made the Congress a widely acknowledged success and provided the stories that are analysed in the pages that follow. Among the many who made the Congress possible, we acknowledge in particular the assistance of Mayor George V. Voinovich, President Walter B. Waetjen of Cleveland State University, and Thomas Vail, publisher and editor of *The Plain Dealer*, as co-convenors; the 26-member planning committee; H. Richard Taylor, Jr., of the Cleveland Clinic Foundation, for his resourcefulness and his travels to cities from coast to coast in search of the best success stories; Karen Lieske, Laurie Caylen, Jean Standish, Barbara Langhenry, and Madelaine Fletcher for managing the logistics; Tom Hallet for press relations; Susann Bowers for publications design; and David F. Garrison, director of the College's Urban Center for counsel and help in many forms. We are indebted, too, to Maxine G. Levin, whose endowment of the Albert A. Levin Chair of Urban Studies and Public Service facilitated the preparation of the book.

A $25,000 grant from the U.S. Department of Housing and Urban Development made it possible to obtain the contributions by urban scholars to this book. We thank Alan R. Siegel and Howard J. Sumka of that agency for their confidence in the prospects for the Cities' Congress when its planning was still in an early stage.

Paul R. Porter
David C. Sweet

Contributors

Dale F. Bertsch is professor of city and regional planning, Ohio State University.

Jay Chatterjee is dean of the College of Design, Architecture, Art and Planning, University of Cincinnati.

Carol Davidow is coordinator for schools of the Cincinnati Business Committee.

Rolf Goetze is a consultant on neighborhood redevelopment and resides in Belmont, Massachusetts.

Robert C. Holland is president of the Committee for Economic Development.

Norman Krumholz is director of the Neighborhood Development Center, College of Urban Affairs, Cleveland State University and former director of planning for the city of Cleveland.

James E. Kunde is director of the urban affairs programs of the Charles F. Kettering Foundation and former city manager of Dayton, Ohio.

Donald E. Lasater is chairman of the Mercantile Trust Company in St. Louis and chairman of the Community Economic Development Policy Board of the American Bankers Association.

Larry C. Ledebur is director of economic development programs for the Urban Institute, Washington, D.C.

Joel Lieske is associate professor of political science, Cleveland State University.

Eugene H. Methvin is a senior editor in the Washington Bureau of *Reader's Digest*; he covered the Cities' Congress for the magazine.

Robert Mier is the commissioner of Economic Development for the City of Chicago. When his chapter was written, he was the director of the Center for Urban Economic Development and an associate professor of Urban Planning and Economics of the University of Illinois at Chicago.

Paul R. Porter is Albert A. Levin Professor of Urban Studies and Public Service, College of Urban Affairs, Cleveland State University; recently visiting scholar, University of Aston in Birmingham, England; author, *The Recovery of American Cities* (1976). Before beginning a study of cities as a retirement interest he had been a trade union official, newspaper editor, diplomat and president of an international company that licensed patents and manufacturing knowhow. He contributed to the concept of the Marshall Plan and was its assistant administrator.

James W. Rouse is chairman of The Enterprise Development Company; chairman of The Rouse Company; developer of the new city of Columbia, Maryland, revitalized multi-purpose centers of distinction in Boston, Baltimore, Milwaukee, Norfolk and other cities, and over 30 suburban shopping malls.

T. Michael Smith is director of the Center for Community Development and Design, University of Colorado in Denver.

David C. Sweet is dean of the College of Urban Affairs, Cleveland State University; Chairman, American Economic Development Council, 1983–84; former director of economic development for the State of Ohio and former member of the Ohio Public Utilities Commission.

June Manning Thomas is associate professor of urban affairs, Michigan State University.

Preface

Paul R. Porter

The grim side of cities is much better known than their upbeat side. For more than a generation the grim side has dominated discussion of cities in the media, universities and the Congress. It was their worsening condition that made news, engaged scholars and generated rising demands for federal aid. Since every literate person is now reasonably well informed about the grim side, the agenda of the Cities' Congress on Roads to Recovery was reserved for the side that not many people know.

When David Sweet, Dean of the College of Urban Affairs at Cleveland State University, and I decided to organize a meeting that would feature city successes, we chose the idea of an old-fashioned fair as a model. The people responsible for the successes—mayors, developers, lenders, community leaders—would be invited to come to Cleveland at their own expense to tell their stories for the benefit of people eager to learn from them. They in turn would learn from others. And that is what happened.

A conference devoted to discovery cannot have the same rules as one in which a representative sample of events is discussed by trained independent observers. We chose to introduce scholarly discipline by asking the U.S. Department of Housing and Urban Development to make a grant so that a group of urban scholars could attend the Congress and evaluate the success stories in a book. The request was approved. The scholars were chosen to ensure a diversity of opinion, including opposition to the recovery concept. Their academic affiliations are identified in the list of contributors. Besides their chapters, the book includes chapters by James W. Rouse, Donald E. Lasater, and Robert C. Holland which are adapted from their addresses to the Congress. We include also a reprint of a *Reader's Digest* article by Eugene H. Methvin who attended the Congress on behalf of his magazine. A concluding chapter considers the potential of a compact between cities and the nation to promote the cities' recovery, rigorously defined.

The stories told at the Congress were chosen to meet three criteria. Each could be deemed to be a success in that it was a substantial achievement of a defined goal; each was a product of cooperation between public and private sectors; and each in some degree and manner was a contribution toward the recovery of the city in which it occurred.

A growing cooperation between the public and private sectors represents a recognition that the tasks of redevelopment are too large and too complex for either sector to accomplish them alone. In the mood of our times, some people maintain that government can do few things right; others are equally distrustful of the private sector. The Congress organizers proceeded from the premise that both can be foresighted and competent as well as fallible, and that in working together each is challenged to bring forth its better qualities. As used here, the private sector is considered to be all that is not government.

Each of the success stories illustrated, in part, a "road to recovery," although none appears to have been influenced by a purpose that broad. They had their origin in an intent to correct a particular local trouble, but nonetheless each contributed to a larger effect. The Congress planning committee, in an attempt to establish a long-term perspective, sought to invest the word "recovery" with a meaning more specific than is conveyed by such words and phrases as "revitalization" or "upgrading the urban environment" which are inherently elastic in meaning. In the prospectus announcing the Cities' Congress, the planning committee defined recovery in these words:

> Concretely, recovery means three things: a city's regained ability to compete with suburbs as a place to live; a regained favorable climate for investment and a consequent growth of jobs; and as a consequence of these two, a regained independence from external subsidies.

The recovery concept used in this book began with a casual study of cities as a retirement interest. Cities are too fascinating for a study of them to remain casual for very long. Their absorbing and varied stories gradually drew a bewitched layman into making comparisons among ten cities chosen for their diversity and, more rashly, into trying to diagnose and prescribe. The book I wrote then was titled *The Recovery of American Cities*.[1] It cost me my retirement. At the invitation of the College of Urban Affairs at Cleveland State, I began an academic career.

This bald statement suggests that the book evoked a larger interest than it did. Except at Cleveland State, the interest was slight and transient. But it did lead to the creation of an Urban Recovery Project at the College, financed by the Cleveland Foundation and the George Gund Foundation, with myself as director. The project allowed an opportunity to organize the Cities' Congress.

When I first put forward the idea of recovery as a proper long-term goal of urban policy, the details of the 1970 census had only recently become known. They showed large and apparently accelerating losses of population by most cities of the Midwest and the Northeast and indications of future losses by some Sunbelt cities. It is useful always to bear in mind that every city at sunset is a little different in its human and physical composition from what it was at sunrise. When differences of the same kind accumulate, they disclose a trend that may be expected to continue until the conditions that cause it are altered. It seemed to be a reasonable supposition that the population losses of older cities would continue and probably accelerate. If so, their power to affect allocations of the national budget would shrink. (Even growth at less than the national average would diminish their influence.)

More speculatively, it also seemed to be plausible that public resistance to the recent large increases in federal aid to cities would emerge and grow unless the aid resulted in tangible improvements in the condition of cities. Both suppositions have become realities. The basic political situation of most cities in the older industrial areas then is this: At the very time that their claims for external aid have increased, their ability to assert and defend their interests is shrinking. This political reality overshadows all other contemporary urban issues and it will not end soon. Continued population losses must be expected, and with them a further decline in the political influence of cities.

A permanent dependency of cities could occur in the absence of a practical alternative, but it is unrealistic to suppose that dependency would be accepted willingly by the rest of the nation, nor would it be in the best interest of any city to downgrade its expectations to the status of a permanent dependent on the grudging and uncertain support of other parties. Prudence alone favors a policy of self-reliance irrespective of its other virtues. A recovery policy based on a fuller use of a city's human and physical resources is an appropriate alternative to permanent dependency.

Recovery does not mean a return to any past condition of cities except one. That one is good health, defined to mean a quality of living as good as will be found anywhere else.

The Cities' Congress success stories are steps in the right direction. Their greatest promise is that broad-based community efforts are making some cities more appealing places in which to live. The condition of the local economy is less subject to local control. In large measure, it is determined by national and, increasingly, by international conditions of production and trade. The Congress organizers were not able to find successes in job generation comparable to successes in neighborhood redevelopment.

Nonetheless, it is still the responsibility of cities—public and private sectors working together—to adapt to new conditions and to position themselves to take advantage of more favorable national policies when established. Cities can become competitively hospitable to new industry and services, and will need to if they are to fulfill a recovery objective.

A more difficult part of the recovery idea to accept—probably the next-to-most-difficult of all—is the proposition that cities should eventually become independent of external subsidies. The reluctance stems in part from a conviction that it is the duty of the federal government to give aid where it is needed combined with a disbelief that the stated preconditions of independence—a regained competitiveness with suburbs and a regained favorable investment climate—can ever be realized. But the reluctance also arises from a confusion of subsidies with federal (and state) grants. Correctly defined, subsidies are an unearned and non-repayable transfer of economic resources from one community (or party) to another.[2] A substantial, though unmeasured, portion of the grants that cities receive are not subsidies at all, but are a return of taxes collected in the same city. Present accounting practices do not make a distinction between the two and a precise distinction would be impractical, but a reasonable approximation would suffice. The eventual elimination of external subsidies would of course require a workable distinction between true subsidies and the non-subsidy transfers which would be continued.

The recovery concept does not ignore a need for subsidies in a long transitional period. Without them, a transition is unlikely. The basic policy issue is not whether there shall be external aid, but whether it will become a permanent condition.

Doubt about its practicality is probably the most formidable obstacle that proponents of the recovery concept must overcome. The American people, it may be said, think pragmatically, not conceptually. Their concerns are short-term, not long-term. Or, it may be said that the recovery concept expects too much from mutual effort by diverse elements of the community who have their own overriding and conflicting priorities.

There is a partial truth in each of the reservations. If a city's recovery were to be projected as a single grand event, then the doubts would be amply justified. But that is not the way a city's recovery comes. It will come as a hundred successes on a dozen fronts. Probably none will ever conform to an ideal model, since each will be shaped by circumstances that are partly unique to it.

Here is the larger significance of the success stories recounted in this volume, a significance that transcends a particular neighborhood or a particular city. The success stories in differing ways and importance are elements of a recovery process that is taking form in localities in response to local needs and local goals. The process, at this time, owes nothing to the recovery concept that initiated the Cities' Congress.

Can the concept help the process in the future? It is too early to know. The recovery process at this time is still rudimentary, consisting of local separate undertakings, largely unrelated to each other, and with goals no larger than the success of the individual undertaking. If the process is to mature and to broaden, it will need larger goals—goals as large as the full recovery of cities. To reach its potential, this fledgling process must acquire a conscious purpose.

Beliefs are not irrelevant. A belief in the inevitability of permanent dependency will tend to be self-fulfilling. A belief in the practicality of recovery will help to generate needed energies, prepare local and national leadership and inspire inventive ways to make fuller use of physical and human resources. In any older city, some derelict land and some idle buildings can be returned to use. Community leadership can be broadened, its goals elevated. It is not beyond human ingenuity to devise ways to enlist people in conserving a city's decaying structures or in providing neglected services.

Human energies are dynamic or passive broadly in proportion to a society's faith or lack of faith in its own capabilities. The conclusion is perhaps not provable by existing methods of social science. But it finds support in history. Twice in the memory of some now living, the nation rose to performances that only a short time earlier were widely thought to be impossible: the immense productive effort of World War II and the undertaking and fulfillment of the Marshall Plan. Exactly how great energies are released to turn the impossible into a reality is something of a mystery, but in at least these two cases high performance was associated with visionary leadership. Readers of ensuing chapters will obtain glimpses of the kind of visionary leadership that gives promise of progressively eliminating the grim side of cities.

I
Some Cities Report Successes

1

A Few Who Made a Difference

Paul R. Porter

Six To Be Remembered

The people who told their success stories at the Cities' Congress shared a common conviction. Even just a few persons, they believed, could make a real difference in the quality of living in their city. They *could*, that is, if they were strongly motivated and went about their task the right way. It seems fitting, therefore, to introduce a review and appraisal of their accomplishments with an account of the careers of six people who in their time and in their own way did make a difference—a big one—in affecting the urban environment of one or more cities.

The six chosen for this purpose are Frederick Law Olmsted, Daniel H. Burnham, Henry E. Huntington, J. C. Nichols, Robert Moses, and James W. Rouse. The last is still living and still making history. He has contributed the next chapter in this book.

Their contributions were of different kinds, differently motivated, and strongly influenced by individual personality. Each of the six was or is a man of his time, sharing with his contemporaries the dominant cultural attitudes of the day, but each also transcended his time by virtue of a vision that he perceived more clearly or pursued more resolutely than did his contemporaries. Posterity—characteristically—has been unsure in its judgments of those now dead, especially the best known, Olmsted, Burnham, and Moses. The reputations of those longest dead, Olmsted and Burnham, have experienced revisionist depreciation and neglect and recently a post-revisionist rediscovery and new respect. The sequential ideas and works of the six are an outline of the evolution of cities and suburbs since the middle of the 19th century.

It should be said that, having willed change, they changed the nature of cities much less than did a dozen or so men who altered them profoundly without any particular intent to do so. The paradox, however, has nothing to do with willpower or competence; it merely records the fact that modern nations have thus far been more successful in creating new technologies than in mastering their side effects. In large measure, the preoccupation of most of the six was to enable cities to benefit more advantageously from the new technologies—especially those invented in the fabulously inventive last half of the 19th century—while ameliorating unwanted side effects. So, before telling their stories we should pause to consider the origins of the paradox.

The history of machine power is rich in antecedents that allow choices in dating the beginning of particular periods, but probably the most relevant early event in its effect on cities occurred in 1774 when James Watt and Matthew Boulton established a partnership to manufacture Watt's improved steam engine in Birmingham.[1] The effect came more slowly in America. However, when the Baltimore and Ohio railroad began operations in 1830 it carried more than passengers and freight. It became itself a locomotive of change. The most revolutionary change in the nature of cities was probably Thomas Edison's invention in 1878 of the incandescent lamp, or electric light. It made illumination safe, plentiful, and cheap. By creating artificial daylight on a grand scale, it permitted land and capital to be used for a longer part of the day—a matter of some moment in the cost of producing goods. Although gas might still serve to illuminate homes and offices, the electric light is inseparable from present-day transportation. Even traffic is regulated by it.

Almost as revolutionary, surely, was the invention of the telephone two years earlier by Alexander Graham Bell, which allowed the human voice to be heard in conversation anywhere. The Edison effect and the Bell effect reach everywhere, but they could not without the Faraday-Brush effect. Michael Faraday, a British physicist, constructed an experimental dynamo in 1831 about the same time as did Joseph Henry, an American scientist; Faraday is credited with being the first. The growing use of the electric light and the telephone created a demand for the central generation of electricity. Charles Francis Brush, a Cleveland engineer, designed a dynamo practical for the need.

Credit for the revolutionary high-rise building must be shared among at least three men. Until about a century ago, the height of buildings was limited by the strength of their load-bearing walls and the stamina of people for climbing. Six stories were a common limit. The maximum was probably achieved in ancient Rome. The poet Juvenal, describing contemporary tenement houses in the second century, A.D., wrote:

Behold the mansion's towering size
Where floor on floor to the tenth story rise.

Understandably, he also said of them that they "shook with every gust of wind that blew."[2]

One of the three was Elisha Graves Otis, a Vermont-born engineer who settled in Yonkers, New York, and invented the safety elevator in 1852. Safety was provided by ingenious clamps that automatically and securely gripped guide rails if the elevator's descent was not controlled by its lifting cable; to convince skeptics, Otis had an assistant sever the cable of an elevator while he stood triumphantly in it at a high position. His first commercial elevator was installed in a New York City department store in 1857 and was powered by steam.

In 1856 Sir Henry Bessemer introduced in Sheffield, England, the Bessemer converter for making steel from pig iron. The building of railroads created a steel industry, and it became inevitable that sooner or later someone would introduce steel into building construction. Its first introduction was in combination with continued reliance on load-bearing walls. By this measure, a plausible case can be made for crediting Burnham (with his partner John W. Root) or either of two other Chicago architects, William LeBaron Jenney and Louis Sullivan as the designer of the first skyscraper. Perhaps, in justice, the honor should be shared among them. Yet, none came as close to anticipating the modern glass-sheathed building as did the French engineer Gustave Eiffel, best known for the tower that bears his name. At the same time that the Chicago architects were feeling their way to the independent steel frame, Eiffel was designing the interior structure of the Statue of Liberty and thereby revealing that an exterior need be no more than a drape. It is not inappropriate to describe contemporary skylines as the Otis-Bessemer-Eiffel effect.

Finally, the automobile. In 1886 Gottlieb Daimler, a German, created an internal-combustion engine light enough and powerful enough to propel a 4-wheel vehicle which he named the Mercedes. Henry Ford made the horseless carriage an affordable product for almost everybody. Drivers stuck in traffic on a city street may call it, if they wish, the Daimler-Ford effect.

Such are the effects of technology that engaged the talents of Olmsted, Burnham, Huntington, Nichols, Moses, and Rouse, whose stories are told in sequence.

Frederick Law Olmsted

Before his unlikely appointment as construction superintendent of New York's pioneering Central Park, Olmsted, a man of "scattered enthusiasms,"[3] had been, since leaving school at 18, an adventure-seeking sailor, a gentleman farmer, a European traveller, a writer of modest but growing reputation, and a partner in a bankrupt publishing company. He was then, in 1857, 35 years old and had not pursued any of his ventures diligently enough to become independent of his indulgent father's financial support except during his two-year voyage to China.

In his new post, in which he was subordinate to the engineer who had created the park's original plan, he displayed managerial competence and, in partnership with a professional architect, prepared a boldly original new design that in a field of 33 contestants won for the new firm of Olmsted and Vaux an exclusive contract to manage the construction of the park. It was the beginning of a career in which he became America's foremost designer of public parks, father of the new profession of landscape architecture and a forefather of urban planning.

William Cullen Bryant, the poet and editor of *The New York Evening Post*, had begun a campaign for a large city park with an editorial in 1844. After nine years of mounting public support, the state legislature authorized the city to buy the site that became Central Park. By 1857 it had been bought for $5 million and construction was proceeding slowing in the face of political bickering and inadequate funds. Expressing its distrust of the Tammany-dominated city government, the state legislature, controlled by the new Republican party, appointed a park commission composed of Tammany Democrats, reform Democrats, and a Republican majority. It was under insistent public pressure to proceed with construction of the park in order to provide jobs for many destitute workers who had been made jobless by the financial panic of that year.

At a chance meeting with a commissioner, Olmsted learned that the commission was seeking a non-political superintendent. He quit work on a new book he was writing on the slave economy of the South (his third) and began an energetic campaign for the job. He obtained endorsements from nearly 200 prominent citizens, including Bryant and the painter Alfred Bierstadt. He cited experience in managing laborers and gardeners on his farm and a knowledge of English parks gained as a traveller. Washington Irving, then America's most eminent man of letters, assured the commission that Olmsted was not too literary to be practical. An Olmsted biographer suggests that Irving's advice was decisive in the appointment.[4]

In its natural condition, the long rectangular site consisted of rock outcroppings, rivulets, and swamps and was largely barren of trees. At the time Olmsted began his job, it was "rubbish-strewn, deep in mud, filled with recently vacated squatters' huts and overrun with goats."[5] The potential for a great park existed, but "anything beautiful on it would have to be created, literally, from the ground up."[6] In later years, when the role of Calvert

Vaux, his partner, was often overlooked, Olmsted insisted that they had been equal partners in design, but acknowledged a difference in concept. Vaux gave emphasis to the park as a work of art, Olmsted to its use. In 1850 the census count for Manhattan Island was 515,000. Olmsted prophesied that it would reach 2,000,000. The park, he argued in the Olmsted-Vaux bid, would need to accommodate crosstown traffic and for this he proposed the novel principle of grade separation. Sunken transverse roads would provide passage for "coal carts and butcher carts, dust carts and dung carts" beneath gracefully arched overpasses.[7]

Central Park was America's first large park. In its design Olmsted was strongly influenced by English parks. During a 5-month walking tour of England, he had been fascinated with the royal parks that had recently been opened to public use and in particular with a new park especially created for the public, at Birkenhead across the Mersey River from Liverpool.

The reputation he won as manager of the park's construction led friends to propose, when the Civil War began, that he should direct the Sanitary Commission's operation of military hospitals. He accepted the post and served two years with results no more distinguished than Lincoln's generals were showing before Grant was placed in command. For another two years he managed a gold mine in California, again not impressively. Only then did he settle into the one occupation that brought forth his exceptional talents. In partnership with Vaux and then younger men, he planned parks in a score of cities including Baltimore, Boston, Brooklyn, Buffalo, Chicago, Cincinnati, Kansas City, Louisville, Milwaukee, Montreal, Philadelphia, and Rochester. He planned the grounds of the Capitol building in Washington, college campuses, and estates for the wealthy. He helped to initiate the first national park at Yosemite which had excited him during his interlude as a mine manager.

In letters and conversations, he offered a general philosophy, never fully developed, that history was a continuing contest between civilization and barbarism, and that cities fostered both.[8] One student of his life says that he felt helpless to improve directly the wretched housing of the poor, but "did deal with the slums at one remove by presenting parks as a palliative, an alternative to the gin house and a temporary escape from the congested misery of Chatham Square and Park Row."[9]

Olmsted was a prophet and strong advocate of suburbs, although this aspect of his career is less well known than the planning of parks. He welcomed the emergence of railroad-linked suburbs and proposed the planning of whole new communities that would correct the faults of the haphazard growth of cities. He wrote:

Probably the advantages of civilization can be found illustrated and demonstrated under no other circumstances as in some suburban neighborhoods where each family abode stands fifty or a hundred feet or more apart from all others. . . There is no reason except in the loss of time. . .why suburban advantages should not be almost indefinitely extended.[10]

Olmsted planned in 1868 a new community west of Chicago that was built and called Riverside. For the benefit of commuters, he proposed a six-mile parkway (a word he coined) to the city, with one set of lanes for carriages and another for horseback riders, but the land company that developed Riverside held that rail travel would be sufficient.[11]

He encountered frustration as often as success. He suffered from insomnia and numerous physical ailments. Shortly before an onset of mental illness brought his intense work to a close, he chose the site and planned the landscape of the World's Columbian Exposition in Chicago in 1893. Burnham said of him at a banquet in his own honor:

Each of you knows the name and genius of him who stands first in the heart and confidence of American artists. He it is who has been our best adviser and common mentor. . . .As artist he paints with lakes and wooded slopes; with lanes and banks and forest-covered hills; with mountainsides and ocean views.[12]

The environmental movement of recent years has brought a large revival of a lapsed interest in Olmsted. Books concerning him published during the 1970s included two excellent full-length biographies by Laura Wood Roper and Elizabeth Stevenson, a short but perceptive and informative tribute by Elizabeth Barlow, and several lesser works.[13]

Daniel H. Burnham

The Columbian Exposition which marked the close of Olmsted's career lifted Burnham, its director of works, from being one of Chicago's three or four best known architects to national fame both as an architect and a grand-scale urban planner. The Exposition was conceived as a commemoration of the 400th anniversary of the discovery of America. Chicago partisans cited the city's central location and its advantage as a terminus of 38 railroads and argued that nothing better typified "the giant young nation" than "the marvellous growth of Chicago from a frontier camp to the active city of more than a million souls, with a corresponding advance in commercial, industrial and intellectual activities."[14] In April, 1980, President Harrison signed an act of Congress approving a national exhibition to be held in Chicago.

The firms of Olmsted and Codman and Burnham and Root were retained as consultants, their joint plan was accepted, and Burnham was made manager. The sculptor, Augustus Saint-Gaudens, described the architects and artists assembled by Burnham as "the greatest meeting of artists since the 15th century." Louis Sullivan, the distinguished Chicago architect who designed the Transportation Building, said that "Burnham performed in a masterful way, displaying remarkable executive capacity. He became open-minded, just, magnaminous."[15] (In his embittered old age, Sullivan harshly condemned Burnham and the Exposition). The Exposition became a patriotic celebration of a frontier society coming of age. Its buildings inspired the City Beautiful Movement.

According to Burnham's biographer:

> No contemporary expressed a completely negative reaction. . . .While amazed and bewildered. . . .by the heterogenous "babel" inherent in all world's fairs, Henry Adams appreciated the relative sense of unity and direction that the White City demonstrated.[16]

Henry Demarest Lloyd, a well-known journalist of the time, expressed a typical reaction:

> [The Exposition] revealed to the people possibilities of social beauty, utility and harmony of which they had not been able even to dream. No social vision could otherwise have entered into the prosaic drudgery of their lives, and it will be felt in their development into the third and fourth generation.[17]

The temper of the people was favorable to its success. Many of the nation's most distinguished architects contributed to the design. Few, if any, however, besides Burnham could have brought to its organization his combination of bold imagination, persuasiveness, organizational competence, sensitive respect for colleagues, and zestful faith in the capacity of art and planning to transform the environment.

He was born in 1846 in Henderson, New York, where his parents had been active in the Swedenborgian religious community—a faith whose services Burnham conducted in his home in later years. While he was a child, his parents moved to Chicago where his father became a prosperous wholesale druggist. Burnham failed entrance examinations at Harvard and Yale and became a salesman, apprentice draftsman, and silver miner in Nevada before deciding in 1871, just before the great Chicago fire, to become an architect. The immense reconstruction task may have stirred him to think boldly.

After a brief apprenticeship, he entered into a partnership with John W. Root. They progressed from houses for the well-to-do to railway stations to

churches to office buildings. Their 10-story Montauk building in 1882, says
Thomas Hines, "was probably the first building ever to be called a skyscraper." By the time of the Exposition, their 22-story capitol building was
the tallest yet built.[18]

The year following the Exposition, Harvard and Yale conferred honorary
degrees. The recognition forecast the public role he would have until his
death in 1912. The City Beautiful Movement was linked in a loose way with
the emerging Progressive Movement. The first would improve cities
through design and planning, the second through a variety of reforms.

The City Beautiful Movement had its first big success in the nation's
capital. When Olmsted landscaped the Capitol grounds in 1874, he proposed extending the work all the way to the White House, but Congress
refused.[19] At the beginning of the new century, the Mall was "a common
pasture, a lumber yard, and the railroad center of the city, dissected and
cluttered by railroad tracks and depot buildings."[20] In 1901 a Senate committee asked Burnham to head a planning commission for the District. His
commission proposed clearing the Mall of all structures except the turreted
Smithsonian building, lining it with galleries and museums, introducing
trees, fountains, and a reflecting pool, and extending the whole to the
Potomac where it would terminate with a memorial to President Lincoln.
Beyond, an impressive memorial bridge would lead to Arlington Cemetery.
A new railway station would be built at its present location (which was done
to Burnham's design). Today's Mall is the product of his commission.

He designed Cleveland's civic center, adapted City Beautiful concepts to
a major redevelopment of Manila, and prepared a major plan for San Francisco that was sidetracked by the earthquake and fire of 1906. His last
grand-scale urban plan was for his home city. It envisaged a "redevelopment of the whole Chicago area within a 60-mile radius of the city's center,
including an elaborate system of outer parks and radial and concentric
boulevards, an aesthetic and useful lakefront park system 20 miles along
Lake Michigan," and numerous other proposals.[21] In his introduction
Burnham wrote:

> Thoughtful people are appalled at the result of progress; at the waste of time,
> strength, and money which congestion in city streets begets; at the toll of lives
> taken by disease when sanitary precautions are neglected; and at the frequent out-
> breaks against law and order which results from narrow and pleasureless lives. So
> that while the keynote of the 19th century was expansion, we of the 20th century
> find that our dominant idea is conservation.[22]

With symbolic intent, the plan was made public on July 4, 1909. Burnham declined compensation for his work, as he did in the case of all work
done for governments, city or federal. Although the more ambitious pro-

posals were not enacted, "Burnham's Chicago Plan formed the basic outlines of the city's development and expansion in the 20th century."[23]

A revisionist appraisal of Burnham's work began with Sullivan's mean-spirited attack in 1925.[24] It coincided with a post-war cynicism typically expressed in the "debunking" writings of Mencken and Sinclair Lewis. Sullivan's credo that "form follows function" had the crispness of an advertising slogan and was seen as a brilliant anticipation of the architectural style introduced by LeCorbusier and the German Bauhaus school in the early 1920s.

The tide now runs against the revisionists. Hines, although critical of the neo-classical Beaux Art style favored by Burnham, has written a sympathetic biography. The slogan of "form follows function" is now viewed by architects as less confining than Sullivan intended; if pleasing the eye is one of the functions of architecture, then an adorned form that pleases does no harm to the doctrine. A more tolerant view of adornment accompanies the contemporary support for conservation prophesied by Burnham.

Burnham's own words characterize him best:

Make no little plans, they have no magic to stir men's blood. . . .Make big plans, aim high in hope and work, remembering that a noble, logical diagram once recorded will never die, but long after we are gone will be a living thing asserting itself with ever-growing insistency. Remember that our sons and grandsons are going to do things that would stagger us.[25]

Henry Edwards Huntington

Huntington was 50 years old before he showed any recorded interest in urban development. He pursued his new career only from 1900 to 1909. In that time he built and operated the largest mass transit system—1,164 miles of track—that the United States has had, and in doing so he created the dispersed structure that metropolitan Los Angeles has had ever since. His transit system lost money in all but eight of the 59 years it operated; it was, in the language of merchandising, a "loss leader" supporting Huntington's primary interest which was the sale of real estate he had acquired in areas now known as Huntington Park and Huntington Beach as well as in Glendale, the San Fernando Valley, Seal Beach, Olinda, and downtown Los Angeles.[26] According to the Encyclopedia Britannica, "much of the city's astonishing growth in the early 1900s was due to the superb interurban transit system provided by the big red electric cars of railroad tycoon–art collector Henry E. Huntington."[27]

The city's crescent of suburbs was securely established in a decade when only a few people could afford the automobiles being newly marketed. Huntington told how it was done in an interview published in 1904:

> It would never do for an electric line to wait until the demand for it came. It must anticipate the growth of communities and be there when the home builders arrive or they are very likely not to arrive at all, but to go to some section already provided with the arteries of traffic.[28]

A local historian, Spencer Crump, has given this account of the transit-land relationship:

> When Henry E. Huntington began building his trolley empire, he also bought large land holdings; values skyrocketed when interurbans made the properties easy to reach. . . .When the Big Red Cars finally rolled into the realm of history, they left a sprawling City of Southern California built precisely as it was because rail lines had encouraged just that development.[29]

There appears to be general agreement that Huntington's transit system provided very good service during his regime and afterwards. The system was not confined to radial lines from downtown, but consisted of a network of connecting lines. It served more than 300 residential districts in four counties and at its peak in the 1920s it carried 2,700 trolley runs daily. An author of an essay about Huntington reports that in order to maintain a 5-cent fare, he declined to collect interest on company bonds that he owned.[30] It would be consistent with the objective of subordinating transit profits to the more alluring real estate profits.

It may be inferred that the transit system would never have been built, at least by Huntington, if he had not lost a contest for control of the Southern Pacific railroad when its president and his uncle, Collis P. Huntington, died in 1900. Henry Huntington was then its vice-president, but a group of stockholders led by E. H. Harriman denied him the presidency. He thereupon sold his holdings to them for a reported $50 million[31] and with it bought Los Angeles real estate and several small trolley lines in the area which he consolidated and expanded into the Pacific Electric.

"I am a foresighted man," he told a reporter, "and I believe Los Angeles is destined to become the most important city in this country, if not in the world. . . .We will join this whole region into one big family." He forecast a population of 6,000,000.[32] The city's population at the time (1900) was 102,000.

Huntington was born in 1850 in the village of Oneonta in central New York where his father and Uncle Collis owned a general store. The uncle left to join the California gold rush, prospered in the hardware business, made shrewd investments, and by 1861 had enough capital to start building the railroad that became the Southern Pacific. Young Huntington migrated to New York without attending college and began work as a floor sweeper. He initially declined assistance from his uncle, but accepted a second offer which was to manage a West Virginia saw mill making railroad ties. Later he became construction superintendent for a railroad owned by his uncle in Kentucky and progressively moved into the top rank of railroad management.

At one time he was a director of 60 corporations. He retained some of his business interests after selling his holdings in the Pacific Electric Railway in 1909, but his principal interest thereafter until his death in 1927 was in collecting paintings and rare books, especially the latter.[33] The Huntington Library and Art Gallery which he endowed has one of the most important collections of rare books in the United States.

The story of the Pacific Electric Railway contradicts a popular belief that the automobile created suburbs. Rail transit did. Even earlier, suburbs were growing along rail lines in other cities.[34] Olmsted, dissatisfied with New York, moved his home and office to Brookline, a suburb of Boston, in 1881. "I enjoy this suburban country beyond expression," he wrote a friend.[35] Long before he owned a car, Burnham chose to commute from Evanston because he did not wish to raise his children in Chicago. Probably suburbs would have flourished less if the automobile had never been invented, but their challenge to cities as a place to live became inevitable when machine technology shortened travel time. The Pacific Electric began to lose patronage in the 1920s, recovered strongly with gas rationing in World War II (when the company had its most profitable years), and then went into a rapid decline.[36] Symbolically, its losing competition with the automobile was signaled earlier. Huntington retained his private trolley car when he sold his holdings in the company and it was his custom to board it on his estate each morning for the trip to his downtown office. In 1913 he abandoned it for an automobile.

Jesse Clyde Nichols

The Country Club Plaza in Kansas City, according to a brochure of the J. C. Nichols Company, is "America's Original Shopping City," built in 1922 as "the first major shopping center to be constructed to cater to people who arrive by automobile rather than by trolley."[37] There appears to be no reason to question the claim.

The Plaza has other distinctions as well. It was conceived as a support for recently built and planned nearby neighborhoods. All buildings on its 55 acres have a unifying architectural style, "a blend of Old Spain, Mexico and

Southern California.'' The Plaza, with its 188 shops, was a ''festive market-place'' long before the phrase entered today's vocabulary; an art fair has been held at the Plaza every autumn since 1932. There are eight movie theaters and 20 restaurants. The landscaped grounds contain a profusion of tasteful statuary, fountains and a waterfall 54 feet wide, and twelve towers that rise above red-tiled roofs, one to a height of 130 feet. The Plaza is the city's largest tourist attraction. One of the tourists, the distinguished French author, André Maurois, wrote:

> Who in Europe, or in America for that matter, knows that Kansas City is one of the loveliest cities on earth. Why? Because a man wished it so and insisted upon it. For it was just the man, J. C. Nichols, who in 20 years created this new city.[38]

Nichols himself wrote, ''Cities are handmade. Whether they are physically bad or physically good is largely a responsibility of the realtor.''

Unlike Olmsted and Burnham, Nichols lost no time in deciding upon a career. He was born at Olathe, Kansas, in 1880. He sold vegetables door-to-door to help support himself as a student at the University of Kansas from which he graduated with Phi Beta Kappa honors and a scholarship to Harvard. At age 24 he began his own real estate business, briefly in Kansas City, Kansas, and thereafter in Kansas City, Missouri. When 26, he bought a 10-acre tract just south of the city limits and began its development as a neighborhood that ''offered a little more than all others.'' The little more included such suburban novelties as plumbing and trash collection. The first Nichols development included a drugstore and a meat market. It was the beginning of a practice of concurrently building homes and stores to serve them.

According to a commemorative publication of the company's 75th anniversary in 1980, Nichols ''worked long hours at many jobs. He and his salesmen built wide wood sidewalks in the morning and then put on their coats and sold homes in the afternoon.'' He met buyers at the end of a trolley line and drove them in a horse and buggy to the new homes. As the new developments flourished, he ''provided electrification of the Dodson Rail Line so that it could be extended out to his properties, initially to 51st, then 63rd, then past Waldo.'' By 1908, the company controlled 1,000 acres beyond the first development. ''Streets curved along Kansas City's gentle hills rather than lay flat in a checkerboard pattern. The company invested in statuary and art objects, placing them at intersections and curves.''

As automobiles came into use, the company ''planned entire communities setting aside space for schools, churches, parks and country clubs. . . Each neighborhood had its shopping center.'' The company bought land for a parkway, constructed it, landscaped it with trees and gardens and gave it to the city, which progressively annexed the new developments on the Missouri side. Some spread across the state line into Kansas. There the company provided its own water supply, fire department, and sewage treatment.

The rapid growth of the area persuaded Nichols that a major shopping center could be created on unpromising swamp land between the first development and what had then been the city line. It was there that the Plaza opened in 1922.

Today the company operates 20 shopping centers that it has built, including the Plaza. It has 27 office buildings, four hotels, two industrial parks, more than 2,000 rental apartments, a mortgage loan and insurance business, and 1,500 employees. During the Depression years it retained all of its employees although losing money in all years but one. Nichols was a founder of the Urban Land Institute and in the 1920s was a member of the National Capital and Park Planning Commission. He died in 1950.

Nichols' particular talent as a developer was to anticipate, enhance, and efficiently supply the residential aspirations of the upwardly mobile middle class, particularly young families, and to invoke in them a pride of neighborhood—much as the new towns of Columbia and Reston do today. He was successful enough that the company was able to claim justifiably on its 75th anniversary:

> Nichols' developments have not experienced transition or turnover because proud homeowners and shopowners have maintained standards, quality and a better way of life in Kansas City for three quarters of a century.

The company has also been fortunate in enjoying community support. The influential longtime publisher of *The Kansas City Star*, William Rockhill Nelson, was an ardent champion of beautifying the city. The newspaper's enthusiasm for the aesthetic quality of Nichols' developments had a promotional value for the company that no amount of advertising could have purchased.[39] The city itself has one of the finest park systems in the nation. Nelson brought Olmsted to Kansas City to help plan the park system and his protégé, George E. Kessler, continued the work.[40] Henry Van Brunt, a local architect, was a close associate of Burnham in the Columbian Exposition and later a leader of the City Beautiful Movement.[41]

In the 1970s the Plaza began to lose patronage to newer shopping centers. The company's response was to undertake a $25 to $30 million new construction program and to raise rents, causing Sears and Woolworth's to leave. In their stead, the Plaza management brought in Saks Fifth Avenue and other high-fashion stores. The action has caused some dissatisfaction among old patrons. Miller Nichols, son of the founder and the present

chairman of the board, justifies the action by saying that Sears and Woolworth's products are readily available in other centers, whereas the high-
fashion stores are expected to attract patronage from Tulsa, Denver, and
other cities. The company's philosophy, he said, was, "You either go forward or you go backward."[42]

Robert Moses

Moses (who had no middle name) is the best known and the most controversial of the men discussed in this chapter. He was an entrepreneurial
civil servant who for 44 years managed simultaneously an array of public
corporations (authorities) that designed, built, and operated great park
systems, city expressways, bridges, public housing, a huge hydro-electric
power installation, and a world's fair. During 34 of the 44 years, he represented both the state of New York and its largest city. Before being forced
into retirement in 1968, a few months short of his 80th birthday, he had
planned and built public works having an estimated value of $27 billion in
1968 dollars.

How does a young civil servant become a one-man conglomerate operating big corporations whose revenues are independent of both legislative al-
location and market competition?

Pleasing a popular governor is a good start. Just five years home from
Oxford with a Ph.D. degree (after Yale), he was hired to help prepare plans
for administrative reorganization in the first administration of Governor
Alfred E. Smith. They became good friends despite (or perhaps partly
because of) a generation's difference in age and still greater differences in
social background and formal education. During a two-year interlude following a failure to be re-elected, Smith often called him to his home for an
evening of conversation and barbershop quartet harmonizing.

Moses meanwhile pursued an idea of his own which was to create state
parks on Long Island that city residents could enjoy. Experienced cam-
paigners for public parks had concluded that even a small park on the island
was not possible because of the strength of the political opposition.[43] Moses
dismissed their opinions. Imaginatively and boldly, he prepared a plan for a
whole *system* of parks—on the wealthy north shore, the lightly settled south
shore and in between—all linked to each other and the city by landscaped
parkways.

Breathtaking boldness, then, was one essential element in becoming a
one-man conglomerate. It was not the Moses temperament to make little
plans. Boldness was matched by thorough preparations. He methodically
traced the ownership of the many pieces of land required by the plan. He

discovered that large and strategically placed tracts were actually owned by the city. They had been bought by Brooklyn, when still an independent city, for a water reservoir that was never built. For a half century the land had been idle and its ownership unknown to its owner except for a few clerks. To Moses, it was a lesson in the use of neglected resources that he later used with great effectiveness.

Returned to office in 1922, the governor informed the legislature of the park plan, but cannily did not endorse it. It was an idea, he said, of his assistant, Dr. Moses, which might merit consideration in another year. The tactic worked. Enthusiastic park advocates mobilized public support and the opposition was caught off guard. In 1924, the legislature approved a Moses-drafted bill creating the Long Island State Park Commission and a $15 million bond issue. Smith appointed Moses to be president of the commission. Within five years, everything promised in the plan was completed and in use, including the famous Jones Beach. Moses was applauded in editorials throughout the nation as a public servant who knew how to make government work for the people.

A second episode is also an important part of the story of Moses's rise to fame and power. When Fiorello La Guardia, a maverick Republican, was elected mayor of New York in the year following Roosevelt's election as President, he urgently wanted Moses to take charge of the city's public works. A split among Democrats, with rival candidates on the ballot, had enabled La Guardia to win with 40 percent of the vote. He wanted Moses's reputation to bolster his own position, and mistakenly, he believed that Moses was close to Roosevelt. (In fact, they disliked each other; Moses was a Smith loyalist). But most important:

> La Guardia knew that a key reason for Moses's success in obtaining federal money was that Moses had plans for huge public works ready at the moment the money became available. To get plans, you needed first a large staff of engineers trained in building such works. He knew that the city departments did not have such staffs and he knew that Moses did.[44]

Moses was willing to accept the position, with conditions. The five separate borough park departments would have to be consolidated with him in charge. Also, he would retain his four state jobs. This condition required special legislation, which he prepared. It provided that an *unsalaried* state official (which he was) could also serve as an *unsalaried* city official (which he became). The legislature speedily enacted his bill. Inherited wealth (from merchandising) was also an element in his rise.

Renovation of the city's neglected parks was the first task. With federal funds, 68,000 men were already working in a desultory way and without plans; the purpose was to provide them with what was then called "work relief." What they did was incidental, and in fact, severely limited by a rule that no one, including architects, engineers and supervisors could be paid more than $30 per week.

Moses insisted upon and won permission to hire 600 architects and engineers at $80 per week (six out of seven architects were then reported to be idle); 1,300 were invited by telegram to report the next day for interviews. Moses persuaded building contractors to lend supervisors at the contractors' expense. Soon, the 68,000 relief workers were working in three shifts around the clock. By May 1, "Every structure in every park had been repainted. . . .38 miles of walks repaired. . . .678 drinking fountains repaired. . . .22,500 benches reslatted. . . .every playground in the city resurfaced."[45] Not in many years had the city's parks been so usable.

Moses made an inventory of all city-owned unused land. Over strenuous objections from other department heads, he obtained a transfer of nearly all of it to his park department. "Within four months after taking office, the new park Commissioner had obtained in slum areas in which there had been no significant park or playground development for at least half a century, no fewer than 69 separate small park and playground sites." It was just a beginning. "When Robert Moses began building playgrounds in New York City, there were 119. When he stopped, there were 777."[46]

If Moses had concluded his career with the building of parks and playgrounds, he might have remained a hero. His decline in popularity and his eventual fall from power began when the city of New York put him in charge of its urban renewal program. He did what the federal government then wanted done in accordance with the Housing Act of 1949. He cleared slums and he built public housing in their place. With his driving energy, he and his disciplined staff executed so well the federal programs then considered to be wise and humane that by 1957 the value of public housing built in New York City was twice that of all the rest of the nation.[47] And the number of people uprooted was approximately in the same proportion.

Moses also built federally supported expressways—16 of them. They, too, caused a displacement of residents and brought more traffic into a congested city. Praise for "America's greatest builder" declined and criticism mounted.

In the words of biographer Robert A. Caro, "The press. . . .had been awakened by its reporters, not by its famous reporters but unknown staff writers scheming together to force publishers and editors to do what the young men felt was their duty."[48] Caro was one of the young men.

Moses struck back, angrily and clumsily, and fell further in public esteem. In 1962, Governor Nelson Rockefeller forced him out of the four state park positions he held then and in 1968 into final retirement (from his job as head of the Triborough Bridge and Tunnel Authority). He was given an advisory position that added to his humiliation. His mind remained active and his spirit restless, but the memoranda he wrote were acknowledged by low-level employees or ignored altogether. (He lived to the age of 92).

In his biography, Caro makes a persuasive case that Moses was arrogant, made enemies unnecessarily, and was often vindictive. One must respect Caro's industriousness and an evident intent to report faithfully what he learned. The faults are of a different kind. Relentlessly, for 1,162 pages of text, he expounds a simple thesis that Moses was a flawed idealist who was so corrupted by power that nothing else mattered, and his use of power caused an undefined "fall" of New York. His language is extravagant and his perception is apocalyptic. A fair judgment of Moses must await a biography that is more objective.

James Wilson Rouse

The annual meeting of The Rouse Company's shareholders on May 29, 1979, was a special occasion. It marked the company's beginning in Baltimore 40 years earlier as a mortgage banking institution consisting of Rouse, a partner, and one secretary. The meeting was also Rouse's last day as chief executive officer, although he would continue as chairman of the board. After brief remarks in which he reiterated the company's philosophy, he delivered to Mathias J. DeVito, his successor, three symbols of office. The first was a Bible. The second was a framed message that read, "When life gives you lemons, make lemonade." The third was a card that had long stood on his desk and that bore the full statement of Burnham's words which, in part, read "Make no little plans, they have no magic to stir men's blood. . . .Make big plans; aim high in hope and work. . . ."

Earlier, DeVito had reported financial results of 1978 to more than 500 shareholders present. Net earnings were $5.9 million. Every operating division had broken its own record. Conservatively estimated current value of assets was $662 million. Shareholders' equity on a cost basis was $27 million; on a current-value basis it was $196 million.[49] In 40 years, the company's work force had grown from three to 3,000.

During his boyhood in the small town of Easton on the eastern shore of Maryland, Rouse suffered from infantile paralysis. He was 16 and the youngest of five children when both parents died within a few months of each other. A bank foreclosed on the Rouse home. "An almost-penniless teenager" in the midst of the Depression, he took a ferry to Baltimore, worked as a parking-garage attendant for $13.50 a week, and attended night classes to obtain a law degree.[50] For a short while, he worked for the Federal

Housing Administration that Roosevelt's New Deal had recently brought into being. The civil service, however, did not have for him the appeal that Robert Moses found in it. At 25, he quit to become an entrepreneur in the mortgage banking business.

The business was interrupted during World War II by naval service at a command post in Hawaii. He returned to it and prospered, but it alone was too limited in scope for his restless spirit. As a sideline, he organized a small consulting company to advise shopping-center developers. In 1954 he bought out his banking partner.[51] He was 40 that year and it was at a time when he had begun to display in his private business and in a newly found public role the Burnham counsel to "make big plans; aim high in hope and work."

The public role began when a pessimistic report on the future of Baltimore's downtown spurred him to help organize the Greater Baltimore Committee from which came Charles Center—the first stage in "the Baltimore miracle"—and, nearly a quarter of a century later, Harborplace.

He was challenged no less by the decay of neighborhoods. Even then he was proclaiming that the city must be seen and dealt with as an entity. Besides serving as chairman of the Greater Baltimore Committee, he became chairman of the Citizens' Advisory Committee to the city housing bureau.[52] The opportunity to elaborate his ideas on reviving decayed neighborhoods came when the commissioners responsible for the government of the nation's capital (before the city was allowed to elect its government) asked him to advise them on urban renewal. His report was given in a booklet, published in 1955, which he wrote in cooperation with Nathaniel S. Keith. Its title was *No Slums in Ten Years: A Workable Program for Urban Renewal.*[53] The report proposed the replacement of the worst one-quarter of the city's housing. The prevailing objective of urban renewal then was massive slum clearance to be replaced with public housing. Rouse accepted the given premise. The report, however, expressed some concepts of neighborhood well in advance of their time. The following are some excerpts:

> The most important element in urban renewal is the people. The object is to provide a neighborhood, not of houses, but people. . . .
>
> A neighborhood renewal committee should be formed in each renewal neighborhood. . . .
>
> Urban renewal. . . .means making the city into a community of neighborhoods where people want to live and raise families; where there is the opportunity for a neighborhood consciousness and a spirit of neighborliness; where there is reason to care about the house, the block, the playground, the school. . . .
>
> Urban renewal in order to be effective must go deep enough to reach the attitudes of the people and reach those attitudes along with the dwellings in which they live.

Rouse's career as a developer began more or less concurrently with the creation of the Greater Baltimore Committee and the writing of *No Slums in Ten Years*. He concluded that if developers were willing to pay for his advice, he could become one. His first shopping center was in his hometown of Easton (population, 8,000). He wanted to protect its retail center from being undermined by roadside shops on the town's outskirts. He found land within two blocks of the principal street intersection and there he built the center he called Talbottown, "a small collection of retail shops along the architectural lines of the town's old buildings."[54] He must have sensed then that his idea would not succeed—the location was not suitable for convenient parking. Thereafter, The Rouse Company built suburban shopping centers. Harundale Mall, the first enclosed shopping center in the United States, was opened in 1958 in a Baltimore suburb. More than 30 others followed which produce most of the earnings of The Rouse Company.

The Rouse Company assembled the land (22 square miles), and planned and built the new city of Columbia, Maryland. It was begun in 1967 and now houses a population of 60,000. Some 35,000 people work there. Like its smaller counterpart at Reston, Virginia, it is considered a model of new-community planning and draws admiring visitors from all over the world.

Rouse's heart, nonetheless, is in restoring cities to health. While not the inventor of the "festive marketplace," he has produced the most exciting ones: Quincy and South Markets (contrasting parts of the Faneuil Hall Marketplace) in Boston, the Gallery of Market Street East in Philadelphia, Harborplace in Baltimore, and more recently, the Grand Avenue in Milwaukee. They are, in the words of *Fortune* magazine, "warm, human, exciting,"[55] and they have brought new visitors in throngs to downtowns. The acclaim has not been universal. One architectural critic has complained that the Harborplace buildings "are a mash of clichés. . . .not well reconciled to each other, nor resolved in themselves."[56] So continues an old story of what the people like versus what purists think they ought to like: Olmsted vs. Vaux; Burnham vs. Sullivan. But clearly, Rouse has revived stagnant downtowns by offering what people like.

Taking downtown lemons, he made lemonade. Can he do so with neighborhood lemons? A later chapter (Chapter 7) tells the story of Jubilee Housing which has had Rouse's support from its beginning. After retiring from active management in The Rouse Company, he organized a new one, The Enterprise Development Company, a for-profit real estate developer like The Rouse Company except for two differences. It develops smaller projects than The Rouse Company. The second difference is that it is a wholly owned subsidiary of The Enterprise Foundation, "a charitable corporation which works with non-profit neighborhood groups in cities across the country to improve housing for the very poor and help them to become self-sufficient."[57] Jubilee Housing was its inspiration. The first full year of operation was 1982. A Norfolk project, the Waterside, opened in July, 1983 to "rave reviews."[58] A similar development is underway in Toledo, and feasibility studies have been concluded for others.

Purposes and Strategies

Reflection on the careers of these few who made a large difference may help others who aspire to make a difference. The hope that it may be helpful is a reason why this chapter was written. But whether or not it has this result, the careers of these men make a fascinating story of how purposes grew and strategies (the organization of means) were devised in response to major urban problems. This account does not tell enough—we do not know enough. Even the best biographies, those about Olmsted and Burnham, are weak with respect to their strategies. There is no biography of Nichols, which is a pity, because he was a creative person. Although we do not know as much as we would like, we can draw some provisional conclusions pending fuller studies by others.

By looking at the careers of the six together, differences are accented which give new insights concerning each. Only Nichols built his career in urban affairs on what he set out to do originally. He seems to have known from the time that he completed his formal education that he wanted to be a real estate developer. His strategy of building for the upwardly mobile class by offering something "a little better" (shopping convenience and aesthetic appeal) was evident quite early.

The others seem to have had the careers by which we know them best thrust upon them. Olmsted, after concluding that there was no future for him in managing a mine, thought of returning to journalism before his former partner persuaded him to return to New York to help plan Prospect Park in Brooklyn.[59] He was then almost 45. Rouse was past 40 before he became a developer. Burnham already had distinction as an architect when he became manager of the Columbian Exposition, but it was only afterwards that he became an urban planner. Moses was 35 when he began his entrepreneurial role, and he appears not to have sought it.[60]

Huntington was a special case. At an age (50) when retirement was not attractive to a self-made man, he was out of a job with, however, a large fortune to reinvest. Correctly foreseeing a rapid and large population growth in the Los Angeles area, an investment in real estate in strategic locations had the potential of a high and early return on his money, provided that he could make development of the land attractive to builders. Once this conclusion had been reached, his strategy unfolded with classic simplicity.

There would be no need for him to become a developer, a business in which he had no experience. Others would build. A transportation network was the way to make his land suitable for development. Since it was a business he knew, it should be a low-risk operation. It was not even necessary that it be profitable; the big money was to be made in enhanced real estate values. As a by-product of Huntington's search for a good investment opportunity, Greater Los Angeles obtained a high-quality interurban system and a dispersed metropolitan structure.

As professional men, Olmsted and Burnham had fewer resources to work with than those who obtained substantial amounts of capital (public capital in the case of Moses). Yet, simply by the quality of their ideas and work, they built reputations which grow again in public esteem.

When the career of Moses is compared with that of the others, a surprising conclusion emerges. Despite his acknowledged brilliance and his inventiveness in using a civil servant's base to become one of the biggest entrepreneurs in this century, he seems to have been the least curious about the adequacy of the goals that went with his jobs. Had he been more questioning about ends, the gifted contriver of means might have avoided some of the accomplishments in urban renewal and expressway building for which he was later condemned. Or will future historians place the responsibility with legislators who created the policies he executed?

Rouse, too, it must be concluded, is a special case. The view he fervently expresses in the next chapter he has voiced many times—all the way back to *No Slums in Ten Years* and the Greater Baltimore Committee. When he retired from active management of The Rouse Company, he said that his primary goal had been "to improve the physical environment and the quality of urban life available to people in the United States."[61] He is entitled to be believed. The transit business was Huntington's strategy for a private goal. The development business is Rouse's strategy for a much larger public goal.

2

The Case for Vision

James W. Rouse

A New Tide of Hopeful Purpose

There is an enormous need, a crying need, in our cities for new life, new structure, new institutions, new ways of doing things. And we have a huge potential for meeting that need—this society with its wealth, its leadership, its power, its management capability, its capacity for analysis and solution.

It is frustrating that we should stand wringing our hands before the problems of our cities where our whole civilization is both nourished and deprived.

It is frustrating that we do not recognize our capacity and begin to work for the recovery of our cities with the determination and the commitment that should be transcending in our lives and in our businesses.

There is a great tide running in America now. It can be seen in the Committee for Economic Development report on public-private partnerships, in the President's Task Force on Private-Sector Initiatives, and in meetings like the Cities' Congress on Roads to Recovery. The people who have come to Cleveland to learn from each others' success stories have risen up to a new awareness, a new fire, that things do not have to be the way they are, and that they can change.

In 40 years of living and working in the American city—sometimes as a developer and sometimes in the public, national and local ways that many of us are called upon to work to improve the life of the city—in 40 years of this, I truly believe that this is the most hopeful period in the history of the American city. There really are new forces at work, forces that have the potential for massive transportation of the city. I think there will be more significant change than we experienced in the 1950s, 1960s and 1970s—in the explosion that led to the suburban sprawl and highway clutter that we have now come to lament.

There is new spirit and purpose. I have attended several hundred meetings in the last 40 years that were focused on helping the American city be a better place. In the past it was an exhortation of unwilling people. You felt that you had gained an inch at the beginning of a meeting, but you knew you had lost it when the meeting ended. It is different now. Today's meetings are coming out of the people and their local leadership. There is a new sense of purpose, commitment and urgency.

Some years ago we were working on the program for a New England city and its metropolitan area. We finished an exhilarating meeting. Everyone reached agreement on how to move forward. As we walked to the elevator, the staff man who was to be responsible for the program turned to me and said: "Well, we are going to get there. I don't know where we are going, but we are going to get there." There is something of that determination today. If we really are determined to move, we will find out where to go.

The Unnecessary Deterioration

The deterioration of the American city did not just happen. There were forces at work which we did not see at the time—but we could have. And there are reasons for the revitalization that is occurring now. It is important to see both the forces at work in the deterioration and in the revitalization of the city, because if we see them, it will help us to deal with them more rationally.

The first devil in the deterioration piece was the automobile. It came upon us after World War II. We did not appreciate then that we were fashioning an entirely new way of moving people about. The automobile hit the cities which were unprepared to accommodate it. It poured into the heart of our cities and congested our streets. We did not manage its movement or its parking. We made one-way streets which became torrents of automobiles pouring through residential and business areas. We built new highways on the edge of the city; widened the old roads; cut back the front yards, created places for service stations and hot dog stands. When that became crowded and cluttered, we built new freeways and where they intersected the highways, we created shopping centers, office parks, and industrial parks. In all of this we were drawing life out of the center city, and doing nothing to help the center city accommodate to this new demand for moving about.

At the same time, there arose the American Dream for a way to live—a quarter-acre lot, picket fence, station wagon, golf course, outdoor barbecue—these became the picture of the good American life. And we did everything to enable it. In the outlying areas we provided 30-year mortgages at low interest. In the inner cities we redlined areas and refused financing or required short-term amortization and high interest rates—not out of prejudice, but out of a belief that there were not sound long-term economic values there. Each of these separate actions drove down the center city and encouraged suburban development.

Then we experienced the world-wide, farm-to-city migration which, in America, became a movement of people who could be labeled by color. We made them live in the center of the city within rigid boundaries. We pushed the black people into the center of the city and built walls around them; congested the center city; allowed the services to decline, provided second-rate schools and a general lower level of services. We built urban jungles for black people to live in and grow.

We built the slums. *We built them!* They did not just happen.

A Wealth of Opportunities

Now there are new forces at work. They are very different and are favorable to the center city.

First is the cumulative impact of many little pieces of action in the center of the city that add up to a new thing. There are better highways into the center city and there is better parking. It is easier and faster to get to the city center from the outskirts than it was 25 years ago.

We have built public squares, built or expanded institutions of all kinds, concert halls, hospitals, universities, museums, theatres; built new office buildings. There are more jobs in the center of cities today than there were 15 or 20 years ago. This had all happened piecemeal. It has not been well ordered, but it has happened. And it is important.

There are tremendous economic development opportunities at the center of cities. We need to stop thinking about the center city as problems and look for the opportunities. Job growth is no longer in manufacturing. It is in services which are concentrated in office buildings or office-type buildings. They do not require large sites; they are well served in the city if we create the proper environment.

Big business is not what we should be seeking in economic development for the city. Eighty percent of all new jobs created in America in the last decade have been in businesses employing less than 100 people.

The opportunity to create jobs is not restricted to the Sunbelt. The Rouse Company is developing a new city, Columbia, Maryland. Thirty-five thousand jobs have been created in Columbia in 15 years; two new businesses a week—an average of more than 100 new businesses every year. This is not the Sunbelt. Columbia is 20 miles from Baltimore and 30 miles from Washington.

Not long ago I was in Washington to attend a meeting on Enterprise Zones. I do not believe they provide a significant answer because they are based on a wrong premise. Enterprise Zones assume that business does not want to come to the center of the city, and the only way you can get it there is to pay it to come; give it some special benefit.

But that is not the way to attract business. We must create an environment that is attractive to business—that uses the resources of the city so well that business wants to come. But typically we do not create the kind of office and industrial centers at the heart of the city that we build in the suburbs.

Before going to the Enterprise Zone meeting, I called the man in charge of business and industrial development in Columbia. I asked, "What would happen if we built in Baltimore an industrial center comparable to the ones we build in Columbia?" Those in Columbia are attractive and well planned. We build buildings with space suited to small businesses needing 5,000 to 10,000 square feet—businesses that will grow. "How," I asked, "would an industrial center in downtown Baltimore compete with those in Columbia?" Without a moment's hesitation, he said it would be the fiercest competitor we could have.

I asked him why. He said, "Look at the assets of the city. It would have public transportation for the biggest labor force that is available in the area. It would have the amenities of the center city available to its workers, its office staff, and its management. It would be the toughest competition."

But we are not creating that kind of environment for job growth at the heart of our cities.

At a recent meeting in Boston I spoke about the resources of New England. I asked, "Who would rather live in Texas than in New England?" Texas is hot, dry, dull compared to New England with its ocean, beaches, and lakes. You can sail or go to the mountains to ski, hike, fish. And you have the joy of the seasons. Think of the advantages of New England compared to Texas. Yet, these advantages are not being marketed. New England is too conscious of its problems rather than its opportunities.

I will make a prediction—by the turn of the century New England will be a more vibrant place for economic growth than the Southwest. The same opportunity exists in the Midwest. New England and the Midwest have skilled workers, extensive cultural, educational, recreational opportunities, the richness of established communities, fine old buildings. Cities in New England and the Midwest are burdened today because many of their people are unemployed. But that labor force is a resource of people available to work. It needs to be seen that way. There are great cities in the Midwest and

New England and we need to see them as an enormous opportunity to unfold for American business.

Another force enormously favorable to the center city is the change in lifestyle in America. That American Dream of a quarter-acre lot and the picket fence is not the dream of most American households today. Sixty-five percent of the households in America have two people working. Fifty percent have no children. Only 20 percent of the households represent a man, a wife at home and two children in school. These households with two people working and no children—where is their life better lived out? In the suburbs or in the vitality of the central city? These people are saying over and over again that it is in the center city. They just want the opportunity to get in.

In Baltimore in the last seven years, there have been over 7,000 houses rehabilitated and restored within ten minutes of downtown. This is happening all over the country — wherever the opportunity is created. Baltimore's city government created that opportunity with a homesteading program that made badly deterioriated housing available for $1 on the condition that it be brought up to prescribed standards. As the houses in the homestead areas were renovated, they brought new life to adjacent rundown houses. As more people come, services improve, values escalate.

The future soft spot in real estate in America is the suburb. The future dynamic spot is the center city. The life, the vitality, the favorable economics will be at the heart of the American city.

Other forces favorable to the center city are the three E's—Environment, Energy and Economics.

Environmental requirements have made it more difficult and more costly for developers in the suburbs. They must obey new disciplines and new constraints. At the same time, the force of historic preservation has made us appreciate the value of the existing housing inventory; has preserved for rehabilitation housing that in earlier years would have been demolished. Rising costs have people spending money more carefully, thinking about efficiency in moving about, not spending all that money moving by automobile over great distances. That is favorable to living in the center of the city. And you can get more square feet of living area by rehabilitating an old house or a loft in the inner city than by buying a new house in the suburbs. And financing is at least as favorable in the inner city today—sometimes at lower, subsidized rates.

Last, and perhaps most important, is the progress in race relations in this country. At long last, it is becoming possible for people to live wherever they want, regardless of the color of their skin. We built the segregated ghetto at the heart of our cities. As we break down those walls so that a black family can live wherever it wants, we open up the city.

Vacancies occur in the center city because there are families who now can move out but have previously been unable to. At the same time, young white couples come into the center of the city and live alongside black families. That is a big change. It would not have occurred 10 to 15 years ago. As young white people come to the center of the city and black people move to the suburbs, we begin to create an open society for the first time in our history.

In Columbia, we are a very open city—about 20 percent black. It is a city of 8 villages. A study was made by the people of one of the villages to determine the motivation of those moving to Columbia. Sixty-three percent rated open occupancy in housing as "most important" or "important" in their decision. Thus, in the marketing of Columbia, racial openness was a positive advantage—not a disadvantage.

Add up these forces:

- The accumulation of separate center city projects over the last 30 years,
- The special economic development opportunities which are available to the center of the city,
- The change in life style of millions of young couples,
- The environmental and historic preservation forces, energy conservation and lower cost for more space in rehabilitated center city housing,
- And the marvelous change in our understanding of race.

They make the center city a vital place with tremendous opportunities.

We need to understand this new potential. We cannot go on railing against the same old past. There is a new situation today. We must marshall the new forces to help the city be what it best ought to be.

Every city in the United States has resources it is not using and a potential it is not realizing. We need to identify those resources—different in every city. The waterfront is often a special resource, perhaps the most neglected in America.

We are beginning to understand the value of our waterfronts. Our new company, The Enterprise Development Company, is developing a festival marketplace on the waterfront in Norfolk. We are working on a similar project in Toledo. By developing the waterfronts into festival marketplaces we create new vitality in the center city, thousands of new jobs, many for the unemployed and minorities—new personality and new excitement at the heart of the city.

People should be seen as a resource—not as a burden. An IBM executive told me recently that when they opened a plant in New York City, they did it primarily for social purpose. They felt that they ought to help people there who did not have jobs. They struggled with the plant. At first, it was in-efficient. It did not have a favorable earnings ratio. But, he said, today that has changed. "We now know how to train the people and it has become one of the most efficient plants we have. We are doubling its size." That is a lesson for American business. People who are unemployed need work, are capable of learning, and are a resource to be put to use.

But we cannot find solutions for the city by working on a building-by-building, project-by-project, block-by-block basis. We need a new way of thinking. We must stop looking at the city as problems to be attacked, situations to be patched up, and leap beyond the problems to new solutions. We have to raise up rational images of what the city could be—and then work toward them. Cost the program, schedule it. Lay it out over a period not of 100 years, but 10 years, maybe 15. You can almost do anything in the city in 10 years. But we don't yet build those images, and because we do not, we fail to stimulate the kind of support that it takes to make them happen.

By building an image of the possible, we not only leap over a lot of road-blocks that would defeat us, we also generate a whole new constituency of people who want to see that image realized. By creating the image of the rational potential of a city, we generate the power to carry it forward. With-out vision, there is no power. Piece-by-piece, project-by-project, never harnesses the power that is available to the city.

The Exciting Story of Baltimore

Baltimore, the city I know from personal experience, is an example of what can be. A miracle is occurring in that city. Of four cities that are much alike—Baltimore, Pittsburgh, Cleveland, and St. Louis—Baltimore was once the least among them. It did not have the wealth nor was it the home-office headquarters of companies. It had a predominantly blue-collar ethnic and black population. It did not have powerful department stores. It was a worn-out city, little was expected of it. People use to say, "The only time I see Baltimore is when I go through it on a train."

In a handful of years, Baltimore has become a new city. It is a tourist center today. In the space of a week *New York* magazine had Baltimore on its cover as one of six places recommended for New Yorkers to spend a weekend. *Southern Living* had a cover story on Baltimore as a place to spend a vacation and the *Philadelphia Inquirer* had a two-page spread in its magazine section headlined: "Holy Crabcakes, Look What's Happened to Baltimore!"

In 1952, a study was made of the city by a business group that analyzed where the city was headed—the growth in its assessable base and in the cost of services. It drew trend lines that projected the future. It concluded that: "Unless radical action is taken, the municipal corporation faces bankruptcy within a generation."

A small group of young business men went to work to take that "radical action." They created an organization called the Greater Baltimore Committee. It formed a Planning Council to make a new plan for the center of the city. The business community put up the money and the Planning Council set out to replan the 500 acres of the center of the city.

After a few months of work, the planners said, "This is hopeless. We can't find any businesses in Baltimore that have any intention of expanding in the center of the city. How can we produce a rational plan for the future of the center of the city when we cannot find any energy, any hope?"

Finally, it was decided to do the largest, most dramatic, most do-able project that could be designed. Thirty-three acres were carved out of the very heart of the city to become Charles Center. It was planned, announced, given to the city council and passed unanimously. The business community had put its money in it and was providing the leadership. The ordinance to condemn the center of the city was passed. The state legislature, in special session, authorized a bond issue. The voters approved the bond issue and Charles Center went forward.

It was under way when a new mayor was elected. He said, "I want to do the inner harbor"—250 acres immediately adjacent to Charles Center. The planning council was reconstituted and made a plan for the inner harbor. Those two plans covered 283 acres of the center of the city and accounted for 20 years of growth. Despite the original attitude that "my grandchildren will never live to see it," the program gathered momentum. Those big images became believable.

In the past 20 years—in this city that wasn't going anywhere—22 new office buildings have been built and occupied, providing over 8 million square feet of space. There are three new hotels, over 2,000 new apartments, and 7,000 rehabilitated dwelling units. At the center of the city, there has been an expansion of the Peabody Conservatory of Music, the Maryland Institute of Art, the Walters Art Gallery, the University of Maryland, the Mercy Hospital. A new Science Center, a new $50 million Convention Center, one of the finest in the country, and a new National Aquarium have been built and a new "Inner Harbor" has replaced the tumbled-down wreckage of rat-infested docks. The harbor area was so disagreeable that it smelled bad. Today, you can swim in it, you can catch crabs in it. And then Harborplace was built. A festival marketplace by The Rouse Company opened in July of 1980.

Eighteen million people came to the inner harbor of Baltimore the first year of Harborplace and the crowds keep coming—day and night. I go downtown and marvel at the crowds, and often I turn to a friend and say, "Everyone knows you can't get people to come to downtown Baltimore at night."

It's a new life—a whole new spirit, and Baltimore has become a tourist city. Over two million visitors came last year from out of the state. Over 35 percent of the people shopping at Harborplace came from outside the state of Maryland. The aquarium, which is one of the finest in America and maybe in the world, projected 600,000 people the first year and drew 800,000 in the first six months, 1,600,000 the first year. It is extraordinary to see the miracle of Baltimore's turnaround.

The real estate taxes from the area where Charles Center and the Inner Harbor have been developed were $1.5 million 20 years ago—they are over $15 million today, and when the buildings now under development are completed, will be over $20 million. There are three times as many people on the streets of downtown Baltimore as there were 15 years ago. Fifteen thousand new jobs were created in that period of time.

It happened for three reasons:

First was the scale of the plans—images big enough to show what the city might be. It was the building of a big rational image that generated the power to execute it.

Second was the relationship between business and city government, a true public-private partnership. An important part of that was building on the private side—The Greater Baltimore Committee—an organization to carry on, to stay in the action, to monitor, to provide continuity. We have had six mayors during this period, 12 bond issues, and three referenda, all of which were won. This could not have happened if the Greater Baltimore Committee had not been there maintaining responsibility for seeing it happen, year after year, through every crisis.

Third was the organization that was established to develop the plan. There was created outside of city government, but alongside it, a servant of city government, a non-profit organization called the Charles City Inner Harbor Management Corporation. It was headed for many years by a retired department store executive as a dollar-a-year man. It is responsible only to the city, but everyone who comes to work there each morning comes for one reason, and that is to carry forward these two plans—Charles Center and the Inner Harbor. They are not diverted by other responsibilities. Their career success depends on the development of Charles Center and the Inner Harbor. Therefore it is happening.

There is a vital new force operating today that is not widely understood. It is the reduced role of the federal government. It has awakened us in the private sector to new responsibilities. It is doing for us today something like the riots did for us in 1968. The riots constituted the most creative force that has hit the American city in our times. It shook up the board rooms, the council chambers, the politicians, and the civic leaders as nothing else had before. It made us see that people who had suffered too long were not going to take the frustrations any longer. As irrational as it was, it made real the state of mind of millions of people at the heart of our cities.

Harm and Promise in the "Conservative Riots"

We are now in the midst of the "conservative riots" of the 1980s. The business community has said loud and often, "Get the government off our backs." America has said it. It did not start with the Reagan administration. It started perhaps with Proposition 13 in California. It spread to 21 states that have enacted new limitations on spending and taxing and to hundreds of towns and counties. The people of the United States have said that they are tired of big, expensive, inefficient, bureaucratic government. That is the voice that has spoken and is the source of the new more limited relationship between the federal government and the cities.

It is cruel and unjust and it is going to exact terrible penalties. Many people are now suffering from the budget cuts. Many volunteer agencies across the country are going to be liquidated. And we will come to lament the loss. Many unfortunate actions are being taken, but out of the pressures created by the new situation is new hope for the city.

It is the hope that we in the private sector will realize that we have basic responsibility for our cities. It is not something that we can any longer push off on the mayor, or the city council, or the federal government. When business said, "Get the government off our backs," it became morally obligated to take on its backs the responsibility for human needs that would go unmet.

We were in bad shape in American cities before there were any budget cuts. We were doing a poor job of meeting the needs of the poor. We are raising more and more young black men and women in the heart of our cities for whom there was no work. Five years ago unemployment rates were as high as 40 percent in the black ghettos. Millions of young people who were not part of the "system" were without jobs and with no prospects of jobs. They were bent to alcohol and drugs and then to crime to maintain the habit. We have built in this country a jungle world that can eat at the very heart of our society, and so far we have shown little creativity, energy, or capacity for correcting it. We lament our schools, we lament the unemployed, we lament drugs and crime, but we fail to say to ourselves, "This is *our* problem."

When some of us developed the Greater Baltimore Committee 25 years ago, we were dealing with the physical condition of the city, and we did something important about it. But changing the physical condition is not enough. The urgent task now is to meet the social needs of our cities. The city cannot possibly manage that alone. Neither, of course, can business. But the public and private sectors together, along with voluntary agencies, can find the answers. Such gatherings as the Cities' Congress on Roads to Recovery are the potential incubators of the vision we need to make our civilization work.

3

A Banker's View of Redevelopment

Donald E. Lasater

Realistic Idealism Does Work

Bankers are not often asked to be a co-author of a book with urban scholars. Nor do many of us encounter the opportunity to take part in meetings so broadly based and forward looking as the Cities' Congress on Roads to Recovery. I did, both as a speaker and as an actor in the make-believe session described elsewhere in this book by James Kunde in which a mayor, a council president, a developer, a head of a hospital, a neighborhood leader, a manufacturer, a trade union official and I played our occupational roles in a spirited debate about a hypothetical redevelopment in a hypothetical Composite City. The make-believe session did not resolve any of the debated issues and wisely did not pretend to. It is not likely either that this book will resolve controversial issues despite the scholastic distinction of my fellow authors and the fact that we discuss real events. I believe, however, that the Cities' Congress and this book as an aftermath may build confidence in the idea that the recovery of our troubled cities is a practical prospect.

The city I know best is St. Louis. I know it from the perspective gained as chairman of the Mercantile Trust Company, a large regional bank headquartered in the city. I know it also from the related perspective of a long-time member and recent chairman of Civic Progress, Inc., a group of chief executive officers of 30 of the city's largest corporations who meet monthly to promote the purpose described by their group's name. In my role as chairman of the Community Economic Development Policy Board of the American Bankers Association, I have also had occasion to be exposed to the problems of many other cities.

Although many cities have heavily lost population, jobs, and capital investment in housing and other construction, I believe that it is possible to redevelop the cities as attractive and prospering places in which to live and work. In my own efforts to promote this goal, I have tried to be guided by two basic principles. The first is a realistic idealism. The second is patience and perseverance. The self-interest of individuals and institutions is not only inevitable; it is desirable because it is a powerful motivating force. But it needs to be disciplined by a vision of what is good for the community as a whole. Because conflicting interests—even conflicting visions—need to be reconciled and also controlled by what is practical at a given time, large results do not come quickly. Anyone committed to redeveloping a city must have the patience and perseverance to stay the course.

As a percentage of its total population, St. Louis has lost more heavily than any other city. At one time when the great rivers were the main channels of inland transportation, St. Louis was the nation's third largest city, surpassed only by New York and Philadelphia. With the coming of railroads that linked the two oceans, it was surpassed by Chicago, but it was fourth in size as late as 1910. It yielded that place in the next decade to the city that quickly emerged as the manufacturing center of the new automobile industry. Nonetheless, St. Louis continued to grow until it reached its population zenith in 1950 with some 860,000 residents. Today the population is about 450,000—the same as it was in 1890. The metropolitan population is 2,400,000. In a familiar tale, the suburban growth greatly exceeded the city's loss.

To understand how the city could lose almost half its population in 30 years, it is necessary to look back in history to 1876. That was the year when our shortsighted forefathers persuaded the Missouri legislature to give the city the status of a county, thereby fixing its boundaries where they have ever since remained. Only 61 square miles in size, the city-county is bounded on the east by the Mississippi River and is otherwise surrounded by St. Louis County, with which it should not be confused.

The aim of our forefathers was to close the door to further annexations and thereby to force new suburbs to look to themselves for municipal services. An unforeseen consequence was to make St. Louis eventually more of an inner city than any other in the nation. Other major cities have also had large inner-city population losses, but because they had continued to annex longer than St. Louis, their percentage loss has been less dramatic.

The most important news about St. Louis, however, is not the magnitude of its population loss, but the number, size and character of its redevelopments. In number at least, and perhaps also in size and degree of private financing, St. Louis probably leads all other American cities. The jolt of the population loss and the civic determination to redevelop aging neighborhoods may both have roots in the city's history of static boundaries. Whatever the initial impetus, the advanced redevelopments in many neighborhoods and downtown make a fascinating story.

A decade ago the six institutions that comprise the Washington University Medical Center and which among them then had nearly 10,000 employees were confronted with a critical decision. Should they escape the unwholesome environment of their rapidly deteriorating area by moving to suburbs, as two other hospitals had done, or should they stay and protect their future by redeveloping their neighborhood? After some agonizing debates, they decided to stay and to redevelop. The Center created its own non-profit redevelopment corporation. Civic Progress supported it with a $1,000,000 low-interest loan. By 1983 a once-fashionable neighborhood that had decayed and was approaching abandonment by its residents was again an attractive place in which to live. Some 800 housing units had been saved by renovation or had been newly built. Nearly 10,000 jobs were kept in the city and some 5,100 more were brought to the neighborhood, of which about three-quarters appear to have been a net gain for the city.

This impressive achievement is beginning to receive national attention. A year before the Cities' Congress, a 45-member delegation from Cleveland, organized by Richard Taylor of the Cleveland Clinic Foundation, came to St. Louis to see it and other redevelopments. To understand it properly, it is necessary to view it as a part of a redevelopment process that had already begun.

The redevelopment of downtown was well under way when the trustees of the Medical Center institutions were faced with their hard decision. The visual evidence of a resurgent downtown with the promise of more redevelopment to come helped create confidence in the city's future and made it easier for those who still had faith to persuade the doubters. Some people believe that a city's downtown and its neighborhoods are locked into a zero-sum contest and that any public incentives to downtown revival and growth must be at the expense of neighborhoods. The empirical evidence of St. Louis refutes them. New investment downtown has stimulated new investment in neighborhoods—not yet in all, but in enough to reveal the potential of much more neighborhood redevelopment to come. A vigorous downtown helps neighborhoods. I can speak with confidence on this matter since the bank I head is a major lender for redevelopment both downtown and in a growing number of neighborhoods.

A Strategy for Neighborhood Lending

We have formulated both a philosophy and a strategy to guide our neighborhood lending. The central element of the philosophy is a firm and substantial commitment to the inner city and the financing of its redevelopment. We have made it because we are the largest bank in the region and we have no intention to move. By helping to redevelop residential and commercial areas, we can attract new business and new residents to the city and thereby enlarge our base of potential customers. Our lending also helps us to comply in good faith with various governmental regulations such as the Community Reinvestment Act.

In support of that philosophy we have developed the following strategy:

1. Take a leadership role in each area where redevelopment is occurring.

2. Act as a catalyst to involve others.

3. Identify leaders in the redevelopment business and then back them 100 percent. The bank's support will greatly increase their prospects for success.

4. Keep informed about all areas and neighborhoods of the city and get to know their leaders.

5. Be active in the process of city government. Get to know how the community development agency works, who makes the decisions, and the policies and goals of the administration in office.

6. From a political standpoint, seek a diversified redevelopment portfolio, including large residential and commercial projects, individual rehab projects and projects of not-for-profit groups.

7. Don't be afraid to be creative within prudent lending standards.

This general strategy then needs to be tailored to the peculiarities of each area's existing stock, its market and geographic characteristics, and its political environment. We do not attempt to impose a solution of our own, but we do encourage major borrowers to engage an architect who is sensitive to urban neighborhoods and is experienced in redevelopment projects. The importance of tailoring a strategy to specific characteristics is illustrated by our experience in four diverse neighborhoods.

The 400 or so stately houses on and near Lafayette Square were among the city's finest in the late 19th century. By 1976 almost any could be bought for $500, so bad was their state of disrepair and the seeming hopelessness of the neighborhood. Then young professional people began to buy them and to make big investments of sweat-equity to make them serviceable to their needs. We decided to back their initiative and thereby encourage others to follow their lead. Since 1976 my bank has made several hundred loans to the sweat-equity owners totalling over $4,000,000. Construction financing of this kind of renovation has many pitfalls. Borrowers are inexperienced in construction planning and management; inevitably there are cost overruns. The lender is handicapped by the scarcity of comparable examples to give confidence to appraisals. Yet our lending experience in this neighborhood has been excellent because of the character of the borrowers. They are not only willing to make a major commitment to their own property, but to the neighborhood as well. Shells bought for $500 now sell after extensive renovation for $90,000. So successful has been the restoration of the neighborhood that the construction of architecturally compatible new infill housing is now occurring on lots that had been made vacant by demolition. With the return of neighborhood stability has come new lending opportunities for commercial redevelopment.

Flexible Lending Practices

Soulard is believed to be the oldest intact neighborhood west of the Mississippi. Traditionally it has housed immigrants. Although there are some owner-occupied houses, a large proportion of Soulard's residents are housed in rental apartments. The Mercantile Bank has fashioned its lending policy to assist the redevelopment of both. We have financed a substantial number of homeowner rehabs, but our principal lending has been to developers who renovate investment property on a scattered-site basis. They normally have a waiting list for apartments that rent in the range of $250 to $425 per month. Commercial investment has followed the creation of residential stability. One developer has established offices in a former meat-packing plant.

The Hyde Park neighborhood has physical and social characteristics similar to those of Soulard with two important exceptions. It is located on the Northside and its population is integrated. For these reasons it has not attracted the interest in redevelopment that has become common on the Southside and in the western part of the city. My bank has therefore adopted a third neighborhood approach here with the objective of providing a showcase of the rehab potential of the whole neighborhood. Under a special ruling by the Comptroller of the Currency, Mercantile formed a Community Development Corporation and chose Hyde Park for its pilot program. The development corporation has not offered direct financing services, but its provision of soft services is helping to create a credibility for the neighborhood's future that is a necessary step in stimulating investment. The bank has made loans to joint ventures formed by two community organizations to be used to rehab 60 units of HUD Section 8 housing. The city has cooperated by making substantial infusions of block grant funds so that the rental income covers the debt and expenses. The Hyde Park Partnership, consisting of the bank and leaders of the community organizations, stimulates interest in the neighborhood through a professional marketing, research and information program. Through charitable funding by the bank and other local corporations, an office has been established to provide counseling services to current residents and new homeowners.

Still another Mercantile lending practice to promote neighborhood redevelopment is being successfully demonstrated in a 106-acre tract in the western part of the city known as Pershing Land or DeBaliviere Place. Its elegant apartment buildings and spacious single homes were built in the late 1910s and early 1920s. Trolley cars provided good transportation to downtown. For a generation this neighborhood, close to famed Forest Park on the south, was among the most fashionable in the city and its residents supported prospering commercial strips on DeBaliviere and Pershing avenues. In the 1950s and 1960s the neighborhood fell victim to the widespread exodus to new suburbs. By 1975 few residents or merchants remained. Few wished to in the desolation of boarded-up store fronts and apartment buildings.

In that year Leon Strauss, head of the Pantheon Corporation, then a budding redeveloper of inner-city properties, came to the bank with an ambitious plan. He wanted to acquire enough of the deserted properties to control a redevelopment on a scale large enough to turn the whole district around. We agree to back him with a $3,000,000, five-year revolving credit to help finance his acquisitions and administrative costs. For every dollar of subordinated debt raised by Pantheon (from a local insurance company and individuals), we agree to lend three.

In response to Pantheon's plan and the assured financing, the city's Board of Aldermen in the following year established the Pershing Redevelopment Area in accordance with Missouri Statute 353 and designated the Pantheon Corporation to be its developer. This unusual state law authorizes St. Louis and Kansas City to create special redevelopment districts in which they may grant a two-stage tax abatement for 25 years and delegate powers of eminent domain to designated developers. For the first 10 years the assessed value of property being redeveloped is frozen at the value that prevailed in the year preceding redevelopment. At the end of 10 years the property is reassessed and for the next 15 years is taxed on one half of the new valuation. Buyers of redeveloped properties acquire the tax abatement. While the legal procedures of eminent domain must be observed, the delegated power to initiate them reduces both a developer's uncertainties and the opportunities of speculators to hold out for unreasonable prices on strategically located properties.

Statute 353 has given a major boost to redevelopment in St. Louis. Doubters need look only at the number of projects to appreciate its effect as an incentive. It should be noted that most of the direct beneficiaries are the people who already live in the redeveloped district, move to it, or find work in it. A developer benefits directly from tax abatement only while he owns a property he renovates. Much more important is the profit earned from renovation. The lender's benefit comes from the profit on lending. The city gives up no revenues it is already receiving. It simply defers a tax on value added. By doing so, it activates developers, lenders, suppliers, residents, merchants and through a well-known multiplier effect others as well, and their activities bring other income to the treasury of the city while it awaits the deferred taxes on value added.

Like the example of the Washington University Medical Center, the redevelopment undertaken by Leon Strauss is now receiving national attention, and deservedly so. It has four main elements: rehabbing for rental, condo conversion, new residential construction, and commercial revival. The developer has rehabbed some 700 rental units, with 250 more in progress. Approximately 300 have been reserved for subsidized rental under the HUD Section 8 program. There is a long waiting list for both the subsidized and market-rate rental apartments. Some buildings have been converted into condominiums. More than 100 units have been sold at prices averaging about $54,000. Perhaps the most remarkable event is the start of the first new residential subdivision in the city in more than 50 years. It is taking place where there had been extensive demolition of abandoned properties. The new construction, already well under way, will consist of 100 duplex units around a new park, Kingsbury Square. Prices range from $80,000 for a 3-bedroom unit to $100,000 for a 4-bedroom unit. In this instance too, market acceptance has been good despite the recession.

The need for patience and perseverance has been amply demonstrated in a major downtown project that the Mercantile Bank initiated. In 1971 we were operating our bank headquarters from five separate and highly inefficient buildings in downtown St. Louis. We were located in the retail section near two major department stores, Famous-Barr, a division of the May Company, and Stix Baer and Fuller, a division of Associated Dry Goods.

While the department stores were doing reasonably well, the two retail blocks between them were deteriorating rapidly and the quality of many of the smaller retailers was declining. We needed a new building both for our own use and to stabilize the declining area around us. Since banks are prohibited by law from being in the development business, we sought out established developers as potential partners. After nine months' search, 20 interviews, and a number of on-site examinations, we succeeded in attracting a highly successful developer then operating primarily in Atlanta, Texas, and Florida. A partnership agreement was signed, architects engaged, and the planning completed. In October of 1972, we announced a redevelopment plan for six blocks in the retail area of downtown St. Louis. The plan included a 36-story Mercantile Bank tower, a three-level atrium retail mall covering two blocks between the department stores, two office buildings, and a major hotel.

Construction began on the office tower in 1973 and it was completed on time and on budget at the end of 1975. One of the best hotel chains in the country gave a luncheon for 150 St. Louis leaders to announce plans to construct an 800-room world-class hotel. Unfortunately, our timing was exactly wrong. The real estate crisis of 1975–76 roared in and there was no institution interested in financing a new hotel. Our partners had to consolidate their positions to raise cash, and so we bought their interest in the project. Since then a lot of studies and reviews were made, but there was no real action until 1981. Melvin Simon & Associates of Indianapolis, a major owner-developer of shopping malls, entered the project and involved the May Company as a limited partner. They have developed a plan for a retail mall and office combination which, like many other projects of this scale, is extremely complex in its ownership and financing. It is also a classical example of a public-private partnership for the good of a city.

The total project involves three city blocks. One block will contain a 1450-car garage with retail stores occupying 80 percent of the first floor. (This is now completed and occupied.) The garage will be owned by the city's Land Clearance Redevelopment Authority. The other two blocks will be a four-level enclosed retail mall stretching from Famous-Barr to Stix and including some 120 retail shops. Financing for the project involves partners' equity, land purchase by the Redevelopment Authority, an $18,000,000 UDAG grant, a $35,000,000 permanent loan by an insurance company, $3,000,000 in public improvements by the city, and $31,000,000 in 34-year bonds purchased by the city's two largest banks. Construction is now in progress and the Centre is expected to open for business in May of 1985.

The last block in the 1972 Redevelopment Plan will be occupied by the headquarters building of Edison Bros. Stores, Inc. Construction of this 450,000-square-foot office building was started early in 1983 and completion is expected in early 1985. This six-block project demonstrates that redevelopment, whether downtown or in neighborhoods, requires inventiveness.

Teamwork Is Indispensable

Useful lessons can be drawn from the diverse examples I have discussed. The most important lesson is that a team effort is indispensable. Developers, bankers, community organizations, and the city must each do what they are best qualified to do, and unless each performs its function, not much will happen. Within the framework of mutual confidence, developers must take risks. So must bankers, although as custodians of depositors' money we cannot take risks in the same degree. Nor do federal and state laws permit it. Parties that risk incurring losses must be allowed a profit if they make sound judgements and manage their business well. Community organizations representing a neighborhood's residents must be listened to with respect and their cooperation sought. The city government must show its confidence in the neighborhood or other area by coordinating needed street improvements and other public amenities with the private investment. Together, developers, bankers, community organizations and the city government need to create a vision of what a redeveloped neighborhood will be and then persevere until it is achieved. There is also an essential federal role. Until the recovery process is much further advanced, city governments, in order to do their part, will need UDAG and community development block grants or similar assistance. However, the most important stimulus government can give to private-sector risk-taking will be incentives that provide for a sharing of benefits to be created by the redevelopment, such as authorized by Missouri's Statute 353.

There was an exciting time in the history of St. Louis when it was the gateway to the development of half a continent. The soaring, 60-story Gateway Arch designed by Eero Saarinen commemorates that period. For the many of us now engaged in the city's redevelopment, it is again an exciting time. We must give to the effort a special dedication. We must accept frequent frustrations. But when we are able to look back upon tangible achievements, as already we can, the feeling of satisfaction and the comfort of future strength is more than enough reward. I suggest that what is happening in St. Louis today is a gateway to the recovery of American cities.

4

Private Efforts to Initiate
Neighborhood Recovery

Rolf Goetze

Subtle Elements of Equilibrium

In healthy neighborhoods there is homeostasis, a balance of many invisible influences encouraging residents and owners to maintain and fix up their communities. Homeostasis is a medical concept, denoting the balance of many forces joining to maintain an organism's equilibrium, that urban planners should learn more about. Outside forces can only work at the margins, and if they distort expectations—for example through promising more low interest loans than will ever be provided—then they easily derange the many subtle forces that are vital at any neighborhood maintaining itself. Outside interveners must be careful to help, but not upset, the intricate inner-workings of any community.

This chapter looks at neighborhood revitalization from a fresh angle, asking how private corporations can help coordinate the behavior of many diverse interests. In a lasting neighborhood recovery, these interests must collaborate, instead of acting independently or at cross purposes. This chapter first lays out some necessary conditions for a sustained recovery, then illustrates them with two examples of privately spurred revitalization in order to develop some general inferences helpful to promoters of recovery elsewhere. It concludes that the process involves more than the physical restoration that past public approaches pursued. Nor is it enough to promote urban living, market neighborhood image, bring in new residents, and unleash market forces. Existing residents must also be involved in the process, and public subsidies are still needed wherever actual housing costs are unaffordable to existing residents. Above all, private interests must avoid simply replacing the public assistance that has been withdrawn. Instead, they must pioneer new ways to motivate residents towards increased self-reliance in order to achieve a lasting urban recovery.

Necessary Conditions for a Sustained Recovery

A lot of effort is required to maintain communities, ranging from the ordinary—simply cleaning windows, raking leaves, and removing trash—to upgrading and replacing whole dwellings in a timely, efficient manner. To keep neighborhoods healthy, a host of interests at both the macro and neighborhood levels must be orchestrated.

Know-how, money, labor and materials, and the residents must all be brought together in appropriate ways to maintain communities and upgrade neighborhoods. Deficiencies in any one of these ultimately require considerably more to remedy later on. Because ordinary maintenance requires much less effort than substantial restoration, it obviously makes sense to replace a roof before water gets in and damages the internal structure. Yet such timely actions were not often encouraged in past assistance programs; instead these tended towards the dramatic face-lift.

In many urban neighborhoods, a "throw-away" mentality has come to interfere with proper maintenance, causing not only people to treat housing like old cars, but even some people to treat others as trash or "throw-aways." If lenders redline and absentee owners turn into slumlords and disinvest, then those interests have failed to play appropriate roles. Investing and owning must then be modified in ways that restore homeostasis, including more constructive future investment and maintenance efforts.

Neighborhoods are the face of their communities. If they are in ill health as a result of insufficient resident employment, not enough real housing demand, or too many residents who feel unneeded, this cannot long be disguised. Revitalization efforts can achieve little if they address only symptoms like peeling paint, and if they ignore or even mask underlying community problems like a weak employment base poorly matched to residents' skills or a "crime" stigma weakening future demand for living space within a neighborhood. When neighborhoods become unattractive to new residents, existing residents spread out to fill vacancies. As individual household incomes drop, disinvestment worsens. Past public programs too often fostered only cosmetic fix-up which failed to address the underlying problems of inadequate demand and limited household incomes.

Nevertheless, concern is widespread that federal budget cuts harmed the many local revitalization efforts that were dependent on community development block grants. It is more productive to ask what made these communities so increasingly dependent on assistance. To what extent did local know-how, money, labor, materials, or motivation take part in revitalization? Too often the federal assistance provided in past public approaches ignored local inputs. Was past assistance promoting real pump-priming efforts to make these communities more self-reliant, or was it only inducing more dependence on subsidies and below-market loans?

The potential for neighborhood revitalization now increases daily. The rate of creating new suburban subdivisions has slowed, and lifestyles are changing. As new supply shrinks, urban demand is increasing, opening new opportunities. In place of the glut of tract homes and cheap energy of the early 1970s which spurred the "throw-away" mentality, there are now shortages. Many more households have formed, causing existing housing to be revalued. New lifestyles are refurbishing the image of city living, enhancing it over suburbia.[1] As waves of new demand enter existing neighborhoods, revitalization is spurred. The challenge lies in enabling incumbent residents to share in the benefits instead of moving out, only to find that marginal hand-me-down housing no longer filters to them as in the past.

True housing costs are now sobering to any who move, owners and tenants alike.[2] This sobering of expectations will induce many upon moving to choose more European living patterns: closer in, fewer square feet, and more emphasis on durability and quality. Nevertheless, too many deteriorating neighborhoods are still being treated as "throw-aways." There, demand remains weak, residents lack income and know-how, and too many still count on the subsidies promised by the Great Society, expecting government to provide decent housing at one-quarter of household income. Even though the challenge is greatest in the most disadvantaged neighborhoods, this is not the place to begin. Acrimony and desperation there may still increase because the know-how, resources, materials, labor, and motivation are variously lacking and cannot yet be orchestrated towards recovery. However, much can now be learned from some situations where the recovery process is already taking hold.

The following examples were among the cases presented at the Cities' Congress. They can serve as meaningful illustrations to conceptualize effective recovery strategies for similar, run-down urban neighborhoods elsewhere.

For each example the key questions relate to its universality. In what ways is each successful? How is it limited? Could the same be done elsewhere or is it suitable only in particular contexts?

Cinderella, the Brooklyn Union Gas

Since the late 1960s, Brooklyn Union Gas, a public utility, has been fighting for its part of New York—Brooklyn, Queens, and Staten Island—because it could not "pick up its pipelines and run." It has sought ways to encourage private investment and to convince business to move in and grow within its service area.

Park Slope is a prominent Brooklyn neighborhood within its territory that declined after the Second World War. Hard-pressed owners carved up their massive brownstones into rooming houses or boarded them up as their tenants flowed from the city to the surrounding ocean of suburbia. Early in the 1960s newcomers began to trickle in from Manhattan and Brooklyn Heights to the north and even from Queens to the east.[3] Some were architects, with a purist's determination to preserve the past; others saw free-wheeling opportunities in buying and modifying the houses needing more work. Preservationists and renovators did not always see eye to eye, but jointly they began the process of turning Park Slope around.

What makes this section of Brooklyn so desirable? Both its location adjoining Prospect Park and the quality of its original housing, as shortages of good housing close by Manhattan emerged. Already in 1963 inmovers from Brooklyn Heights like Everett and Evelyn Ortner helped form the Brownstone Revival Committee and began promoting Park Slope. Brooklyn Union Gas quickly became their ally. Together the Revival Committee and the gas company attacked the neighborhood's decline on two fronts: image and investment.

In 1966 Brooklyn Union Gas began the Cinderella project by buying an abandoned brownstone for $15,000 on an upper block of Berkeley Place. This was the first of some twenty such projcts in fringe areas, carefully chosen for their potential impact in the neighborhood—and Brooklyn Union's gas sales. Instead of allowing vacant buildings to be leveled, Brooklyn Union Gas chose to demonstrate that structurally sound housing could be transformed from tax burdens into tax producers, without much public assistance, at a cost 40 percent below building from scratch.

Around this time a delegation from the Brownstone Revival Committee persuaded Chase Manhattan to reconsider the mortgage risks of lending in Park Slope, an area redlined by conventional lenders. Then in the early 1970s, the New York City Landmarks Commission designated a quarter of Park Slope, some 19,000 structures, as a historic district. This lending turnaround, linked with historic district designation, spurred a wave of new settlers during the 1970s, not so much family people, but childless couples and singles. As house prices soared, co-ops appeared. In 1979, for the first time, a home sold for over $200,000.

More intent on upgrading "place" than helping people, Brooklyn Union Gas and the preservationists sought to attract tax-paying middle and upper income people back into once fashionable residential areas, to stabilize them and act like a blood transfusion. By renovating vacant and neglected Brooklyn houses into showcases of elegant brownstone living, Project Cinderella opened people's eyes. It was promoted by the local media at just the right time and place to ride the crest of the gentrification wave.

Brooklyn Union Gas was convinced that the need for liveable housing could be met by brownstones improved through private efforts. As a utility, it could not go into the building business, so it chose instead to interest builders, investors, banks, and the media to play the roles to which each is best suited. By the Cinderella approach, fixing up vacant homes and stores—here and there, first in Brooklyn and then in Queens, and again in Staten Island—and turning them into housing or a new branch office, Brooklyn Union Gas selects key buildings that confront people and cause them to reconsider their urban assumptions. Thus, it makes a critical difference. It has also helped the area by developing techniques for retaining and expanding local businesses and attracting new ones.

Consistently, Brooklyn Union Gas has been a mover in presenting a positive image of its territory, building confidence in the area's future, and attracting people, business, and investments. Upon several occasions, the company has even arranged local media blitzes and advertising promotions of Brooklyn in the *Wall Street Journal* and on the local radio networks.

Even though many today deride such efforts as simply "promoting gentrification/displacement," this boosterism by the resident utility has helped Brooklyn's image enormously. It has demonstrated significant ways in which private initiatives can spark vital changes in attitudes, leading to new bootstrap community efforts.

Recently, Brooklyn Union Gas has begun to focus increasingly on helping small businesses already in its territory to expand and grow, as well as to participate in job creation and training initiatives within the local private industry council.

Brooklyn Union Gas makes recovery look simple. While some might argue that it makes things look better than they are, the contribution of promoting positive attitudes should not be belittled. However, in other cities without Brooklyn's favorable situation and demographic tide, achieving a lasting recovery is more complex. In any case, revitalization should involve the residents already there more fully. Promotional names were often chosen in other revitalization cases as well, like Renaissance in Columbus and Jubilee in Washington, D.C. (see Chapters 5 and 7) and this seems effective. However, promoting "a population transfusion," as Michael Teatum of Brooklyn Union Gas calls it, easily results in pushing previous residents aside, making them feel even more "trashed" or "throwed away."

Whenever there is a substantial influx of newcomers, care must be taken to avoid a backlash by existing residents. In the nitty-gritty of urban recovery, it is always important to note whether it is "people" or "place" that is recovering. In Fort Wayne, the business emphasis is on helping prior residents become homeowners.

Lincoln Life in Fort Wayne

Context is important to understand the Lincoln Life Improved Housing (LLIH) program. Fort Wayne, Indiana, is a city of 172,000, losing blue collar employment and rising in unemployment. With 107 formally recognized neighborhood groups, East Central is one of the stronger associations. Even so, this inner-city neighborhood has declined from 10,600 people in 1960, half black–half white, to 4,500 in 1980, four-fifths black. Note that even the total black population has declined. From 1960 to 1980, total housing units dropped by 40 percent from 3,400 to 2,200 units. Currently, only one-third are owner occupied and one-quarter are vacant. Sales prices here average $5,000 in a city where $50,000 is average.

East Central experienced massive outmigration, disinvestment, high vacancy rates, unemployment, and has no public school and little adjacent shopping—only bars and poolhalls nearby. Formerly housing the middle and upper class, the surrounding area acquired a poor public image because of much physical deterioration. Unlike Park Slope, a turn in the demographic tide has not yet begun.

Since 1973, Lincoln National Corporation, the parent of Lincoln National Life Insurance Company and several other U.S. and European insurance companies, has created a program designed to provide resident low- and moderate-income families the opportunity to become homeowners and thereby preserve neighborhoods in Fort Wayne, its headquarters city.

Lincoln National, as a major local employer with considerable corporate clout, decided to make a "visible and lasting impact" in its own backyard. Careful study led to the selection of a six-square block area, East Central, as a demonstration site. The area's 105 single family houses, many in disrepair or boarded up and abandoned by absentee landlords, were mostly still structurally sound. Some were even in good shape despite surrounding neighborhood conditions.

Guided by the notion of capturing some federal tax benefits to offset rehab costs, Lincoln National formed a for-profit subsidiary, Lincoln Life

Improved Housing, Inc. (LLIH), to buy, rehabilitate, lease, and later to sell homes to low- and moderate-income households. Under Section 167K of the Internal Revenue Code, LLIH is thereby eligible for a five-year depreciation tax write-off of up to $20,000 in rehab costs for each rental unit.

Vacant houses in the target area were available for $2,000 to $4,000 from the absentee owners eager to sell property no longer generating any income. LLIH bought these and then negotiated with a local contractor to redo each property from top to bottom after "gutting" the structure down to its studs, roof and outside walls. Installing new plumbing and wiring, new furnace and heating systems, hot water tanks, new siding and insulation, completely modern kitchens and baths, and carpeted living areas typically cost between $18,000 and $22,000.

To help pay for this, LLIH arranged a $500,000 financing pool with the five major Fort Wayne banks, which provided fifteen-year mortgages at lower than conventional rates upon completion, covering roughly half the purchase and rehab costs. LLIH then acts as mortgagor for the first five years, receiving the tax benefits while leasing the houses to carefully selected low- and moderate-income families (average income $8,000 per year) who desire to become homeowners. Their rental payments, averaging $125 monthly, cover the mortgage, taxes, insurance costs, and a maintenance charge. During these first five years, families are only responsible for ordinary wear and tear; major items like furnace, hot water, or roof problems are handled by LLIH.

At the end of five years, the resident household becomes the owner, paying one dollar for the property. It then assumes full responsibility for homeownership and the outstanding 10-year mortgage, but its monthly expenses remain at levels comparable to renting.

By late 1982, LLIH had housed over 70 families (with over 150 children) and half were single-parent households. Forty homes were already under ownership by the tenant-purchaser and LLIH began to expand into a contiguous twelve block area in the center of the city. There has been only one mortgage default, involving a divorce and family split. Here LLIH will take back the house from the bank, pay off the mortgage, restore the house and continue with a new family.

One of the completed homes is the LLIH office, furnished as a model home and also used as an office by Mrs. Howe, a social worker. Mrs. Howe interviews applicants desiring to become homeowners in their current homes, checks on their job stability and then makes recommendations to the LLIH screening committee which, based on her analysis, decides which people will be offered the opportunity to enter the program.

Lincoln National has put $750,000 into the program in the last nine years, which has actually cost it some $350,000 after considering the tax consequences. Beyond that, Lincoln National also provides a full-time social worker, a part-time construction superintendent, and the guiding genius of Harlan K. Holly, conceptualizer of the whole program while general counsel of the Lincoln National Life Corporation and president of LLIH.

Two years after LLIH started its efforts, the city designated East Central as one of its original neighborhood strategy areas, due to its strong neighborhood association. Of the city's annual $2.5 million in community development block grant funds, some $1 million is earmarked for neighborhood capital improvements. For East Central this has meant $125,000 towards repaving, new curbs, sidewalks, street lighting, and putting wiring underground. To further improve the area LLIH prevailed upon local concrete manufacturers to donate materials to provide parking slabs for everyone on one street wanting them, even those not in the LLIH program.

Now the city acquires properties after joint inspection with LLIH and deeds them over to LLIH. It also markets its paint-up, insulation and home improvement loan programs in the area and has promoted neighborhood clean-up to complement the impact of the Lincoln Life initiative. To deal with the vacant lots, the city has created some vest-pocket parks and in one instance intends to move a house from nearby onto a vacant lot in the neighborhood, which LLIH will also rehabilitate.

As the public image of East Central improves, new residents committed to homeownership are forging alliances with private and public interests to handle challenges as they arise. Trust between all the interests involved in maintaining this neighborhood is now growing, putting it clearly on the way to recovery. Nevertheless, each home still costs Lincoln National several thousand dollars in direct subsidies. It is also important to realize that LLIH focusses on helping *employed* families attain homeownership and that East Central is one area where homebuying is still affordable. Without this private backing and the public subsidies, this venture could not continue. Nor can this concept help more distressed families, or people preferring to remain tenants. LLIH's president, Harlan Holly, emphasizes that only "in-between" neighborhoods are suitable to this approach, not the areas "completely deteriorated, beyond rehabilitation."

Lincoln Life ingeniously coordinates a host of interests, using only limited subsidies. Section 167K is utilized well outside the congressional intent which was to induce private investors into rehabilitating multi-family apartments. Here the five-year lease period assures that builder, investor, owner, and residents deal fairly with one another, and do not take shortcuts or use inferior materials. The normal adversary relationship between tenant and developers is transformed because the renter knows he is not contributing to the developer's profits. The Lincoln Life approach also forces out absentee owners, unscrupulous contractors and families not committed to ownership. In all these ways the Lincoln Life approach fosters neighborhood homeostasis — even if it cannot help more distressed areas, create more jobs, or aid those who wish to remain tenants.

Conclusion

We are on the threshhold of a new approach to neighborhood revitalization, linking private, public, and community interests in new ways. These two examples only permit us to glimpse the new directions. For too long, neighborhood health was judged symptomatically, equating new with "good" and old with "bad." Because this oversimplified matters, public attempts to face-lift old neighborhoods with subsidized loans and grants often failed to stimulate a lasting recovery. Instead, they made untreated homes look even shabbier while increasing resident expectations and urban dependence on more assistance.

Confidence is emerging as a critical, but previously neglected, factor in local recovery—both confidence in the overall urban future as well as in each particular neighborhood. This future view involves the hearts and minds of all the affected interests including the present residents. Revitalization that brings in too many new residents without helping those already there, boosts confidence but also raises resident fears of displacement.

Restoring urban housing demand through Brooklyn Union Gas-style promotions boosts that neighborhood confidence, and can help persuade existing owners to stop treating their housing like a throw-away. While this improves the housing it will also raise housing costs. Living in an area of disinvestment costs relatively little only because the main housing expenses are utilities, while maintenance costs are ignored. Proper maintenance costs more, requiring more rent.

Turnover and financing at new values raises housing expenses even more. To the extent that there are newcomers and new ownership, especially in strong demand areas, few previous tenants will be able to afford to remain, and fewer still will be able to buy without subsidies. Tenants are all too easily pushed aside by market forces in such areas unless special provisions for their accommodation are made *in advance*.

In weak market areas, more skilled guidance and technical assistance may enable some to become homeowners, but even here some subsidies are required, as the Lincoln Life Housing example in Fort Wayne indicates. In general, helping residents who do *not* wish to become homeowners requires yet deeper subsidies and more resourcefulness, as the Jubilee example in Washington, D.C. illustrates. In any case, tenants in coming years will be called upon to shoulder more responsibilities for managing, operating, and even buying their housing on a cooperative basis—and to double up to meet true housing costs if new subsidies are not forthcoming.

Private know-how and community participation, coupled with public subsidies and much patience seem the most promising combination for initiating a lasting neighborhood recovery. There are no easier ways. A flood of newcomers entering without subsidies and a lack of resident involvement will only shift and exacerbate the plight of prior residents, revitalizing place but not people. Boosterism, however, when it comes from the community, can help. A credible upbeat image—provided by such names as Cinderella, Renaissance and Jubilee—seems important to persuade everyone including outsiders that recovery is on its way.

Of course, the dangers are that a new name can be created and subsidies applied unimaginatively, without the patient work shown in these examples to carefully and properly orchestrate all the interests. In that case there will be not lasting recovery but only further disillusionment, disappointed expectations, and eventually an even deeper dependence on more subsidies.

New housing demand can be channeled to promote physical regeneration but this will not automatically help prior residents. Few in this country yet grasp how difficult it remains to develop communities that truly involve and support their weaker members. In spite of promising spurts of urban revitalization now occurring in parts of many cities, decently housing the disadvantaged remains a formidable challenge everywhere. It cannot be done without the kind of dedication and sincere commitment shown in these examples, but it will also require substantial public support for new, more flexible forms of housing assistance.

5

Non-Profit Institutions
and Urban Revitalization

Dale F. Bertsch

Elements Specific to Non-Profits

The search for urban revitalization programs that work quite naturally leads to an examination of non-profit or not-for-profit[1] institutions. While churches, hospitals, universities, and foundations have always been a major part of the urban fabric, the importance of these institutions in determining the character and quality of a neighborhood or a city is growing: there are more of them; they have more assets; and they have more physical plants. With the city government and for-profit business, non-profits must be part of revitalization programs.

Three examples of non-profit institutions rising to the challenge are the Renaissance program in Columbus, Ohio, sponsored by the Battelle Memorial Institute; the Yale University program in New Haven, Connecticut; and Washington University Medical Center's role in St. Louis. In each case, these are part of a much broader redevelopment effort. This chapter, however, deals with non-profit organization programs and not the general redevelopment programs of these cities.

The three programs will be examined in light of several important factors.

1. *Replicability*: A major concern with offering these examples of non-profit activities in urban revitalization is that each describes a unique institution with a unique role in its community. Certainly there are no other Battelles. Even Harvard is different from Yale. While the exact situations described here will not occur again, many hospitals, private universities,

and foundation centers occupy similar amounts of space in similar urban settings. What should be of concern here is how non-profits behave, what triggers their participation in such projects, and the distinctions among non-profits and other actors in urban revitalization.

2. *Roles and Characteristics of Non-Profits*: There are several characteristics of non-profits that should be kept in mind in considering their role in urban revitalization.

• *They are not charities and should not be expected to behave as such.* Like a private business, they will be primarily concerned with carrying out their charter, whatever it is, and only secondarily with urban revitalization and only then when it helps and does not jeopardize the institution. Regardless of their wealth, non-profits cannot be expected to foot the bill just because they are wealthy.

• *Their decision-making structures are less complicated and easier than public ones.* It is easier to get a complicated idea or project before the board of a non-profit than a comparable public board or city.

• *They tend to be more anchored to their present location than do businesses.* Retailing can move to the suburbs and manufacturing can move to Korea, but most non-profits are tied to their city and even neighborhood because of their charter, their historical image, or their work. Of the three institutions reviewed here, only one had any real relocation option. The key is to help non-profits build bridges to their community rather than walls that shut them off from it.

None of the organizations described here had to undertake the kind of revitalization program that they did. Indeed, in each case their new role represents a change in behavior and a new concept of the organization's role and responsibility in its community.

3. *The Role of Federal Funds*: One concern in looking at innovative projects of the past 20 years is whether they were dependent for their success on either federal funding or tax code provisions. This appeared to be more of a problem when the Reagan Administration took office than it has turned out to be. While funds have been cut and there is less to aid low- and moderate-income persons, there are still many ways to fund a good and imaginative project.

Indeed, the Economic Recovery and Tax Act of 1981, added many new tools. Some of these, such as sale and lease-back of non-profit facilities are being seriously questioned as to whether they serve a valid public purpose or are merely a treasury raid on behalf of the rich.

Nonetheless, as of this writing, availability of federal funds and programs should not serve as an impediment to designing and implementing a good, non-profit project.

Renaissance, Columbus and the
Battelle Memorial Institute

The Battelle Memorial Institute (BMI) is an internationally known scientific research foundation. It was founded in Columbus in the 1920s through a bequest of Gordon Battelle, a local industrialist.[2] Although BMI now has four major laboratories, two of which are in Europe, its headquarters and major facility is in Columbus, Ohio, on a large site which abuts the Ohio State University campus. The management of the foundation has never wavered from the position that its business is scientific and industrial research and that its activities are to be operated like a business.

In the past several decades, few Battelle employees lived in the surrounding neighborhood. However, the institution dominated a 22-block area immediately south of the Ohio State University campus, east of the Olentangy River and west of Neil Avenue.[3] This is a largely residential area, part of which is called the Near Northside of Columbus. It was developed at the end of the nineteenth century as a prestigious single-family neighborhood. The housing is predominately Queen Anne, Richardson, and Eastlake styles of Victorian architecture. However, in the southern part of this area, architecturally undistinguished, small, wooden frame homes predominate. Many of these cannot economically be brought up to the housing code.

After World War II, like many similar areas across the country, the neighborhood changed from owner-occupied to renter-occupied. The housing deteriorated. By the 1970s, the area was comprised of OSU students and low- and moderate-income families. It was perceived as a high-crime district. Most of the larger homes were subdivided and rented. Tenant turnover approached 80 percent annually.

In the late 1960s, Battelle began to buy properties in the area in order to assure its ability to expand. There was no particular pattern to these acquisitions in either quality, style, or location. BMI simply bought what came on the market. They were in a financial position to do so. If the building was rentable, it was rented. If it was not up to housing code standards, it was torn down and the lot left empty. By the mid 1970s, Battelle owned approximately 65 percent of the low-rent housing in a 100-acre spread adjacent to its headquarters. In 1976 these 533 residential properties were valued at $6 million.

In the mid-1970s, Battelle changed its property ownership policies for the neighborhood. There were several reasons for this. First, the Institute realistically examined its property needs in the area. Second, the properties had become a substantial liability to the organization. In 1975, Battelle had been required, under a court settlement, to distribute most of its liquid assets to local charities.[4] It no longer was in a position to own property that did not pay its way. Finally, the property created an image problem for the laboratory. Rightly or wrongly, it was seen by Columbus residents as being an aloof slum lord. These views were particularly strongly held by residents of the immediate area. Battelle decided to dispose of the properties in a way that was both socially responsible and which would recoup its investment.

In 1976, to carry out this task, Battelle created a for-profit subsidiary— Olentangy Management Corporation. Battelle could have either leveled the properties or sold them. Instead it decided to rehabilitate the property and the neighborhood. The program was dubbed "Renaissance."[5] OMC employed a rehabilitation and construction supervisor, an accountant, a public relations director, a tenant assistance officer, a rental agent, and sale and maintenance forces to carry out the 10-year, $22.5 million project.

The program began with a detailed feasibility study conducted by a private local development firm. Its study indicated that a significant number of the residents wanted to remain in the neighborhood. Moreover, there was a strong prospective demand among the professionals and employees at Battelle, OSU, and other area organizations in the neighborhood if it could be stabilized and improved.

The program required a partnership between public and private organizations. As was true of the housing, public facilities had deteriorated. Parks, street rehabilitation, and cul-de-sacs were needed for amenities and to make the neighborhood attractive to present-day urban residents. Significant public investment in public facilities would be essential. It was also clear that residents and area institutions would have to be involved and that diverse interests and concerns would have to be balanced out. A formal community-participation process began in the first year of the project.

OMC organized community meetings. Suggestions were requested and these were incorporated in a negotiation document. In August 1977, after a year of planning and analysis by OMC and its consultants, and in conjunction with the city government and neighborhood groups, a consensus was reached on a plan of action. The resulting "Neighborhood Development Implementation Plan" identified a two-phase plan for the revitalization of the neighborhood, which included the following objectives:

- partially renovate and insulate 125 Victorian homes;
- fully renovate another 54 Victorian homes;
- pre-sell and build 67 medium-price houses on vacant lots;
- prepare for a 20-acre expansion of the Battelle complex, moving 11 houses, and relocating a street;
- construct a street, improve traffic flow, and landscape public areas;
- develop a shopping center for the neighborhood;

- develop a tenant-purchase program;
- target 79 houses for low- and moderate-income households;
- assist in tenant relocation;
- encourage the development of government assisted housing, including 33 units for the elderly.

Residents and resident organizations had expressed concern that OMC and Battelle's plans would encourage gentrification and do nothing for low- and moderate-income residents. Part of this stemmed from long-standing suspicions of Battelle's motives, not surprisingly in view of its previous property acquisitions and management policies.

The city was neutral. City officials, of course, favored neighborhood improvement, but had not become actively involved in the gentrification issue. Furthermore, with many demands for rehabilitation funds, the city was concerned about how it could provide public improvements needed in the area.

To meet neighborhood concerns, OMC offered to provide relocation payments for those displaced, to donate four houses to Near Northside Housing Corporation as demonstration projects for low-income rehabilitation, and to seek federal funds that might be used to meet both the public-facility needs and permit broader social objectives for the project. The Near Northside Housing Corporation was created in the mid-1970s to assist in housing rehabilitation for low- and moderate-income families. It became a major force in the revitalization program.

The search for federal funds produced a proposal for an Innovative Grant from the Department of Housing and Urban Development. The city of Columbus was the applicant. The proposal was submitted in January of 1978 and approved in September of that year for slightly over $2 million. It was the largest such grant ever made by the federal department. The funds were evenly split between tenant-assistance programs and infrastructure improvements. The tenant assistance was intended to help low-income area homeowners to upgrade their property and to convert some 125 to 150 properties for sale to low- and moderate-income individuals. Funds were also available for relocation assistance.

The low- and moderate-income assistance program encountered difficulties from the beginning. OMC felt the goal of 125 to 150 houses was too ambitious in light of the highly transient population in the area. As a result of the difficulties encountered in carrying out this portion of the grant and protracted discussions among the resident association, the city, the federal government, and OMC, a number of modifications were made in the program, principally shifting away from direct grants to using the Near Northside Housing Corporation as the principal vehicle for assisting low- and moderate-income residents.

OMC moved forward with the major aspect of the revitalization plan involving the clearance and relocation, housing rehabilitation and construction. It acted as an overall management agency using private developers for the actual bricks and mortar work. Now with the end of the six-year project nearly at hand, it is possible to look at what happened. Physically, the results are impressive. The neighborhood has been upgraded and one can see the results. OMC has improved and sold over 200 homes. About 30 new homes have been built on vacant lots. The city has carried out the street-relocation improvement projects. On the low- and moderate-income side of the ledger, the results are equally impressive. NNHC bought 130 homes from the Olentangy Management Corporation, rehabilitated them using the funds from the Innovative Grant and other federal assistance programs, and sold them to low- and moderate-income tenants.

Washington University Medical Center, St. Louis

The Washington University Medical Center's role in revitalizing the St. Louis neighborhood in which it is located was selected as an example of non-profit activities for several reasons:

• Scale: This is one of the largest non-profit projects, involving over 1,200 dwelling units and over 500,000 square feet of retail and office space.
• It is replicable from an institutional standpoint as many larger cities have similar medical complexes in similar urban settings.
• Government funding was kept to a minimum, with the primary government impetus being Missouri's redevelopment law.

The involved area developed at the turn of the century, in part spurred by the St. Louis World Fair.[6] It is west of the city's central business district and originally consisted primarily of large, single-family homes for middle- and upper-middle-income groups. Later, commercial and institutional buildings were developed in the neighborhood. The area is bounded to the west by one of the largest urban parks in the country (1,200 acres).

Like many such areas, decline began in the post-World War II period. The single-family homes were broken up into apartments. Retail merchants moved to the suburbs following the residents of the area. The crime rate increased.

At the same time the complex of medical and medical-education facilities centering around Washington University grew. By 1960 it was one of the largest in the nation.

Also by 1960, some of the medical institutions considered relocating to the suburbs. Indeed, two of the private hospitals did move. The remaining institutions balanced the major costs of such a move and the disastrous impact the loss of 10,000 jobs would have on St. Louis against the cost of revitalization and developed a different answer. They decided to stay and to change the neighborhood.

A key organization in St. Louis's redevelopment efforts was Civic Progress.[7] Organized in 1953, it is a looser-knit and less-formal institution than those which evolved in many cities. It consists of the chief executive officers of principal area businesses and, ex-officio, key government and civic leaders. Civic Progress viewed itself as having two functions: to be a forum for civic action and discussion; and to support a broad-based plan to improve the quality of life in the city.

Washington University played a major role in this public-private partnership. In 1962, under the leadership of Chancellor William Danforth, it formed the Washington University Medical Center, consisting of six of the seven medical institutions in the area—the Barnard Free Skin and Cancer Hospital, Barnes Hospital, Jewish Hospital of St. Louis, St. Louis Children's Hospital, Central Institute for the Deaf, and Washington University School of Medicine.[8] The center now has a budget of over $400 million annually. With between 12,000 and 13,000 employees, it is St. Louis's largest single employer and a major economic force in the city.

The center's role in revitalization was as simple as it was important. It formed a redevelopment corporation—the Washington University Medical Center Redevelopment Corporation. Its roles were to provide leadership and to act as a management arm for dealing with private developers and the community. It also made major capital investments—$100 million—in facilities. This large investment provided the impetus for overall neighborhood renewal. It was a clear signal that not only was the center staying in the neighborhood, but also it had confidence in the area and the city.

The principal public tool aiding the redevelopment of the area was Missouri's Urban Redevelopment Corporation Law, Chapter 353.[9] This provides for the use of eminent domain for private development under certain conditions. It also allows for tax abatements.

The results of the project after nine years are impressive. In excess of 200 acres of the 280-acre area have been revitalized in some significant way. Nearly 600 new residential units have been built; another 660 have been rehabilitated. Seventy thousand feet of residential space have been developed.

Nearly half a million feet of office space has been built, including a new regional Blue Cross headquarters.[10]

Nearly $90 million in private funds has been invested, against $2 million in public funds. The institutional investment provided another $275 million and served as the financial anchor for the entire program.

With a total program investment approaching $370 million, the Washington University Medical Center redevelopment must have one of the highest leverage rates for a large-scale project anywhere in the nation.

Yale University and New Haven

New Haven is 75 miles northeast of New York City and 140 miles southwest of Boston. The city itself has a population of 126,000 people in an urban county of 757,000. It offers a very good test case of what non-profits might do in urban revitalization as six of its seven top employers are non-profit or publicly regulated organizations. It has no single large industry and its economic base, like those of other communities, is shifting from manufacturing to service industries.

Yale University is obviously a key factor in what happens to downtown New Haven. The city was laid out in a grid pattern of nine 16-acre squares, the center square being the Common. Yale University occupies three of the remaining eight squares.

The University's budget is nearly three times that of the city. It has 10,000 students and 8,000 faculty and staff. It is the city's fifth largest taxpayer. Clearly, both physically and financially Yale is the dominant institution of New Haven.

Like similar institutions, Yale felt somewhat besieged in the 1960s and 1970s. It was viewed as a "rich boy's school"[11] and was often asked to undertake projects or programs it felt inappropriate.

Yale University's current role in the revitalization of downtown New Haven grows out of a larger public-private partnership it had a role in founding. New Haven was nationally recognized for its programs in urban renewal in the 1950s and 1960s which were largely city-government-initiated efforts. By the late 1970s, however, both city and private leadership realized that there were new tasks in urban rehabilitation and economic development that called for new organizations and new approaches. In 1978, the mayor, Frank Lowe, commissioned a study of the nine-block core that led to the creation of the new organization, the private Downtown Council. In its three years of operation, it had seen its roles as:

- encouraging public-private partnerships to stimulate economic development;
- stimulating developer interest in New Haven;
- promoting an improved image for the city and the downtown;
- involving a broad spectrum of people and organizations in the revitalization efforts.

Yale was one of the founding organizations in the Downtown Council and assists in its funding. The University's own role was described by the community and state relations director, Ralph W. Halsey, thus: "Yale's future is inseparable from the future of the city of New Haven. . .Yale is not going to pick up and move to Tucson. It's not going to pick up and move anywhere. It would be folly for us to consider ourselves as separate from the city."[12]

Yale has undertaken three major kinds of activities. The first is related to its major mission of research and education. It has opened its enrollment to part-time degree students, making the community much more attractive to high technology industries. It created a special liaison office for private industry. It made a major and very important financial commitment to public school education in the community. Local high school students can attend Yale classes free. While the university has no education college, it assists in the advanced training of teachers and administrators.

The second kind of role Yale undertook was in the creation of a science park. It is a cooperative effort of the city, the Olin Company, and Yale resulting in an industrial park especially tailored to the need of high technology and science-based industries. Each organization contributed land to the project.

The third Yale activity was also in the field of physical development. According to Halsey, the university realized it was not itself a developer. Instead, it views its role as putting underutilized property into the hands of developers that could do something with it. Developers were given such properties for a lease of 20 to 25 years with nominal, if any, rent. The developer invested in the rehabilitation of the property, had use of the property for rental or other purposes, and depreciated the value of his investment. At the end of the lease period, the property will revert to the University's ownership.

Participation in innovative financing mechanisms such as this one where all parties profit in some way is one of the most promising roles for non-profit organizations. As direct federal grants and loans become less and less of a factor in revitalization, local governments and non-profits will need to look for such financing schemes that utilize the incentives of the tax code.

Roles for the Non-Profit Organization

The patterns shown in Columbus, New Haven, and St. Louis indicate the four major parties to a successful revitalization project as the major non-profit organization, the city government, private developers, and residents. The idea for the redevelopment can come from any of the four or even an outsider. However, either the non-profit or the city government must take the leadership role in planning and executing the project, with the other using its tools and resources to make it happen.

The non-profits all had major missions other than neighborhood revitalization—research, teaching, health care. They undertook these projects for a variety of motives, but generally speaking, to improve the neighborhood in which they were located. Battelle initiated the Renaissance project. Yale University and the Washington University Medical Center became involved as a part of a larger community redevelopment effort.

In each case these non-profits did not try to be something that they were not. They were not redevelopers. The direct roles of planning and managing the projects were put in the hands of others. Battelle and Washington University Medical Center created special subsidiaries for the projects.

Non-profits offer certain advantages over city governments in leading revitalization efforts. They have less complicated management and decision structures. They can decide how they will use the major capital and operating resources at their disposal. This gives them a tremendous ability to leverage other investments.

Gentrification and Displacement

The most frequent criticism of urban renewal and revitalization programs has been that they do not benefit the low- and moderate-income people who lived in the neighborhood before the redevelopment program began. At best the people were assisted in relocating to another low-income neighborhood, at worst they were put out on the street.

Upgrading a neighborhood while keeping at least a mix of income levels is one of the greatest challenges facing an organization. Nor can this challenge be ignored. The poor today, unlike a few decades ago, have power. They have spokespeople. There are laws, organizations and public officials who pay attention to their needs and demands. While the poor do not have the power to effect neighborhood change by themselves, they can slow down or even stop a revitalization program that does not take them into account.

To meet the gentrification issue, redevelopers, including non-profits, must commit themselves to a continuous process of negotiation and accommodation. The strength of the neighborhood reaction to the Columbus Renaissance effort is surprising in two respects. First, the neighborhood had an almost 87 percent turnover rate among renters. This should have been a classic case of a low level of neighborhood involvement. However, the residents had strong and vocal professional advocates who frequently represented their interests. They could not be ignored and were successful in helping the project.

If gentrification represents what will happen if a project must entirely meet tests of the marketplace, if the needs of low- and moderate-income families and individuals can only be met by moving, then someone must pay the bill. In the past, this has been done with federal funding through many different programs. Without such funds, there is little a private developer or a non-profit institution can do. Few city governments are in a position to take up the slack, but through using their development tools and innovative financing techniques (such as the Yale program) they may be able to develop some kind of accommodation to the needs of low- to moderate-income individuals.

The Role of Federal Funds

Federal funds were crucial to these projects in two ways. Indirectly, all three institutions received substantial amounts of their income from federal funds. Over one-third of Yale University's $300 million budget comes from federal grants. The federal government is Battelle's major customer for contract research and management services. A disruption or reduction in such funds would certainly mean retrenchment and require such institutions to be less expansive about doing "good things" in their neighborhood. Most non-profit organizations would be in a similar situation.

Second, in this and other revitalization projects, federal funds have been the "glue money" needed to carry the project off. The $2 million innovative grant from HUD for the Renaissance project in Columbus not only allowed accommodation to low- and moderate-income interest in the project, but also was used as a stick to enforce it. Battelle could certainly have carried out some kind of rehabilitation of the neighborhood with its own resources, but it would not have been able to meet the needs and demands of low- and moderate-income people.

Community Development Block Grant funds have also been used to pay for public facility improvements in revitalization areas. These must, under the terms of the law, substantially benefit low- and moderate-income individuals. Most city governments are financially hard pressed and have a substantial backlog of public works projects. These CBDG funds must now be stretched to cover many kinds of projects where federal funding is either being reduced or eliminated. This cannot help but slow the pace of revitalization involving non-profit and other kinds of institutions.

There is also a shift in the federal strategy away from direct grants and loans toward tax incentives. At first blush, this would seem to be a substantial disadvantage for developments where non-profits are the principal actors. By definition, they do not pay taxes and depreciation and tax credits would appeal less to them. But this is not so. First, Battelle is a not-for-profit organization. It operates under the same cost rules as a business organization. If it has profits, it pays federal taxes, and has. It can use depreciation and tax credits. Yale and Washington University are in a different situation, more representative of non-profit institutions. They do not pay income taxes. Here, however, imaginative financing techniques can be used to take advantage of incentives in the tax code. Yale University did this in turning over construction to a private developer who could take advantage of depreciation. Yale, in essence, gave the developer land and buildings in return for the deed for the property once the developer had fully depreciated the improvements he made to the property. If there is to be a substitute for federal funds in the short run, it will have to be in the form of imaginative financing techniques such as this. Such methods allow the project to meet the income tests that private developers must follow at the same time the non-profit can use its resources in a responsible way.

Conclusion

One must not confuse major non-profit institutions, such as research foundations, universities, and hospitals, with charities, or as Senator Sam Ervin liked to call them, eleemosynary institutions. In spite of their enormous wealth, if one expects them to act as general local charities, one will invariably be disappointed. That money is for the major missions of the organization: research, teaching, and health care.

The real lesson from these three examples is not the novel use of development tools nor the architectural quality of the urban revitalization efforts, but rather the change in organization behavior. All three organizations were under pressure at one time or another to do things they felt they could not do. The change in behavior came about when all the parties in a good revitalization program began to work together to find solutions that met the

needs of the non-profit institutions and provided benefits to the neighborhood and the city. City government leaders and civic leaders in other communities that wish to motivate similar kinds of good works, might do well
to search for ways to moderate the more extreme pressures on non-profits
and help them find workable solutions that also provide community revitalization benefits.

6

Cleveland Comes Back*

Eugene H. Methvin

On December 15, 1978, the city of Cleveland, that proud industrial giant on the Lake Erie shore, met the ultimate financial disaster: default. It became the first major American city since the Great Depression to fail to repay its noteholders on time.

But when the crash came, the people of Cleveland put their shoulders together and went to work with a new will and vision. Today, a little over four years later, the city has accomplished the seemingly impossible: its budget debt is largely paid off and its services have vastly improved.

Cleveland's story offers lessons for us all. Says Mayor George Voinovich, "Many cities are in the same shape today that we were in four years ago. As the flow of 'free money' from Washington dries up, their ticking fiscal bombs will explode unless they get moving."

Cleveland's crisis of municipal government and finance reflected a crisis of its soul. In the last quarter-century the city lost half its manufacturing jobs and nearly half its people. (Cleveland currently ranks 19th in population among the nation's cities.) Most younger middle-class whites and corporate and business leaders had withdrawn to suburbia. Left behind in the inner city were the elderly and poor whites, and middle-class, and middle-aged white "ethnics" too attached to their neighborhoods to leave. All were suspicious of or hostile to the blacks who today make up 44 percent of the city's population.

Cleveland's municipal structure at the time was perfectly designed to mirror and magnify this angry mood. The city council had 33 members, making it the nation's third largest. Council members and the mayor were elected every two years, so they seldom stopped campaigning for re-election long enough to think of the city's broader needs. Hard decisions and unpopular stands were political suicide.

In 1970, with fiscal trouble clearly lying ahead, Carl Stokes—a Democrat and the first black mayor of a major American city—named a blue-ribbon committee of bankers and businessmen to study Cleveland's problems. They recommended a steep income-tax hike from one percent—one of Ohio's lowest rates—to 1.8 percent. Stokes sweetened the pill by offering a $17 million property-tax cut. Upshot: the property tax was cut, but voters rejected the income-tax hike.

Leading the charge against "Stokes's tax" was fellow Democrat Dennis Kucinich, a 23-year-old councilman and former newspaper copy boy who understood the media's lust for controversy, confrontation and colorful rhetoric. His well-publicized tirades also suited white Clevelanders' moods perfectly. When Stokes retired in 1971, frustrated and disillusioned, Kucinich led a white Democratic rump movement that helped elect Republican Ralph Perk mayor.

Used to being maligned, Cleveland became the butt of national jokes when Perk set his own hair afire cutting a ceremonial metal ribbon with an acetylene torch. Reporters dubbed his administration "municipal vaudeville," and neither media nor public paid due attention to the fiscal flames.

And burn they did. Perk sold Cleveland's transit system for $10 million and the sewer system for $33 million to regional authorities, and used the money for current spending, including, some said, heavily padded payrolls. Deficits were concealed with such budget foolery as classifying uncollectible bills as collectible. Federal-grant dollars were wasted on such dubious projects as bus placards and billboards—prominently displaying the mayor's name—urging citizens to fight crime. Promising "no new taxes," Perk won re-election twice.

Rampant Confrontation

Some voices of reason tried to caution the voters. One belonged to Republican George Voinovich, Cuyahoga County auditor, who warned that the city must make three changes to avoid bankruptcy: double the income tax, extend the terms of mayor and council members to four years and stop excessive pay hikes. Two Cleveland State University professors published a study forecasting municipal fiscal collapse by 1978.

Undaunted, Dennis Kucinich, then 31 years old, ran for mayor in 1977 and won. In barely a year, the city seemed to fall around his ears. He hired a new police chief from California, and within two days fired him. He quarreled irreconcilably with black city-council president George Forbes, and called Forbes's colleagues "lunatics" and "buffoons." Three times Cleveland voters rejected a school-tax increase, and teachers struck the schools for five weeks.

So it went. Rare among major cities, Cleveland has two electric systems. The Municipal Light & Power Co. ("Muny Light") served 76 city facilities as well as 40,000 residential and 6000 commercial customers. The investor-owned Cleveland Electric Illuminating Co. (CEI) served the other 170,000 consumers and provided a large part of Muny's power because, after years of neglect, Muny's generators were shut down in 1976. The city owed CEI $13.9 million for past light bills. A federal judge ordered Kucinich to pay up, and armed marshals were sent to seize city water-system trucks for the debt. At almost the same time a county judge declared Cleveland's water system so deteriorated that it constituted a danger to health and safety. The judge declared that a $15 million investment by the Water Department in City of Cleveland short-term debt was not appropriate, and he ordered it repaid. (An appellate court later reversed the decision.)

Rock Bottom

With the city near collapse, Kucinich's finance director, Joe Tegreene, discovered a new nightmare: to pay day-to-day expenses, the Perk administration had taken $30 million from the proceeds of long-term bond funds obligated for repairing roads and bridges and for other capital investments. Almost instantly, Wall Street financial experts dropped Cleveland's credit rating to zero. Local banks, which held millions of dollars' worth of the city's short-term notes, demanded an audit. But the state auditor had already pronounced Cleveland's books "unauditable."

Kucinich's response was to accuse the banks of "systematic looting" and "destroying the city." Finally, in a last-ditch plan to avoid default, he called for an income-tax hike—to a 1.5 percent rate—to bring in $38 million in needed revenue. But the council refused to approve this plan unless Kucinich agreed to sell Muny Light—which he would not do. Bankers now refused to extend any further credit unless the council and the mayor agreed on a recovery program. Thus default became inevitable.

Within three months, shocked Cleveland voters approved the income-tax hike by a two-to-one margin, but by the same margin rejected the sale of Muny Light. Then a delegation of top businessmen asked George Voinovich, by now Ohio's lieutenant governor, to come home and run for mayor.

Voinovich laid down stern terms, exacting a promise of cash and expertise to help streamline city government.

In November 1979, Voinovich defeated Kucinich with solid majorities in both black and white precincts. Declared *Cleveland Magazine*, "There was a strong, united voice demanding order and cooperation and an end to chaos and confrontation."

Biting the Bullet

The day after his inauguration, Voinovich began calling in volunteers. Experts from seven major accounting firms and five corporations spent 11 weeks auditing the "unauditable" books and eventually established that the city debt totaled $111 million.

With Cleveland's financial mess on the table for all to see, Voinovich got 22 city-employee unions to agree to curb wage demands for two years. Then he asked voters for a second matching income-tax hike—to two percent. The electorate said no. So Voinovich announced a lay-off of 400 city workers, declaring, "We're going to balance the budget come hell or high water." Three months later, he asked again, and this time voters agreed to the tax hike, thus doubling the income tax within two years. Half the new money would finish restoring the diverted bond funds (a debt that will be fully repaid this year), and then five-year programs to restore the water system, bridges and other crumbling infrastructure will begin.

Voinovich went back to the business and civic leaders who had drafted him for the mayor's job. They provided 89 top executives, supported by $800,000 in foundation and corporate grants, to hire additional outside experts. This task force spent three months combing through 63 city divisions for ways to make them more effective without reducing services.

Task-force members found many hard-working, conscientious civil servants, but they were mired in mismanagement. A secretary bought office supplies with her lunch money because "proper channels" took weeks. Mechanics took auto parts home to repair because they had no workshop. One employee counted and recorded all incoming checks by hand—and left a $10 million federal-aid check sitting unopened for four days.

Selling any municipal property, even a $200 parcel, took 41 steps involving 4 council committees. The task force cut that to 20 steps and recommended selling $1.5 million worth of surplus land. They found City Hall's third floor unoccupied; refurbished, it now houses two agencies that had been renting costly downtown offices.

The executives consolidated 78 city gas stations into 40 and instituted proper fuel accounting. They saved $1 million a year by showing the data-processing center how to get more out of its computers. By centralizing absentee reporting and enforcing policy strictly, they cut municipal employees' absenteeism nearly a third.

The task force made 650 recommendations that could save $37 million in one-time economies, plus $57 million a year. Then its members went to work with their municipal partners, nights and weekends, and within two years had 75 percent of the recommendations implemented—and most of the rest under way.

Only a Beginning

Clevelanders are revitalizing their city in other ways as well:

• Playhouse Square is one of the nation's finest theater restorations, with 7000 seats and facilities for opera, ballet and dramatic productions. The restoration began when a public-school official wandered into three magnificent 1920s movie palaces that were scheduled for demolition. Soon volunteers were refurbishing their ornate interiors. When completed next year, Playhouse Square will draw more than a million people annually.

• Voinovich and business leaders attacked the decaying-city look. Corporations "adopted" whole city blocks in the Cleanland Ohio campaign, landscaping, tidying, painting and improving.

• Forty corporate chiefs formed the Cleveland Tomorrow Committee, launching a high-technology research institute, a seed-capital fund to help young companies start or expand, and a "clout" committee for lobbying Columbus and Washington. Buoyed by new confidence, businessmen have completed more than $100 million in new construction since 1980, and another $442 million is under way.

• The League of Women Voters spearheaded a campaign to reduce council membership from 33 to 21. Two times in nine years voters had rejected the idea. In 1981, Clevelanders approved. Similarly, voters approved four-year terms for mayor and councilmen—after rejecting such extensions eight times in three decades.

That November, Cleveland voters re-elected Voinovich to the first four-year term by a record 77 percent landslide. (Black voters gave him an astonishing majority of over 80 percent.) Four months later, the National Municipal League selected Cleveland as one of ten "All American" cities.

Syndicated urban-affairs columnist Neal R. Peirce summed it up: "If any town ever labored heroically and against odds, it must be Cleveland. A broad coalition of Clevelanders, rising above petty jealousies, finally coalesced to take control of their collective destiny. Politicians and businessmen, neighborhood and civic organizations, banded together. This country, at its grass roots, can still work magnificently well."

7

The Salvation of American Cities

Joel Lieske

Churches and Urban Society

Can we whose souls are lighted
With wisdom from on high
Can we to men benighted
The lamp of life deny?
Salvation! Oh Salvation!
The joyful sound proclaim
Till each remotest nation
Has learned Messiah's name.

    Lowell Mason
    Missionary Hymn, 1824

Over the past two decades there has been a growing concern among main-line Christian churches in the United States with urban problems. In church convention resolutions, council encyclicals, religious tracts, and the public pronouncements of high church officials, American church bodies have repeatedly expressed their concern and dismay over the continuing plight of our major cities. And it is not uncommon for church groups to schedule "urban experience" workshops, as the American Baptist Church recently did during its June, 1983, convention in Cleveland. But it is one thing to express concern. It is quite another to become personally involved and committed.

Without disparaging the many church-sponsored efforts already in place —drug rehabilitation centers, medical clinics, housing for the elderly, and welfare services—it is perhaps appropriate to ask why the religious concerns of American churches have yielded so little in tangible consequences. One explanation can be seen in the primary mission of most churches. Traditionally, church bodies have attempted to serve the long-term spiritual and personal needs of their members. As with other institutions, organizational demands are paramount. And social issues have traditionally taken a back seat in the religious life of the nation.

A second explanation can be found in the growing fiscal problems of American churches. Like government itself, many churches are beset with rising costs, falling revenues, and members who do not pay their way. Third, there is the obvious failure of many government programs themselves. If ambitious federal programs like the War on Poverty, Model Cities, and CETA cannot achieve their objectives, how can church bodies expect their more limited social action programs to succeed.

All of these factors understandably diminish the urban commitments of American churches. However, with the exception of doctrinally conservative and fundamentalist denominations, few churches have denied a social responsibility. Rather, most have asserted it. But instead of assuming the role of the Good Samaritan themselves, most mainline church bodies have established permanent lobbies in Washington to support social legislation proposed by other groups. Thus, many appear content to delegate their social responsibilities to the state as God's surrogate. This delegation represents perhaps the final triumph of the public welfare ethic in American life, whereby the state is assigned most of the social obligations of a purportedly civilized society.

Between 1960 and 1980, three Democratic and two Republican administrations forged a succession of policies and programs ostensibly designed to help reverse the economic decline and social rot of our aging central cities. Unfortunately, the urban problems they were designed to address—poverty, welfare dependency, family breakdown, functional illiteracy, unemployment, crime, central city abandonment, and blight—seem no closer to solution than they did twenty years ago. In fact, many have become demonstrably worse.

If our cities are to be saved, Americans must find answers to two chronic problems. The first is to redeem a large and growing underclass, whose members can only drag down and dilute future recovery efforts.[1] The second is to make our cities good places to live and play, as well as to work. The question is how.

The answer may lie in the organized urban programs of two American churches, who in contrast to most mainline bodies, emphasize personal involvement and commitment. Curiously, the circumstances and background of the two churches and their urban missions could not be more different. The Church of the Saviour is a small ecumenical group of approximately 100 members located in the nation's political capital, Washington, D.C. Its primary urban mission is Jubilee Housing, a self-help housing project in the declining Adams-Morgan neighborhood, less than two miles from the White House. The Church of Jesus Christ of the Latter-Day Saints is a multinational church organization over five million members strong that is headquartered in Salt Lake City, a city originally established as the religious capital for the Mormon Church. Its primary urban mission has been the renewal of the downtown area surrounding Temple Square, a once declining but now radiant setting of fine hotels and restaurants, quality retail shopping, and outstanding cultural amenities.

Redemption in the Inner City

As we came to see more clearly the faces of those submerged in the crushing poverty of our own city, it became obvious that only those engaged in the struggles of the poor were going to be able to speak to them any message of God's reign. . . .It seemed. . . .that the best way to eradicate the creeping blight and decay of the city was to purchase housing in the area, to work with the tenants to upgrade it without raising rents, and then to begin a program of education, literacy, recreation, and counseling that would engender hope and spread to the larger community. . . .

The new mission. . . .took the name of Jubilee Housing, after the Jubilee Year in the Old Testament which was established to "proclaim liberty throughout the land to all its inhabitants." . . . .The members of Jubilee Housing had no less a mission in mind than to put an end to poverty in the city, to secure decent housing for every person at a cost that each could afford, "to proclaim the year of the Lord's favor."

Elizabeth O'Connor
The New Community, 1976

Jubilee Housing is a story of human redemption, set in the changing Adams-Morgan neighborhood of Washington, D.C. An unusually diverse neighborhood of some 70 blocks, it is 58 percent black, 22 percent Latin American, and 18 percent white, with the remainder mostly Middle Eastern.[2] Peopled by every race, skin color and social condition, Adams-Morgan is aptly characterized by Karl Hess as "a small country afloat in a great city."[3]

The shops that line the business district along Columbia Road and 18th Street were fortuitously spared the looting and destruction that devastated the 7th and 14th Street corridors during the 1968 riots. Nonetheless, a number of stores have taken the precaution to use iron grates that can be lowered at night. They offer no protection, however, from the discarded cigarette butts, junk food wrappers, shards of broken glass, old newspapers, dented soft drink cans, and occasional empty liquor bottles that litter the sidewalks and street gutters in front of the stores.

Most buildings in the neighborhood date to the 1920s or earlier, when the area was affluent and respectable, fit even for "housing the diplomatic representatives in Washington," as the original prospectus for the local Ritz apartment building proclaimed. During the 1950s, it took on the character of a quiet, middle-class community, whose median income closely matched the city's. By 1970, with more than 40 percent of the residents below the city's median income, it had become a haven for the poor. Since the mid-1970s, the area has been caught up in real estate speculation and population change as residents adjusted to the pressures generated by the metropolitan housing shortage, the city's 1972 rent control ordinance, gentrification, and the influx of Latin American immigrants. By 1980, unrehabilitated row houses that sold for $20,000 five years earlier were going for $80,000 to $100,000. Deteriorated one-bedroom units that were formerly rented to low-income tenants for $140 per month were being rehabilitated and sold as condominiums for $60,000 to $100,000.

Against this backdrop in the early 1970s, a small group of individuals from the Church of the Saviour decided to provide fit housing in the area for poor people. The Church of the Saviour is a tightly-knit, evangelistic church whose members maintain a strict religious discipline and shun the institutional structures of traditional Christianity. It was organized by Gordon Cosby, its present minister, in 1947. According to church historian Elizabeth O'Connor, "The Church of the Saviour is an attempt to recover in one local expression of the Church Universal something of the vitality and life, vigor and power of the early Christian community."⁴ Toward this end, the church has launched some dozen separate inner-city faith missions, including the establishment in 1960 of the Potter's House, the first church-operated coffee house in the country.

It is here that the vision of Jubilee Housing was conceived. Situated just east of the old Ontario Theater, the Potter's House sensitized church members to the poverty and social needs of the surrounding neighborhood. Many were veterans of the civil rights and anti-Vietnam War movements. They wanted desperately to provide the poor with adequate housing and to start mending the District's shattered race relations. At the same time, they wanted to avoid the pitfalls of paternalism and arrogance.

To get things started, Carolyn Cresswell, a young member of the group, secured a real estate license and began to investigate the deteriorating apartment buildings in the streets behind the Potter's House. She was finally able to track down the absentee owner of two old buildings, the Ritz and Mozart. Both buildings, notes O'Connor, were in an advanced stage of deterioration: "roofs that no longer kept the rain out, plumbing that didn't work, no adequate locks on the doors, steel mailboxes twisted open, urine-drenched halls, chewing gum and graffiti on the walls, garbage piled two floors high in the stairwells, and overrun with rats and roaches."⁵ The buildings belonged to a wealthy octogenarian who lived alone in a hotel room. Finally, in 1973, he agreed to sell.

At this point, O'Connor reports that Cresswell and the group at the Potter's House did not know what to do. The octogenarian had been too shrewd to reveal how badly he wanted to unload the buildings. Cresswell had been too shrewd to reveal that her group had no money. The group's social idealism was shared by James Rouse, the well-known developer and resident of nearby Columbia, Maryland, who had dropped by the Potter's House one night and advanced his own "wild" dreams for renewing cities and providing the poor with decent housing. But he was temporarily out of the country on business. So the group decided to borrow $10,000 to make a deposit on the 60-unit Ritz and the 30-unit Mozart, hoping Rouse would like their idea when he came back. Happily, he fell in with their plans on his return and agreed to arrange a personal loan for the buildings, and Jubilee Housing, Incorporated, was born. Two days after the purchase of the buildings, the District of Columbia slapped the new owners with a three-page list of 947 housing code violations. The violations would take three years and some 50,000 hours of volunteer labor to correct.

Initially, the black residents of the Ritz and Mozart met the Jubilee owners and volunteers with suspicion and hostility. Many feared the new owners would eventually displace them. But slowly, by their constant presence, tangible results, and the recreation and summer camp programs they organized for the residents' children, the Jubilee Christians began to win friends and establish credibility. Even more surprising, the Jubilee volunteers embraced the residents in social fellowship and treated them as equals.

Eventually, the residents themselves became involved in rehabilitating and caring for the buildings. Some even began to assist in the repair work and others were appointed tenant floor leaders. At first, each floor leader was given responsibility for enforcing building rules, reporting maintenance problems, and visiting with residents. For this, each was paid a small amount of money. The theory was to get cooperation from tenants through self-management. "It was a good idea," says Terry Flood, who initially served as volunteer manager for the Ritz and Mozart, "but it never really got off the ground."⁶

The next step was overall building management by a single tenant. Rosa Hatfield, a young black woman with several children who had initially opposed the Jubilee takeover, was made resident manager. She quickly demonstrated management skills and assumed more responsibilities. But the Jubilee leaders were convinced that only total tenant participation could insure quality control and a liveable building environment. To achieve these goals, volunteers began to introduce a cooperative housing concept to the residents in late 1976. They asked interested residents to serve on one of five committees for finance, maintenance, missions and orientation, public spaces, and legal rules. Each committee was assigned a Jubilee support volunteer. An overall steering committee, composed of two residents and a Jubilee volunteer from each of the five committees, served as an overall management council. Within a year, all residents of the Ritz and Mozart were required to serve on at least one committee and to contribute five hours of volunteer time per month. Those who did not meet the service requirements were charged a $10 monthly penalty. By November, 1977, the co-op structure was successfully in place. It has served as the organizational model for all subsequent acquisitions.

Between 1978 and 1981, Jubilee added the 32-unit Sorrento, the 16-unit Marietta, the 27-unit Ontario Court, and the 48-unit Cresthill. These acquisitions increased Jubilee's holdings to its present total of 213 low-income units in six scattered buildings.

The new acquisitions also created a need for a professional property manager. Since 1978, this position has been filled by Robert Boulter, a certified property manager and real estate broker in the greater Washington area, with funds supplied by Rouse. As a Princeton University student, Boulter had led student protests against the Vietnam War. Ultimately, his sense of moral outrage had forced him to file as a conscientious objector, and to renounce his family (with whom he later reconciled), his Ivy League education, and the perceived "falseness and shallowness" of his upper-middle-class, suburban Methodist church. His spiritual quest, as well as his professional experience, had prepared him for the Jubilee Housing job. Unfortunately, his privileged background and liberal idealism had also strapped him with some excess baggage: a naivete about the violence of inner city life and a false sense of his own invulnerability.

In July, 1981, his wife, Marla, was mugged. Four months later, he was brutally beaten by car thieves he had boldly challenged. Both assaults occurred in broad daylight less than two blocks from his office. His was the most painful and traumatic. While he was lying prone on the sidewalk, one of the thieves began kicking and stomping his head. At this point, a toughened and savvy street veteran rushed across the street from a pay phone and stood protectively over Boulter. "Who (the hell) do you think you are?" demanded Boulter's assailant. "I'm nobody," the man evenly replied, "but you've robbed him and hurt him bad enough; why don't you quit?" Refusing to be intimidated, the good Samaritan stood his ground until the attackers left and help arrived.

Boulter required two operations, one to set broken cheek bones and later a second to insert a tiny plastic device for correcting a hearing loss and con-

stant ringing in his inner left ear. Though he is now almost fully recovered
from his physical ordeal—a slight ringing persists—Boulter is a chastened
and different man. For a time, he anguished over the attacks, and even
questioned his faith and social ministry in the neighborhood. Now like the
apostle Paul, he believes the pain and suffering he endured has only served
to strengthen his Christain faith, his empathy for the poor, and his resolve
to help them. At the same time, he is more aware and accepting of his personal limits, and the need to be less a "point man" and more a team player
in working out their social salvation.

Towards this end, the Jubilee leadership has created a set of social-service
support facilities. Intended primarily for Jubilee residents, though not
restricted to them, the facilities include: (1) Columbia Road Health Services, a health center which operates on a sliding fee scale basis and serves
over 20,000 patients annually; (2) a Montessori pre-school program; (3) the
Washington Work Association, a cooperative that employs residents in
manual service jobs such as finishing floors, cleaning apartments, tending
parking lots, and baking; (4) a Community-of-the-Arts, a home for Christians living with retarded adults; (5) the Committee of Compassion, which
distributes about $3,000 each month in donations to fellow residents who
need emergency financial assistance; (6) Jubilee Jobs, an employment
counseling service for very low-income people; and (7) the Family Place, a
pre-natal service center opened in May, 1981, for expectant mothers and
mothers with children up to the age of three.

Boulter views the services they provide as an integral part of a holistic
ministry to the neighborhood. "They make communities out of a housing
program," he said, and "that is why they are essential."

The City of God

It is our desire to build a beautiful city to the Lord, which shall soon become the
pride and ornament of the whole earth.
                            Brigham Young
                            Epistle from Salt Lake City,
                                Great Basin, North America, 1848

I

Brigham Young is said to have had two visions of Salt Lake City, one
before he actually saw the Great Basin, the second when he lay deathly sick
in a carriage that paused at a high vista overlooking a secluded mountain
valley in the summer of 1847. Both visions had shown him the "future glory

of Zion." When the second had passed, Young reportedly turned to his close friend, Wilford Woodruff, and said, "It is enough. This is the *right* place. Drive on."[7]

The place that Young had selected as the Mormon homeland was dry and barren, cold in the winter and often hot in the summer. At its best, the Great Basin could be "an extremely pleasant and exhilirating country."[8] But farming was possible only in a few, favored irrigated valleys, and most of the area was uninhabitable. The frontiersman, Jim Bridger, had confidently bet Young that the Mormons would never be able to grow corn in such an inhospitable environment. Yet Young firmly believed that the Valley, "if liveable at all, would be the best location."[9] The saints had stubbornly lived by their beliefs and had suffered and died for them. As the American frontier expanded, other Americans who felt threatened by their close-knit communalism and prosperity had driven them successively from Palmyra, New York; Kirtland, Ohio; Independence, Missouri; and Nauvoo, Illinois. Now they had the necessary isolation to build their city of God. To be successful, they needed only faith, hard work, persistence, and discipline.

Today, Salt Lake is a beautiful, clean, and thoroughly cosmopolitan city of some 160,000 residents. Nestled along the western slopes of the Wasatch Range, it is the cultural, commercial, and recreational center of the Inner-Mountain West. The heart of the city is Temple Square, a ten-acre complex that includes the famed Mormon Temple and Tabernacle plus other shrines that commemorate the struggle to establish Zion in the mountains. As a visitor to Temple Square, I soon perceived that the Mormons are a people of destiny who share an acute sense of history and their place in it.

In the shade of the Assembly Hall, a neo-Gothic stone structure that once housed the Utah State Legislature, a young guide, escorting a group of German tourists, stops in front of the Seagull Monument. He has clear blue eyes, close-cropped blondish hair, and is dressed in a conservative blue suit. In fluent German, he explains how early Mormon settlers were saved from starvation by seagulls that devoured an infestation of locusts in the summer of 1848. Feverishly, the farmers tried to stop the swarming insects. They set fires, opened irrigation flood gates, and even flailed the locusts with their rakes, but to no avail. Finally, realizing that only a miracle could save them, they reportedly dropped to their knees as one, and fervently prayed for deliverance. At this point, the story goes, great flocks of seagulls arose from the Great Salt Lake and began devouring the insects. Repeatedly, the gulls would gorge themselves, regurgitate, and gorge again. Though crop losses were substantial, the saints had been spared enough to carry them through the winter.

Another guide positions his group before the Handcart Monument. He is a successful, middle-aged construction contractor from Phoenix. In straight-forward language, he tells how later settlers, too poor to own horses or oxen, pulled wooden handcarts loaded with their possessions across sun-blazoned prairies and snow-covered mountains. Many perished along the way. But most made it, and gathered together, they built the new Zion.

The Mormons constructed the Temple by hauling blocks of granite, stone by stone, on mule-drawn carts from a mountain quarry 23 miles away. Started in 1853, it took forty years to complete. To build the 6,000-seat Tabernacle, the pioneers hauled timber from the mountains and made huge arched trusses out of beams lashed together with rawhide. The Tabernacle is home for the renowned Mormon Choir, now heard weekly over 1,000 radio and television stations around the world.

Just to the east of Temple Square lies another block of church-owned buildings—the five-star Hotel Utah, the old and new church administration buildings, and Brigham Young's family and official residences, the Beehive House and the Lion House. Interspersed throughout the block are immaculate English-style flower gardens, arranged in crisp, symmetrical quadrangles. Like the Temple and Tabernacle, the buildings on East Temple Square were designed and constructed as permanent landmarks.

Built of white enamel brick, the ten-story Hotel Utah is rococo in style. In 1976, it was enlarged and refurbished to accommodate rising numbers of tourists, many of whom still prefer it over the newer Mariott and Hilton hotels. "The church spared no expense to make sure the new addition perfectly matched the old," said the city's planning director, Vernon Jorgensen. Pointing with obvious pride, he added, "Even the filigreed cornices along the roof line blend together. To achieve this effect, we had to locate the original forms which someone had fortunately stored away."

A devout Mormon and former ward bishop (the Morman equivalent of a lay minister) for ten years, Jorgensen regularly tithes of his time and income. In addition, he and his wife assumed the entire financial burden of supporting four sons who served as lay missionaries, each for two years. Upon completing a six-week language course at Brigham Young University, three of the four served abroad in foreign countries. The fourth proselytized in backsliding Boston, the New England seat of the Puritan culture from which Mormonism sprang during the Second Great Awakening of the 1820s.[10]

The old church administration building is a white marbled edifice of three stories, reminiscent of a Federal Reserve Bank at the turn of the century. Though it is still used by high church officials, most offices are located just to the north in the new 30-story administration building. Dedicated in 1972, the new corporate headquarters is suitably off-set from the street to conform with the city's strict zoning code. A relief map of the Western and Eastern hemispheres spans the entire front of the building, pinpointing the fifty some countries in which the Mormons have established active churches. With each of its young lay missionaries reportedly winning 9-10 converts on the average, the Mormon Church is the fastest growing church organization in the world.

The Beehive House is a classic New England frame in bright yellow with white trim. The Lion House is French-Norman with a subdued gray-stucco finish. Both pioneer homes are preserved to show visitors that the Mormon settlers had come to the Great Basin not only to practice their religion, but to establish a self-sufficient and civilized way of life. This impression is also effectively reinforced by attractive and gracious tour guides who recount the life and times of the Young family.

"Brigham Young always believed that if you give something for nothing, you take away a person's self-respect," a chic young matron cheerfully informs her group. This is why everyone, including unexpected visitors, were required to contribute to the household duties, she explains. Young was also responsible for initiating the Mormon family custom of gathering together, at least once a week, to talk and enjoy each other's company, she said. A reformed Haight-Ashbury flower child of the 1960s, she had returned home "to marry a Mormon man she could *trust* and respect."

The woman, like other guides in the Temple area, is a lay volunteer called by the church. Over two million people visit Temple Square each year, making it the most popular tourist attraction in the Rocky Mountains, including Yellowstone Park. However, it is the simple and credible personal testimonies of faith by each volunteer guide that may be the real attraction.

II

Following Young's vision, every street in the city is referenced to Temple Square. Most are 132 feet wide and bound ten-acre blocks. Originally, they were designed to handle irrigation ditches and the broad turning radii required by horse-drawn wagons. Now, they easily accommodate the city's vehicular and pedestrian traffic. Unlike the streets of many cities, they are generally safe at night and free of litter during the day.

Despite its large blocks, Salt Lake has all the charm and amenities of a European walking city. In the downtown area, the city has begun constructing graceful pedestrian promenades and dotted them with small trees, fountains, brick hexagons, and brightly colored flowerboxes of pansies and marigolds. To break up the large blocks, the city has begun developing small interior parks, courtyards, and cobblestone streets and alleys. Recorded birdcalls, installed for the convenience and safety of the blind, trill changes in traffic lights. Canaries beckon all-clear for east-west crossings; whippoorwills signal safe passage for north-south transits.

Radiating south of Temple Square, the central business district contains almost all of the major amenities one might expect to find in a much larger metropolitan area. All lie within a short walk of the Square. Across from Temple Square are two new shopping malls—the ZCMI Mall and the Crossroads Plaza.

The ZCMI Mall is an extension of the old ZCMI Department Store. ZCMI is an acronym for Zion's Cooperative Mercantile Institution. Founded by Brigham Young in 1868, ZCMI was America's first family department store. At the north entrance to the mall, the church has erected a bronze monument to celebrate family life. It shows a young boy eagerly running from the protective arms of his mother to the outstretched arms of his father, and bears the inscription: "The nation is only as secure as the family." The Mall itself contains two million square feet of space and accommodates 65 stores and shops. On most days, it is filled with throngs of happy faces. When completed in 1975, it became the largest source of funding for the Salt Lake Development Agency. Following the successful example of Los Angeles, the city uses the tax increment as a major source of income.

Besides some 19 first-run movie theaters, Salt Lake's downtown recreational amenities include the Salt Palace, a modern coliseum and convention center; a new symphony hall; and the restored Capitol Theatre, home for Utah's opera and ballet companies. Within this same area are 4,500 hotel rooms, most built in the last decade, and a new 15-story high-rise of luxury condominiums. "All of the condo units were sold in one week," reported Salt Lake's Redevelopment Director, Michael Chitwood. "The developers feel the demand is so great they have made plans to construct a second building next to it."

The most impressive feature of Salt Lake, however, is its clean and well-kept residential neighborhoods. For the most part, it is a middle-class city of property owners who take meticulous pride in the appearance of their modest homes. Despite the semi-arid climate, the lawns are uniformly green and weed-free, even in the heat of summer. Most homes are decorated with neatly trimmed shrubs and variegated flower beds. According to Raymond Gastil, a student of America's regional cultures, over half of the city's population has Northern European, as opposed to native American, origins.[11] In the tradition of their English, Scandinavian, and German forebears, Salt Lake residents evidence a preference for cleanliness and ordered beauty.

Near the central business district, one may find one or two houses in a block whose structures and lawns are not kept up as well as the rest, or a couple of blocks of houses that are over-crowded. But overall, there are no areas of slum or abandoned housing in the city. There is also no significant underclass to destabilize the housing market.

Beautiful, cosmopolitan, clean, well-ordered, and civilized—Salt Lake is unquestionably a great American city. There are minor problems to be sure: What to do about occasional outside drifters and derelicts who sometimes panhandle on downtown streets. Or how to deal with the squalid living conditions of Southeast Asian refugees dumped on the city by the federal government and their former sponsors. But these problems seem inconsequential to those confronting most other American cities. This has not always been the case.

With the exception of southern migration streams that largely by-passed the city, the national currents that changed American cities over the past 50 years—the automobile, rising affluence, and the postwar push to the suburbs—also changed Salt Lake. And as suburban malls lured increasing numbers of shoppers from the downtown area, decline began to set in near Temple Square and some of the older neighborhoods. By the early 1970s, the downtown was in decline and deterioration around the old Union Pacific Station began to push the central business district north and east into The Avenues.

There is nothing inevitable, of course, about urban decline or recovery. History unfolds because men and women will it, either by their action or inaction. In Salt Lake, the monied interests were doing nothing to reverse decline. If anything, they were making investment decisions that would only accelerate the decline. Brigham Young had built his city of God on the basis of a heavenly vision. To reclaim the city, his spiritual heirs would have to reclaim the vision as their natural birth right.

It is therefore perhaps fitting that the Mormon Church spearheaded Salt Lake's restoration. But the city's recovery is also a story of urban visionaries, committed men and women whose imaginations were fired by dreams and plans beyond economic self-interest. Working in tandem, they provide Salt Lake with a unique resource for the city's long-term survival—a guardian class that cares.

III

Howard Dunn is an unpretentious businessman in his mid-50s, who occupies an imposing executive office in the ZCMI Tower. For the past 15 years, he has been president of Zion Securities, a subsidiary of the Mormon Church that buys, sells, and manages its considerable property holdings. Conservative estimates place its Salt Lake portfolio at several thousand acres alone. Despite the church's power and wealth, Dunn prefers to play down its impact on the economy of the city. But when pressed, he does acknowledge its leading role in spearheading the revitalization of the downtown area.

Historically, the Mormon Church has followed a policy of encouraging religious and cultural freedom, Dunn emphasized. This commitment goes back to the establishment of Salt Lake City as a refuge for Mormons from religious persecution, he said, and is reflected, for example, in Brigham Young's grant of land to Catholic settlers for building the Cathedral of the Madeleine. At the same time, the church has a vested interest in controlling land use around its Temple Square headquarters. It is this interest, Dunn said, that is responsible for the church's willingness to accept lower rates of return on its investments.

The turning point for the city appears to have been the development of the ZCMI Mall during the mid-1970s. In building and underwriting this shopping center on church-owned land, church leaders offered retail firms from 5- to 25-year leases with options to renew in exchange for a nominal four percent rate of return. With the success of this project and the expansion of new church buildings on Temple and East Temple Square, other projects the church had been quietly pursuing quickly fell into place. After patiently assembling land over a 12-year time period, the church had accumulated enough by 1978 to begin construction of the Crossroads Plaza shopping mall. To guarantee success of this project, the church worked in tandem with private developers to offer favorable 50-year-plus leases with options to renew.

To promote the cultural development of the downtown area, the church signed a long-term lease with the county for six acres of church-owned land that was necessary to complete construction of the 22-acre Salt Palace, Symphony Hall, and expanded Convention Center. The token lease of this land for one dollar per year gives the county the option to purchase at original value plus a nominal interest of four percent per year. The church is guaranteed the option to use the complex for two conferences per year at the prevailing market rental rate, and the Utah Symphony is provided free use of the symphony hall for half of its concerts. According to Chitwood, these developments have made the central business area very attractive to upper-income residents who value the cosmopolitan life-style advantages of downtown Salt Lake.

One of the most exciting and imaginative projects being planned for Salt Lake City is Triad Center, a 26-acre mixed-use development in the city's historic Gateway District near the Union Pacific Station. The master plan calls for a nine-story broadcast studio, several atrium office towers that will soar from nine to forty stories, a 2600-room grand hotel, luxury condominiums, an international bazaar, multiplex cinemas, a 450-seat live theater, a 2500-seat amphitheater, an ice skating rink, and parking for 9000 cars. Perhaps because a nurtured remembrance of the past looms large in the religious and cultural life of the city, the center will surround a refurbished historic mansion, the old Devereaux house, set in a garden park with belltower. With a red brick motif running throughout, the center will be linked to Temple Square and the rest of the downtown area by a yellow brick road and old-fashioned trolley cars.

Triad is owned by the Khashoggis—a Saudi family with corporate offices in Los Angeles, New York, Houston, Salt Lake, and Saudi Arabia. According to Triad's Steve Angebauer, the Khashoggis like the city because it "reminds them of their own homeland—their people, their culture, and their moralistic way of life." These cultural ties have been cemented for almost two generations. Triad Board Chairman Essam Khashoggi played a pivotal role in Triad's enormously successful decision to develop the Salt Lake International Center west of the airport. This complex of four major industrial parks laid out in spacious lakeside, garden settings has attracted a diverse and growing clientele of corporate businesses, including many Fortune 500 companies engaged in light manufacturing, research, and development.

Jorgensen believes that most new firms are attracted to the area because of the honesty and work ethic of its labor force. Greater Salt Lake also ranks first out of 243 metropolitan areas on a composite index of economic and social indicators considered important to businessmen.[12] One major attraction appears to be the number and quality of college graduates in the labor force. Surprisingly, the Mormon region—an area that includes all of Utah and parts of Idaho, Wyoming, Colorado, and Nevada—boasts the highest number of college graduates per capita in the nation. Since the early 1970s, the church has actively supported economic development and job creation programs to retain its educated young. Most college graduates want to remain in the area, said Jorgensen.

In contrast to many Sunbelt cities, Salt Lake's leadership has also taken pains to preserve the city's character and culture. "We are not at the point where we are fighting to have new industry or development in Salt Lake," said City Council President Sidney Fonnesbeck. "Growth management has become very important to us because there is a very deep sense that to grow is not enough. Growth has to be lived with. We do not want to make mistakes that perhaps other cities have made in allowing any growth at any time in any place and then feeling sorry or resentful a few years later."

Fonnesbeck represents The Avenues, a professional, upper-income area that is undergoing gentrification and restoration of its Victorian-style homes. It is a short 10-minute walk northeast of Temple Square into the Wasatch foothills, where deer can sometimes be seen in wooded canyon cul-de-sacs. Fonnesbeck has been a leader in preserving and protecting the neighborhood's character and traditions. "We have been fighting to keep out the cute boutiques, and keep it a good middle-class neighborhood," she said. Recently, when a young couple bought and restored a century-old brick home, they contracted in the purchase agreement never to displace a basement tenant or raise his rent. "We have interesting restrictive covenants," she chuckled.

A new breed of leader in the city, Fonnesbeck is a school teacher by profession, a mother of two children, and a Mormon. Several years ago, she won an upset election and then forged a council majority with other newly elected members to protect neighborhoods from unwanted development. Sometimes, early in the morning, she will walk to her city hall office dressed in blue jeans before she heads over to Robert Redford's Film Institute where she drafts grant applications. "My film studio associates would think I was putting on airs if I didn't show up in jeans," she modestly explains. Later, she is attired in a fashionable, but conservative, solid blue dress for her official afternoon and evening duties. In style, Fonnesbeck is a soft-spoken, down-to-earth person who believes in gently persuading her colleagues on council to make the right decisions. But sometimes her uncompromising integrity has forced her to oppose church policy, as when she urged locating the church-backed Crossroads shopping plaza near City Hall and away from Temple Square. This location, she noted, would have helped stabilize and anchor the southern part of the central business district.

Perhaps the senior diplomat of Salt Lake's guardian class is Wendell Ashton, publisher of the church-owned *Deseret News* and President of the Utah Symphony Orchestra. In the Mormon religion, "deseret" means work. The *Deseret News* is a family-oriented newspaper dedicated to defend the Mormon faith; to uphold the Constitution of the United States, which orthodox Mormons believe to be divinely inspired; and to produce "a quality metropolitan newspaper that presents news accurately, fairly, and at *reasonable* profit."

"The church has tried to maintain a viable downtown and a good moral climate," Ashton observed. This dual role as civic booster and moral watchdog has sometimes cast his newspaper in an adversarial position with the *Salt Lake Tribune*, as in 1968 when the *News* successfully fought the *Tribune's* advocacy of liquor by the drink. Even today, Salt Lake's cocktail lounges are allowed to serve only beer, wine, and set-ups. While the city's dry ordinance is a source of irritation to non-Mormon "gentiles," it has also spared the city from most of the social problems often posed by derelict bars.

However, Ashton believes that the real secret of Salt Lake's success lies in its people. "The greatness of a city depends on the greatness of its civili-

zation," he declared. And Ashton impresses you as a man who has dedicated his entire life to building great people. In the waiting room to his office, there is a plaque which seems to summarize his business philosophy.
It reads: "If you concentrate on building a business and not the man, you
will not achieve. But if you concentrate on building the man, you achieve
both."

"Mormons are unique in how we see life," observes Neal Maxwell, the
youngest (in his late 40s), and most recently added elder to the church's
governing Quorum of the Twelve. "We take our values seriously." Hand-
some, athletic (an avid tennis player), tanned, and well-groomed in his corporate pin stripe suit, Maxwell perhaps embodies the Mormon ideal of a
sound mind and body. A former political science professor, Maxwell is the
resident intellectual of the Mormon Church and author of some dozen
books on the Mormon religion and culture.

What attracts people to Mormonism, Maxwell concluded, is its ability to
connect "a belief in God with a plan and purpose in life." Perhaps to re-
mind himself and his visitors of this fact, Maxwell has placed a framed inscription in his office, which reads: "The long view of history is never
longer than when it is glimpsed through the lens of the gospel." Like other
Mormon faithful, the daily lives of Jorgensen, Dunn, Fonnesbeck, Ashton,
and Maxwell appear to be governed by Christ's promise: "Seek ye first the
Kingdom of God and all these things will be added unto you."

The Beginning of Wisdom

As you believe, so you live.
As you live, so you die.
As you die, so you go.
As you go, so you stay.

German Religious Proverb

I

How do you evaluate the Jubilee and Salt Lake experiences? For over a
century and a third, Mormonism has exercised a dominant influence on Salt
Lake City. The impact of the Church of the Saviour in the Adams-Morgan
neighborhood is less evident. But Jubilee Housing is less than a decade old,
and the people who occupy its 213 apartments are a small fraction of the
neighborhood population. Moreover, the venture began, not with a clean
slate, but with almost all the pathologies of urban life arrayed against it.
Nonetheless, change is evident in the cleanliness and orderliness of the

Jubilee buildings and grounds. And the older residents seem different from what they would have been without the patient and selfless contributions of the church activists who created Jubilee and its supporting social services. However, I wonder whether these changes will persist.

There are, of course, many varieties of religious experience.[13] But are they all equally authentic? And do they all necessarily lead to personal and social "salvation?" In his book, *The Smallest Part*, Elder Maxwell advances an absolutist notion of religious moralism that runs counter to prevailing pluralist conceptions. "The gospel of Jesus Christ," he argues, "calls our attention to the reality that there is an aristocracy among truths; some truths are simply and everlastingly more significant than others! In this hierarchy of truths are some which illuminate both history and the future and which give to men a realistic view of themselves—a view that makes all the difference in the world. In this context, one can see how being 'learned' (by simply indiscriminately stockpiling a silo of truths) is not necessarily the same thing as being wise, for wisdom is the distillation of data—not merely its collection and storage."[14]

This statement, perhaps better than any other, illustrates the underlying basis for the fundamental differences in religious doctrine and methods between the Mormon Church and the Church of the Saviour. The Jubilee model, for example, is liberal in orientation and based on modern behavioral and social-psychological assumptions. It tends to view people as the products of their environment and their behavior as the expression of underlying economic and social needs. Thus, if individuals are preoccupied with issues of physical survival and personal security, it is because they have little time or inclination to concern themselves with higher-order needs such as love, self-esteem, and self-actualization.

Are the poor themselves to blame for their poverty or are they the victims of society? On this issue, the Rev. Gordon Cosby is unequivocal. Casual in dress, professorial in bearing, and his kind, fatherly face visibly lined with the cares of the world, he has dedicated most of his urban ministry to the poor of the Adams-Morgan neighborhood because he believes they "are caught up in a system, one devised by those with power. As a result," he argues, "these people [the Jubilee residents] get what is left over—what is left over for schools, health care, and jobs."

To date, 95 percent of the mothers seeking pre-natal assistance at Jubilee's recently opened Family Place have been Hispanic. Fifty percent are illegal aliens from El Salvador. Why are their parenting skills so poorly developed? It is because they are preoccupied with the primary needs of housing, food, and companionship, says Delores Aroyo, pediatric coordinator for the Family Place. "The baby gets what's left over." These "at risk" children develop social and learning problems, like juvenile delinquency, and the whole vicious cycle repeats itself, she explains. "As the young twig is shaped, so it grows."

The Mormon approach, by contrast, is conservative in outlook and tends to view people and their behavior as the products of their beliefs. Sociologist Thomas O'Dea, a student of the Mormon culture, has characterized Mormonism as a uniquely middle-class, American religion.[15] The middle-class prescription for worldly success has always stressed the virtues of honesty, hard work, self-sufficiency, self-discipline, and persistence. In Mormonism, these values have been elevated to religious principles that virtually guarantee temporal as well as spiritual happiness. "It has always been axiomatic with Mormons," states a church tract on welfare services, "that a religion that cannot save people temporally and make them prosperous and happy cannot save them spiritually and exalt them in the life to come."[16]

A second major difference between the two churches is their policies on membership. The Church of the Saviour has a strict prohibition against nominal members. As in the early Puritan settlements, church membership is an exclusive matter and secured only with difficulty and yearly renewal. Consequently, the life of the church is divided first, into strictly religious activities and programs that bring together its active members; and second, into its separate inner-city faith missions, such as Jubilee, that put them in touch with residents of the Adams-Morgan neighborhood.

This separation between the strictly religious and secular life of the church can also be observed in the reluctance of many Jubilee volunteers to force their religious beliefs on the people they help. Though a spiritual counselor is available upon request in the Columbia Health Services Center, personal witnessing does not appear to be an integral part of Jubilee's inner-city mission. The Family Place provides free lunches every day and two free dinners every week. Yet, no effort has been made to institutionalize prayer or daily devotion.

The Mormon Church, by comparison, actively proselytizes and accords new church members all rights and privileges, including participation in temple ceremonies provided they are "temple worthy." Elder Maxwell could not see the church involving itself in a welfare-style housing project such as Jubilee. But it would surely not fail to proselytize, he insisted. "We would want to share our belief of life. Not to do that would be to deprive people of something very special."

The two churches differ also in their views on social welfare. Though Jubilee has not fully worked out its welfare philosophy, there are strong internal peer pressures to identify with the struggles of the poor, to accept them unconditionally as social equals, and to treat welfare as a free gift from people who care. The city's poor "have become 'our people,' " affirms Elizabeth O'Connor.[17] "We have to be sure that we are not viewing

[them] as somehow inferior to ourselves. Their problems are the same as ours—for we all share in the human condition. We come up with acceptable solutions not because we are better or know better, but because we have worked them out together with those who are more involved than we."[18]

For many Jubilee activists, the ultimate solution to poverty appears to be some variation of Christian socialism. "The people of Jubilee," writes O'Connor, "are convinced that all the walls that stand in the way of a better life for people housed in tenements, in filthy inhuman jails, overcrowded mental institutions and dilapidated nursing homes will be brought down, and the people shall walk into a new land where there is color and light, plenty of space, and singing, caring people."[19] Until this millenial stage is reached, however, she feels the members of Jubilee will be a sharing people, "sharing our resources so that no one is in need."[20]

A revisionist and perhaps more realistic view of Jubilee's evolving welfare philosophy is provided by Boulter. He is currently wrestling with two difficult problems: (1) how to implement a mutual housing association plan, and (2) how to evict problem tenants. The mutual housing plan was to have been initially tested in the Mozart apartment building and would have provided tenants permanent resident status, a share in the governance of the building, and membership equity equal to two times their monthly rent. Because of a re-emergent drug and crime problem in the Mozart, with male live-in companions of female tenants openly soliciting drugs on the street, Boulter and the Jubilee leadership have been forced to put the mutual housing plan on hold.

The tenant eviction problem stems from overly protective legal safeguards in the District's 1972 rent control ordinance. "In order to provide low-income housing, it is necessary for laws to protect tenants, owners, managers, and developers," said Boulter. "But there is abuse on both sides." Boulter has a list of problem tenants that he has unsuccessfully filed in the District's Municipal Court on eight separate occasions. "Traditionally, church and nonprofit organizations have been very lax in enforcement," he noted. "But as long as you enforce them [the rules] consistently, they are essential. True compassion demands strict enforcement."

In emphasizing the responsibilities of individual tenants, Boulter's views seem to be more in line with traditional Mormon welfare philosophy. Mormons believe that responsibility for a person's temporal well-being rests upon himself, his family, and the church, in that order. The church provides aid only when individual and family resources are considered insufficient to sustain a person or family through sickness, old age, economic depression, or major disaster.

The primary aim of the church's welfare service system is to help those in need to help themselves. From its earliest days, the church has drawn a sharp distinction between "welfare" and "welfare services." "Welfare" has been seen as an undeserved dole that takes responsibility away from the individual, depriving that person of his or her dignity. "Welfare services," by comparison, is seen as a system for enshrining the principle of work, discouraging idleness, abolishing the evils of the dole, and inculcating the virtues of industry, thrift, and self-respect.[21]

Here is the way the system works. The church maintains an extensive network of bishop warehouses that provide food and clothing to needy members. The bishop in each ecclesiastical ward, about 600 members in size, is responsible for identifying those in need and providing assistance in a direct, personal way. He is assisted by priesthood quorums, men who are assigned to visit each family in the church every month. As in their missionary efforts, the men go in pairs and report to the bishop when a family is in need. These lay Christians and their families also provide voluntary labor, usually once a month, to produce the goods and services distributed by the warehouses. For this purpose there are church-owned farms, canneries, ranches, and laundries.

The warehouses are organized like modern grocery and department stores, with food, clothing, and other items attractively arranged on shelves and display racks. All of the goods are quality merchandise and are *new*. There are no hand-me-downs. And the personal touch is always visible, from brightly colored labels on canned goods to English-style smocking on dresses for little girls. In exchange, members who receive aid are expected to volunteer work, as they are able, in the warehouse system until they again become self-sufficient. In effect, the system gives church members the opportunity "to earn their bread" and keep their self-respect.

Non-members are left to rely on the state welfare system. "The church is better at helping its own than helping the larger society," admits Elder Maxwell. At the same time, one advantage reaped by all residents is the significantly lower public welfare costs. Expenditures on public welfare per capita in the Mormon region are the lowest in the nation.[22]

A fourth major difference between the two churches concerns the place of religion in people's lives. In the Church of the Saviour, religious beliefs and practices are celebrated primarily for their instrumental value. Thus, the church becomes the institutional means for providing Christian love, reconciliation, and community fellowship. "It [the Church of the Saviour] was founded on the conviction that the greatest contribution the church can make in any time is in being the church—a fellowship of reconciled and reconciling men, a community of the Holy Spirit, a people in which Christ dwells, a people who have a newness of life and who are transmitters of newness," observes Elizabeth O'Connor. "Whatever we do, however, must be done with an ever-deepening consciousness that the people inside the churches and the people outside the churches are asking in epidemic proportions the question, 'Am I loved?' ''[24]

Church members are expected to pray and read the Scriptures daily, worship weekly, become actively involved in one of the church's mission groups, and give proportionately, at least a tenth of their income. All of these practices are considered "marks" of a liberated Christian community, one whose members are truly committed to their religous beliefs. as an authentic "Guide to Life."

Mormon theology, by comparison, tends to emphasize religious beliefs and practices not so much for their instrumental value, but as an end in themselves. In essence, Mormons see their religion as a total "Way of Life" that exemplifies the "crowning principles" of Christianity; namely, love for one's fellowman, service, the salutary benefits of work (happiness, self-esteem, and prosperity), self-reliance, consecration and sacrifice, and stewardship.[25]

But the key to the Mormon way of life is self-reliance. Mormons are constantly enjoined to avoid becoming dependent on others; to become skilled in reading, writing and mathematics; to choose careers that satisfy future economic needs and provide personal satisfaction; and to tithe, set financial goals, and avoid debt. In addition, they are expected to maintain gardens, sew and make household items, and, where possible, to store a year's supply of food, clothing, and fuel. Finally, they are urged to practice sound nutrition; keep physically fit (each ward meeting hall, the Mormon equivalent of a church or synagogue, is generally equipped with a full-size gymnasium); and as frequent objects of ridicule, to build inner emotional and spiritual strength through daily devotion and prayer, service, and righteous living.[26]

II

In their private lives, most Americans regularly weigh the consequences of religious and cultural differences. These differences affect our choice of friends, neighbors, schools, churches, social clubs, civic organizations, and the cities and regions of the country in which we live. But as a "nation," we tend to discount or deny them. For the "educated," religious and cultural differences are, at best, irrelevant or a source of embarrassment. Certainly, they do not comport very well with prevailing secular norms. At worst, they are often viewed as suspect or even potentially dangerous because they may lead to intolerance and an excessive in-group versus out-group identification, thereby threatening the fragile social fabric of American pluralism.

The dominant sociopolitical value system, if one can be identified, is secular pluralism.[27] To the extent it stands for anything, it stands for the propositions that "nothing is sacred" and "truth is relative." Few have suggested that these new truths are also dogmas. Neither do many dare to link the icons of the new creed, mainly materialism and individualism, with the present urban malaise.

For most of our history, we have believed that we could build civilized and democratic communities of free men and women who would be united by the bonds of economic self-interest and material progress. American cities were always regarded as the land of unbounded economic opportunity. But collectively, they and their residents have suffered from this myopic vision. Human experience confirms that "man cannot live by bread alone." Neither can people easily grow and thrive in a society of selfish, irresponsible individuals.

The German sociologist, Ferdinand Tonnies, has specified two necessary conditions for transforming a collection of individuals into a functioning community. The first is *Gemeinschaft*; i.e., the common beliefs, values, attachments, and commitments that create and maintain a "sense of community." The second is *Gesellschaft*; i.e., the social and economic institutions of society that promote interdependence. Structurally, Tonnies saw a "sense of community" as the necessary social mortar that binds individuals and their economic and social institutions together.[28]

If accurate, this definition has far-reaching implications for the rebuilding of American cities and the place of religion and culture in American life. What large cities seem to lack most is a unifying sense of community. This may be why most metropolitan residents prefer the suburbs as a place to live, why suburbs are often culturally homogeneous, and why all but a handful of metropolitan areas are politically fragmented.[29] But urban scholars have generally been reluctant to accept this reality. For many, the "ideal" city is still one that is large, dense, and heterogeneous.[30] Never mind whether it is desirable to live in, conducive to human scale, or socially feasible.

To conclude, the basis for any community, religious or secular, is a unifying social ethic. Thus, to rebuild their cities, Americans must first learn to build a common cultural identity. As the Jubilee Housing and Salt Lake experiences demonstrate, religion in general, and Christianity in particular, can provide an important basis for this task. For in contrast to most other belief systems, Christianity has always identified itself on the side of self-improvement, universalism, and a deep commitment to the welfare of others over self-gratification.

True, religion is not necessarily the only basis for developing a unified community. But as many cultural scholars have observed, religious belief systems are generally at the root of most civilized and enduring cultures.[31] As you believe, so you live.

8

Schools and the Private
Sector in Partnership

Jay Chatterjee and Carol Davidow

A Need for Outside Help

If we are to accomplish the change and innovation in our cities that is
clearly needed, outside intervention must be coupled with inside commitment in the public sector to generate ideas, involve people, make changes,
and institutionalize new processes for change.

"The technique of local public-private partnership aimed at community
improvement is the best alternative option left—and it is probably the only
option that is capable of being expanded a great deal in the contemporary
environment. That's the reason for interest in public-private partnerships
and why we're seeing successes," said Robert Holland at the Cities' Congress on Roads to Recovery.

An underlying premise of the Congress was that as most cities continue to
lose population, their ability to influence the allocations of the national
budget will wane, and they will clearly need to find ways other than the
federal government to address their problems. The Congress convened participants in local efforts which were succeeding in releasing sources of
human and physical energy which had not been tapped before.

Common threads ran through the success stories. They depended on self-
reliance, creativity, and cooperation of sectors which had not previously
worked together. They are not bounded by city limits nor to professionals in
city or school government. They are responses of leaders in significant positions who believe that the vitality of their city is intertwined with the vitality
of their own companies and institutions. They are responses to city needs

93

which people from non-governmental sectors felt they had expertise to help alleviate, in concert with the responsible administrators.

Yale University began its partnership with New Haven with an analysis of what Yale is and is not, matching its strengths in teaching and research to the needs of New Haven schools and businesses. With the school system, Yale did not enter into teacher training in which it had no expertise, but instead offered academic courses to New Haven students, citizens, and businesses. In defining its assistance to leaders in the school and business sectors, it worked with the understanding that whatever benefitted New Haven would benefit Yale and vice versa.

In Cincinnati the business community organized itself to give the kind of help it could give best and offered its assistance to the superintendent of schools and local government administrators. It felt strongly that whatever benefitted the city schools benefitted the economic vitality of the city.

For school-business cooperation, this was a new direction, well beyond business's traditional role of providing some on-the-job experience for work–study students or participating in career days. Leaders in business and industry in Cincinnati now play a participatory role in better management processes, and in high technology, mathematics, and science provide better ways of learning. Along the way, they have moved to a deeper level of participation in career awareness and vocational education—recognizing that only they can provide a realistic understanding of the working world and the attitudes and skills needed to succeed in it.

A Background of Isolation

Public primary and secondary education in America does not have a tradition of cooperative ventures. Prior to the twentieth century, public education was academic in orientation and a majority of Americans were not formally educated in public schools.[1] In early twentieth century cities, schools were run individually within the city-ward structure.

With the professionalization of education (the requirement for teachers to have a college degree in education), public school educators assumed control of the schools and began to set the direction of education alone. Government, education, and business went their separate ways and did not interact concerning education to any significant degree. Yet, the result of the direction which public education has taken affects life in all the other sectors.[2]

Through the 1930s, 1940s and 1950s, public education meshed reasonably well with middle-class expectations and needs, and educators strengthened their hold on what happened in the schools. Concurrently, the move of middle-class families to the suburbs increasingly left public schools in the cities to the children of the poor. Their parents often had different cultural backgrounds and value systems than those held by the middle class and taught within schools. These children did not succeed as well as middle class children had succeeded within the public schools.[3]

As cities were drained of a viable economic base, jobs, and a reasonable quality of life, many urban residents rebelled in the sixties against the quality of the schools as well as other facets of their lives. As achievement scores dropped, frustration, despair, and hopelessness spread throughout school systems. Blame was attributed to several "other" sources: teachers, parents, students, bureaucracies, unionism, funding, television, racism, society.[4]

The serious financial troubles of New York City, Cleveland and Newark captured the attention of the nation, including its business leaders. Many looked at their own cities with new awareness and serious scrutiny. The cities belonged to them, as well as to other city residents. Corporate taxes heavily supported cities. Company work forces were dependent upon the quality of life in the city and were educated within its schools. The future of corporations was inextricably woven into the fabric of cities.

Aristotle said, "All who have meditated on the art of governing mankind have been convinced that the fate of empires depends on the education of youth." And yet, there has never been a broad-scale debate on education's purpose in America.

In 1903 Charles W. Eliot, president of Harvard, led "The Committee of Ten" which set policy in the primary and secondary public high schools in favor of traditional academic study devoted to the pursuit of knowledge and training of the intellect. Its goals were aimed at the mastery of subject matter and intellectual skill.[5]

"As studies in language and in the natural sciences are best adapted to cultivate the habits of observation; as mathematics are the traditional training of the reasoning faculties; so history and its allied branches are better adapted than any other studies to promote the invaluable mental power which we call judgement," reported the committee.

In 1918 that direction was changed. The basic educational goals which have shaped American education since that time were set by the National Education Association (NEA) Commission of the Reorganization of Secondary Education. That Commission developed the Seven Cardinal Principles which have set the guidelines for colleges of education and curriculum in schools throughout the nation to this day.[6]

"This government best-seller is a significant document which has served as a guideline for the development of thousands of curricular programs. It has encouraged a shift in the purpose of American secondary education from college preparation for the few to life preparation for the many. Teachers, colleges, and schools of education came to expect graduates to know the Seven Cardinal Principles as a base for the many," said Richard Gross.[7] These principles were reaffirmed by the NEA in 1976.

The Seven Cardinal Principles are Health, Command of Fundamental Processes (basic skills), Worthy Home Membership, Vocation, Civic Education, Worthy Use of Leisure, and Ethical Character.

The U.S. Commissioner of Education sat on that commission along with 26 other professional educators. No academicians (other than professional teacher educators) or persons from other occupations served on the commission, which eliminated from the chief goals of education traditional academic study and the training of the intellect. The shift to other purposes, directed to social adjustment rather than to the achievement of academic goals, addressed the fact that schools were not serving well large numbers of American children who failed to enroll, or left school early without skills. Presently, schools are still not serving well large numbers of American children.

Educators and philosophers are proposing alternatives to the system built on the Seven Cardinal Principles. Mortimer Adler in *The Paideia Proposal: An Educational Manifesto* has recently advocated a sweeping, nationwide, twelve-year, single track academic program with virtually no electives and no vocational training.[8]

Otto Friedrich writes that the fundamental goals of education are "truth, knowledge and the understanding of the world." He says that the basic questions of education reach deep into every aspect of life—what is essential to learn, to know, and why? He finds five interesting patterns among myriad answers—that education means careers, transmits civilization, teaches how to think, liberates individuals, and teaches morals.[9] This definition differs in significant ways from the Seven Cardinal Principles, as well as from Eliot's goals and Adler's proposal.

There is widespread awareness that there are problems with public education but not agreement on where the most serious problems lie. Richard Mitchell, in his book *The Graves of Academe*, decries the influence of the Seven Cardinal Principles. He states, "We have accepted the determinations of a teachers' union as to how America should be educated only because the job of designing an educational system is so hideously boring that only those whose self-interest is clearly at stake will undertake it. Our corporate self-interest, to be sure, is also very much at stake but not *clearly*, at least not clearly enough for the ordinary citizen."[10]

Jill Kerr Conway, president of Smith College, blames the cold war and sputnik for what she calls utilitarian education and a lack of classical roots.[11] Chester Finn in the *Wall Street Journal* says the most obvious conclusion to be drawn about American education is "how little it needs Uncle Sam to chart its course, define its problems, validate its ideas and pay for its betterment." He adds further, that "school standards are ultimately the responsibility of ordinary mortals, not Washington's wizards."[12]

In an effort to develop standards to measure students' achievements, many state legislatures have required minimum competency tests for students.[13] By 1978 Florida and North Carolina requested tests, and a majority of the fifty states had already mandated some sort of competency testing, either through legislation or action by state boards of education.

Why Business Became Involved

The growing involvement by business leaders adds a new dimension of interest in public education that has not surfaced previously. Some business leaders began to see schools as a basic cornerstone of economic development. Schools were building blocks of a democratic society based on the free enterprise system. Their success (and the development of a productive citizenry) or their failure (and its reflection in crime, unemployment, poverty, poor health and attendant costs, and a work force lacking skills to succeed on the job) were viewed as central elements in the local quality of life and in the development of a competent work force.

A recent study by the New York Stock Exchange of Japan's high productivity, attributed Japan's success to its education system "which brings the average capability of the entire population to the highest possible level" (particularly in mathematics and sciences). William M. Batten, chairman of the Exchange, says, "All Americans, not just corporation executives, have a stake in the quality of their educational system. But to use a term businessmen are fond of, the 'bottom line' is nothing less than the future vitality and competitiveness of the nation's economy."[14]

Lee Hamilton, Assistant Vice President of the National Association of Manufacturing, said there are three major reasons for business involvement in education: (1) corporate citizenship; (2) financial investment; and (3) employee supply.[15]

In many cities, direct business involvement in schools was prompted by implementation of desegregation decisions. Business leaders were asked to participate; judges and school officials sought the assistance of top local business leaders in constructively implementing court orders and designing remedies for systems. Many systems developed magnet schools (special purpose schools such as a technology school or school for creative and performing arts) as voluntary tools to lessen racial isolation. For magnet schools to attract integrated populations and provide educational excellence, they needed hard work from parents, teachers, administrators, companies with expertise in that magnet school's specialty, and other community and city leaders. When those interested participants worked together, higher than expected achievement often resulted. At Cincinnati's Schiel Bilingual School, the students reflect the black/white ratio for the school system. Its proportion of poor students is greater than that of most schools. Yet, the students significantly exceed the average in reading and mathematics test scores and attendance rates. The teachers, too, have a higher attendance rate than their colleagues in other schools. These differences seem to link the alternative nature of the school to student, parent, and teacher choice, and commitment.

As for school leaders, Willard Wirtz, former U.S. Secretary of Labor, has this advice. "Schools that become isolated from the rest of the community become isolated from the knowledge of what it takes for youth to participate in those other institutions, from how employing establishments view the development abilities provided by the schools, from the resources throughout a community for enriching and extending the educational process, and from the reserve of good will potentially existing for furthering educators' objectives, recently buffeted by public discontent and criticism."[16]

The mutuality of interest caused the National Assembly of State Superintendents of Education to invite a high-level business executive to be its keynote speaker in 1982. In his speech to them, W. Wallace Abbott, senior vice president of Procter and Gamble Company said,

> Schools are where business must look for its future employees—and the future of any business depends most importantly, in the end, on the quality of its work force. Beyond that narrow self-interest, however, there is a broader self-interest—a recognition that the health and vitality of our total society depends on the continuing reinvigoration of its human resources. This process, of course, is fundamentally what our schools are all about.
>
> We expect basic literacy. Along with basic skills, we believe it proper to expect graduates of our schools to have learned something about good work habits and accountability. We expect them to know that people are regarded in our society for results achieved—not for efforts expended or time served. And we expect the schools to instill some appreciation for the importance of integrity and follow-through on commitments.
>
> There is potential for great synergism for schools working closely with business and vice versa. [Business people] can bring a fresh perspective to the problems which school administrators face—and they can bring insight to students and teachers alike about the world of work which most students will face upon graduation.[17]

The growing phenomenon of business support for city schools has assumed a variety of forms. Dallas has been a leader among cities in which federal desegregation orders involved the business community. In 1976, a federal judge directed the business community to develop magnet schools cooperatively with the school system and to develop and lead an extensive community-involvement network benefitting the schools.

In Dallas there was already a history of public-private sector cooperation in economic development and in schools. In 1968, the Chamber of Commerce had assisted the school system in creating the Skyline Career Development Center, in designing courses for it, and in forging strong business and industrial links to its program. It also spearheaded the local bond issue campaign which funded the Skyline Center.

Following the 1976 court order, Bloom Advertising Agency developed a campaign to recruit students for the magnet schools which had been ordered and to let the community know that top corporate leaders were involved in assuring that desegregation would lead to a higher quality of education for Dallas students. In the fall of 1977, four magnet schools opened, with strong business participation. John D. Miller, president of Sanger Harris Department Stores, chaired the Career Education Advisory Council which oversaw that task.

In 1978, the Dallas school system signed a $108,000 contract with the Dallas Chamber of Commerce for services rendered through the Career Education Advisory Board, Magnet School Task Forces, Adopt-a-School Program, and Talented and Gifted Programs. Three Chamber employees worked full time to provide business assistance to Dallas schools.

Because Dallas was in the vanguard, the school system received questions from around the nation. In 1978, the director of the Chamber program, Renee Martinez, asked two paramount questions: Why did the business community get involved, and why were educators so willing to accept help from it? Martinez said the answers to both were a combination of community pride, business's long-standing track record of successful involvement in key affairs of the city, the quick and realistic recognition on the part of the educational community of the crisis caused by the 1976 desegregation court order, and their joint conclusion that Dallas public schools were salvageable.

The awakening hope that city schools and the students they house are salvageable is a key element in public-private partnerships. In cities around the nation, the success of such partnerships depends on the commitment by top administrators and top business leaders. This element is also key to substantive assistance, implementation of changes, and continuity of relationships. System administrators respect top-level business leaders and understand that to maintain long-term interest, participation in planning must replace predetermined plans, and results must occur.

The Indianapolis public schools and the Chamber of Commerce have developed cooperative programs in a widening number of areas. Partners-in-Education provides direct links between companies and schools. When the system was forced to lay off significant numbers of teachers, the Chamber provided out-placement counseling for those teachers. One special project provides architects, builders, real estate professionals, attorneys, and others to help students in a high school construction program to build a house within the time frame of a single school year. The Chamber provides public relations and communications assistance to the schools as well.

The Pittsburgh Experience

The Allegheny Conference on Community Development, an organization of top business leaders founded in 1944, is a corporate "think tank" applying corporate planning strategies to problems in the Pittsburgh region. In the 1940s, it addressed issues of flood and smoke control. Through the decades, it formed a regional industrial development corporation, worked with lower and moderate family housing, attracted foreign investment, and spurred downtown development. In the 1970s it became aware of the importance of public schools to the corporate community.

The first step was small. The superintendent of schools asked a business leader to address a meeting of superintendents of large city school districts. Meetings thereafter developed awareness that the Pittsburgh public school budget of about $150 million had not been published for ten years and its operations were vague to outsiders. Fewer than 18 percent of all Pittsburgh residents had children in its public schools. The only formal communication link with the community was a part-time public information officer who generally fielded calls from irate parents.

The Allegheny Conference provided a Public Information Advisory Committee which gave professional assistance. It raised money to design, print, and distribute an annual report to 55,000 citizens. It developed communications tools to encourage parents to enroll their children in individual Pittsburgh public schools. It offered a grant program for use by those schools to mail newsletters, fund neighborhood events, or to underwrite whatever marketing effort that school community chose.

The next step was more publicly visible and risky. Magnet schools were being formed as part of a desegregation plan. There was disagreement within the school board about their value which caused public controversy. The Allegheny Conference provided a staff member for six months to work in the school system to form a Citizen Magnet School Advisory Committee. The Conference raised $80,000 for a professional public information campaign to sell the magnet schools to potential students. Magnet schools got off to a good start.

A private "Education Fund" was developed to provide financing for many other needs in the schools. The Conference began a Partnership-in-Education Program matching companies with schools for projects helpful to the schools. A summer camping program and after-school activities designed to provide smooth development of a middle school formed for desegregation purposes were funded. As remaining middle schools were developed, the school system repeated the successful initial program. A parent from the first school wrote a book describing steps to take and the Conference published and distributed it.[18]

The "Fund" provides mini grants for Pittsburgh teachers who compete to develop their ideas for writing courses or enriching the curricula. It provides a small discretionary fund for the superintendent who is sometimes limited by school district or state policies in small ways (like providing coffee for principals' meetings).[19]

David Bergholz, deputy of the Allegheny Conference, told the Cities' Congress that it was hard to believe how isolated the school system had become from the rest of the community. He said that the morale change of teachers and administrators and the hope that has accompanied the interaction may be as significant as the infusion of funds and expertise. The schools project a better image within the community as a result of the joint efforts.

The Evolution of a Large Role in Cincinnati

A second success story about schools that was told at the Cities' Congress was that of Cincinnati. It provides a strong example of many cooperative ventures between the schools and the business community, and also between the schools and other citizen groups. The school system and business community cooperated first on task forces, working with the central office. Individual school and business partnerships followed. Next, the cooperative venture was extended to the problem of unemployable youth in the city. The schools and citizenry cooperated to pass a school tax levy, following which local school councils were developed to help set the school's priorities, review its budget and make suggestions, and work cooperatively with its community and other support groups it could generate. Local school councils include the principal, school staff members, parents, community leaders, and others interested in the school. They range from 10 to 22 in size.

Close cooperation with the business community began in 1977 with the formation of the Cincinnati Business Committee (CBC), an organization of 24 chief executive officers from major corporations. Within the public school system, the financial base had seriously eroded, school board members were quarreling publicly, and there was distrust of the system with charges of waste and mismanagement in financial reporting. The CBC offered assistance to the superintendent of the Cincinnati public schools for projects in which it could be helpful. It also offered assistance to the city in areas of local government and downtown development.

Original co-chairmen of the CBC were Edward G. Harness, Chairman of the Procter and Gamble Company, and Ralph Lazarus, chairman of Federated Department Stores. Chairman of the original Schools Task Force was William N. Liggett, chairman of the First National Bank of Cincinnati.

"In 1977 when we met to discuss how to shape CBC," said Harness, "everyone around the table automatically agreed on the importance of primary and secondary schools. When schools deteriorate, the community does. Each of our companies has an enormous stake in our community. Early on, we decided to work in areas in which business brings knowledge and expertise: finance, computers, reporting lines within administration. We really know something about these things." Harness described some key elements which have proven workable:

1. Chief executive officers choose company people who are willing to go into schools and donate their skills. Many people (company and other) are willing to do so because a chief executive asks and makes it clear that schools hold a high priority with him.

2. Assistance is offered in a manner that assures the superintendent and school board that it is helpful and supportive of their goals so they are willing to seek it. It is low-key and cooperative with school system managers.

3. CBS has resisted the temptation to spread its efforts too thinly. It prunes requests to those with the highest priority and those which business has special expertise to deliver.

Harness said that frustration was plentiful and triumphs were small at first. Trust and mutual understanding were built when results began to be apparent. He observed that schools can only succeed if the general population agrees that they are worth supporting. "In a time when school systems are often discredited, business can play an important role in heightening their credibility and calling attention to the positive existing in schools. Schools need neutral, respected citizens to praise and publicize their successes."

The superintendent of schools, Dr. James N. Jacobs, welcomed the assistance offered by the business community and promptly provided several requests. CBC provided appropriate experts from their companies to work with school system managers in financial operations, plant and maintenance procedures, energy conservation, food services, purchasing and warehousing, administrative organization and school consolidation. School and business people became teams, with the system managers providing invaluable information on problems, constraints, and history. The expertise given was not purchasable by the system for any price; company people were not selling the system anything; their advice was neutral.

Cooperative public school–business efforts have grown as a cadre of top managers have become knowledgeable about an area of school management. They remain consultants to school staff with whom they worked. The standard procedure for task forces is that the school manager and his staff work with business managers whose expertise lies in the field of school management that is under study. Together they define the problem, analyze it, and develop solutions. Many school system managers, formerly teachers, came to their jobs without the benefit of training in their administrative area of responsibility. The coaching they receive is invaluable. Advice is given quietly and results can never be attributed specifically to business experts; this could not happen without responsible involvement of school system people and their commitment to institutionalizing the changes mutually wrought.

The superintendent meets routinely with top business leaders to discuss topics of interest and to bring requests for assistance. Currently, task forces are working on an office systems study, on real estate advice (evaluating surplus buildings), on communications and public relations, and on brainstorming future mathematics and science problems and how to use computers properly for education and for the management system.

In addition to working with public primary and secondary schools, CBC offers assistance to the Archdiocesan parochial schools. Cincinnati has a large Catholic population; 26 percent of school children attend parochial schools. The well-being of that system, too, affects life in the city. In 1977, several issues divided the school communities and the media highlighted the divisions.

CBC and the superintendents of the two systems recognized their many common interests, and recognized that both were vital in providing education to residents. In addition to helping each system, CBC worked with both to build better relations between the systems.

CBC task forces examined parochial school buildings for energy conservation and building and maintenance needs. It trained Archdiocesan principals in record-keeping and in financial and time management. School-business partnerships were initiated between three companies and Archdiocesan schools and between two Catholic universities and public schools.

Biennially, CBC sponsors a joint dinner for administrators of the two systems. Principals of schools in a single neighborhood sit together to share knowledge. Individuals who have grown to know each other are willing to discuss issues before they become divisive. Business assistance is given in areas where that might help defuse or avert problems.

Aid with the Nitty Gritty

In the public school system an early request for assistance with financial management resulted in a major reorganization of financial systems and data, which took four years to complete. The business–school team still meets to refine its work and address new concerns about school finance. During two unsuccessful tax levy campaigns in 1977, CBC participated in the campaign effort, including giving attention to citizen distrust of the schools—particularly distrust of what was seen as an arbitrary distribution of money to schools and a misunderstanding of the annual budget.

Theodore Emmerich, managing partner of Ernst and Whinney, chaired the financial reporting task force. It included the superintendent, clerk-treasurer, school board finance committee chairman, and top managers from companies and accounting firms. The administrative structure of financial management within the system was changed; a new computer and software were purchased; and 3,000 man hours of accounting time from several major firms were donated to work with the system budget office and system principals to develop data, building by building, throughout the system. Training sessions were held to acquaint principals and central office budget managers with business methods and procedures for budgeting. In 1981, when the computer and software were working, the first school budget document was published. Each school's data (financial and other) are provided on a single sheet.

The Cincinnati public school system has an extensive network of magnet schools which enroll over 10,000 of its 51,000 students. With special education, vocational education, and open enrollment policies, more than 50 percent of its students attend schools other than their neighborhood schools. Costs vary from school to school.

The system gambled that if citizens understood why financial decisions had been made, they would agree with the decisions or argue cogently for changes. In fact, that is what happened—destructive myths faded and the system was widely praised for its openness by the media, community groups and by all who sought information about the school system. The direct involvement of neutral financial experts helped build respect for school system numbers and data which were presented in understandable fashion for school people as well as citizens. Use of the document as a management tool has been successful.

In 1979, Superintendent Jacobs asked the business community to explore an Adopt-a-School program. Mr. Ralph Lazarus (CBC co-chairman) led the investigation since Federated Department Stores' Dallas subsidiary was deeply involved in such a program; its president had provided leadership there. Partners-in-Education is the Cincinnati school–business partnership program which grew out of that investigation. Housed in the Chamber of Commerce, Partners-in-Education served 30 elementary, junior, and senior high schools within the Cincinnati school district in 1982–83. The guiding principles are the same as those between the CBC and the central office: Projects are developed together; trust is built slowly; long-term assistance permits evaluation and improvement. Projects are initiated which are congenial to both school and company, and these lead naturally to others.

As in other cities, partnerships include such substantive career education as job interview workships, tours, visits, speakers, and job "shadowing." They also include in-service training for teachers, curriculum development, and morale building projects. Sometimes they address the school's major goal for improvement.

Three schools are currently working with the assistance of their business partners on improving attendance. At Washington Park Elementary, the Kroger Company provides incentives for perfect attendance. During the last week in September, teachers made posters which said, "Stick to attendance as peanut butter sticks to your mouth." For perfect attendance that week, students were awarded a jar of peanut butter. For perfect attendance each ensuing month, students win other prizes (a sack of apples, a loaf of bread). Teachers create adjunct contests; company spokespersons come and speak about coming every day and coming on time. At Woodward High, a Proctor and Gamble manager developed an attendance monitoring plan. The principal and three other administrators give a major time commitment each week to seeing that it works. The Procter and Gamble manager addressed assemblies of teachers, students, parents, and went to meetings about the project. Some Procter and Gamble volunteers work one-on-one with chronically absent tenth graders. At Hughes High, AT&T volunteers and a teacher developed software for an attendance program which reduced run time from 12 hours to one hour and which was in operation the first day of school. Hughes now has quick access to its attendance statistics.

Teachers and company people have changed some curricula. A drafting teacher at Woodward High redesigned his course to include Procter and Gamble visits, projects, resources, and speakers. A computer teacher at Woodward redesigned his course with the assistance of a Procter and Gamble expert who donated her personal library to update and enrich the class materials. A General Electric manager is reviewing Aiken High's science curriculum to see where company resources might make lessons more relevant to the work world. AT&T people help teach a COBOL course at Hughes High. AT&T employees rotate as teachers, working three weeks each. The course includes a component whereby students must master small segments before going on to the next segment. Whether the teacher eventually teaches it himself or continues to coordinate the course, he and his current crop of students are learning how people at the front edge of technological change work and think.

Making Students Employable

Schwab Junior High approached IBM about its problem with teenage students who could not read. IBM offered a corrective reading program (SRA) produced by one of its subsidiaries, a program used to help illiterate Army recruits. With school staff, IBM instituted a pilot program for 250 students in 1980–81. In 1981–82, they expanded the program school-wide, and in 1982–83, they have institutionalized the program for those students who need the greatest amount of remediation. The program was a significant success.

Procter and Gamble provided in-service training for Woodward teachers on using the resources of business and industry in the classroom and on interpersonal relations. Teachers attended these seminars as volunteers.

In student and teacher surveys, AT&T found concern about the school environment and about the lack of extracurricular activities. Students identified the two cafeterias as the top priority for sprucing up. AT&T organized two Saturday paint parties where employees, students and teachers painted the giant rooms. Some AT&T employees volunteered to sponsor clubs. One was a newly employed immigrant, a former chess master in Russia who volunteered to sponsor a chess club. He plays all comers at the same time every Wednesday. That effort spurred the teaching staff to sponsor one club per department and to co-sponsor some clubs with the AT&T people.

It was always possible for students and teachers to work together on activities. The missing ingredient in many schools has been hope; the feeling that no one cares and the job cannot be done alone. With the addition of outside assistance by individuals who go an extra mile, change is more likely to happen and a sense of community can develop. Failures occur too, but they can be dealt with. The direction changed because of the long-term commitment.

In early 1982, five major Cincinnati corporations, Cincinnati Milacron,

Federated Department Stores, the General Electric Company, the Kroger Company, and the Procter and Gamble Company each funded an on-loan executive to study the serious problems of unemployed and unemployable youth. Of all students who are enrolled in the ninth grade, nearly 50 percent either drop out before graduation or graduate without sufficient skills to hold a job. To date, this effort has generated a "Jobs for Cincinnati Graduates" program based on America's Graduates, Inc.

Governor Pierre S. duPont IV of Delaware chairs this agency set up in 1981 on a model program in Wilmington, Delaware, which Governor duPont also chairs. The program itself is based on the following key features:

• Creation of a public service agency on whose board serve the *key* leaders of business, government, education, labor, and the community who agree to accept personal responsibility for the success of the program.

• Identification of potentially unemployable youth in the junior and senior years of high school—before they become unemployed.

• Assignment of these young people at a ratio of 30/50 to one staff person responsible to the newly created nongovernment agency.

• Motivation of these youth through participation in a newly formed vocationally oriented motivational student organization, their preparation in basic "employment skills" identified by employers for entry level employees, and their orientation to the *real* world of work.

• Intensive identification of known job opportunities in the labor market with special focus on employers of twenty or less.

• Placement of these youths in private sector jobs with continuous follow-up for nine months after graduation.

• To see a significant change in the status of these youths on the job (a promotion or raise) during the nine-month period.[20]

Cincinnati schools are in the initial stages of a program where seniors who are not in college-bound or directive vocational programs are given special coaching. Areas include job awareness skills, application for jobs which have been identified by their job specialist/coach/teacher, and follow-up for nine months after beginning the job on graduation from high school. This program is funded and run by the business community. It is housed at the school system's central office. The job specialists were screened and hired by a joint team of business and school staff. Commitment to success of the program is high on both sides.

This five-company effort, the Cincinnati Resource Development Committee, is now exploring ways to improve the programs in area vocational schools by cooperative efforts between the public and private sectors. It is attempting to identify ways to use computers to remediate young adults more effectively, both those in schools and dropouts served by city agencies. When lack of basic skills precludes funding jobs in the open market, help is needed.

The Emergence of Citizens Groups

In addition to business input, citizens have been encouraged to participate beyond any previous school-community interaction. In Cincinnati, all school tax levy campaigns had failed since 1969. In 1980, G. David Schiering, school board finance committee chairman, used hearings to increase public input, which became the basis for the board recommendations on the size and use of a proposed levy. Neighborhood groups which had traditionally helped in redevelopment of the city, but not the schools, sat down with school administrators and Board members. The slogan "Together, There's Hope" keyed the June 1980 campaign. Neighborhood teams tailored campaign strategy and funds to the needs of their areas. With strong school, business, and neighborhood cooperation, the levy passed.

The citizens group which strongly supported the tax levy remained organized. It changed its name from Cincinnatians Active to Save Education to Cincinnatians Active to Support Education (CASE). Its first supportive efforts were to encourage better state financing; to develop local school advisory councils; and to improve student achievement. To address student achievement, a group of citizens and principals found, on the basis of research, that the key element in increasing student achievement in a particular school was a strong principal with specific expectations.[21]

CASE, in concert with school development staff, obtained foundation grants, hired a consultant, and provided training to thirty system principals and assistant principals (over 25 percent of the total.) These administrators volunteered to take the 80-hour course held in three weekend over-night sessions with small team meetings in between. Administrators were not paid to take the training in how to supervise teachers more effectively.

In 1982, the school board set policy ordering local school advisory councils in every school. The board had recognized that citizen involvement was helpful. Where school-business partnerships exist, businesses provide a member to the council; local universities are working to provide a member to each. Staff, parents, community leaders, and high school students also serve on these councils. Some schools already had local school budget committees which were folded into the councils; by 1982 twenty schools had such committees with some training in the intricacies of school budgets and group processes.

Additionally, Superintendent Jacobs and Dr. Henry Winkler, President of the University of Cincinnati, are working through the Association of Land Grant Colleges under a Ford Foundation grant to explore closer collaborative efforts between local school systems and universities. Building closer ties to local agencies and to the private sector is also an element in their exploratory effort.

In Cincinnati, a growing number of citizens who do not have children in the schools are participating in school decisions (fewer than 20 percent of the citizens have children there.) New ways of thinking, openness, and questioning of the ways things have "always" been done sometimes cause discomfort; to date they have not caused recrimination, blame, or public anger. "Outsiders," interested citizens, have become a strong resource for accomplishing work which administrators and teachers did not dream of accomplishing alone.

Dr. Jacobs discussed his reasons for opening the school system to the community. He said, "The complexities of running an urban school system are so enormous that one is inevitably led to the need for decentralization, shared decision making, and, perhaps most importantly, collaboration with 'other' public and private sectors."

"We are at a point in urban education where the community must participate if the system is to meet goals we all want. It is essential that public and private sectors collaborate and share resources and claim the system to be 'ours'."

Conclusion

Evolution toward more cooperative ventures is never assured; change can move in either direction. Evolution will continue to require commitment by the top leadership of school, corporate, city, and citizen structures. It requires patience and trust in the goodwill of those with whom individuals from the different sectors are not in agreement—as to methods, philosophy, action, or attention to the "bottom line."

Relationships are individual; each city and school system has a different case of individuals who affect what happens and how it happens. Yet, over the nation, there is more interest, more understanding, and some developing track records that bring hope. The new emphasis on voluntarism and cooperation might bring substantive change and become a continuing process.

On April 15, 1983, the National Commission on Excellence in Education published its report, "A Nation at Risk: The Imperative for Educational Reform." This report catapulted public education into public attention and into the presidential election of 1984 as a major issue. It was followed, in May 1983, by a report of the College Board, "What Students Need to Know and Be Able to Do," and in June 1983, by a report on the Task Force on Education for Economic Growth, "Action for Excellence," with several other national studies slated for release before the end of 1983.

All of this attention by nationally respected commissions has focused attention on public schools and recommendations for improvement. What is still needed is close analysis of why schools do what they do and what deters them from being more effective. There is no national consensus on the goals of education; no state or local consensus on goals either. Conflicting directives and purposes contribute to why schools do not and cannot meet all the expectations with which they are charged.

The spotlight, if used constructively, could help improve schools if national, state and local resources were meshed supportively. It will, however, always need close attention locally if students in a given system are to meet the expectations of their families, the local job market, and the city.

Cities can recover best if more of their citizens become productive members of society. Thus, city school systems should warrant a high priority of attention by those who care about the health of cities.

Significant attention to the correlation between the health of cities and education gives reason to hope that more attention will focus on public schools. School administrators must open their doors and find cooperative helpfulness outside. Corporate and city leaders need to commit long-term assistance to a joint venture in which everyone has a stake. Schools are everyone's business.

9

Process Lessons From a Cities' Fair

James E. Kunde

A Gamble

The urban scholars who have contributed chapters to this book also assisted in planning the Cities' Congress. When we met to organize the conference, we had serious doubts that our hopes for it could be realized.

Putting on a conference with no precedent is always a risky business. It's hard to take into account all the details that can spell success or failure. There are seldom the resources to check out the "market" — and, even if there are, the difficulties of timing, sites and dates and lining up funding sources make it impossible to be precise.

Besides, recent times have been difficult for urban places. The Reagan administration's budget cuts were now reality. Government leaders were dreading a long, hot summer, and it was clear in everything from the debates on federalism to the staffing of agencies that the federal government had abandoned any notion of a "national urban policy."

Sometimes leadership operates on hunches. Paul Porter—who once helped launch the Marshall Plan in Europe, and who was now a member of the faculty at Cleveland State—developed the idea for a Cities' Congress. He had a cadre of energetic supporters willing to try his idea. So, in spite of the gloomy outlook for cities and funding problems for a conference, the Cities' Congress on Roads to Recovery came to pass.

Planning the Congress

A fair—yes, it should be like a fair—a real celebration of the accomplishments of communities around the country—something to lift our spirits at a time when all the talk is starting to focus on what we can't do—something to build on what has been happening in our cities right now to encourage people to go out and accomplish things.

With those words, Porter left the planning meeting of the group of urban scholars looking nervously at each other. Questions about the Congress reflected our skepticism about its success. Why would important people take time to come to something that wasn't primarily designed to penetrate analytically into what really happened in urban development projects? Even if they came, why would they stay? There was to be no effort made to structure the presentations so that hard comparable data would emerge. Worst of all, it had been suggested that the conference would end with a giant role-playing exercise in which mayors, developers, and citizen leaders would play out similar roles in a fictitious "Composite City" under the critique of an audience of peers. Would knowledgeable people stay for such a thing? Would sophisticated community leaders give up their time to perform a role-playing exercise? How would they find such participation fulfilling?

There were several major hurdles in the way of a successful effort of the kind that was desired. First, the presenting cities had to be picked somewhat arbitrarily. An effort had been made to carefully screen cities that would be asked to tell their story, but that proved impossible to accomplish without substantially greater funding. So places were selected on the basis of suggestions from Cleveland State staff members and their contacts around the country—in many cases, without first-hand knowledge of the facts. The experience of the National Municipal League and its All-American Cities Program suggests that that can be risky. The National Municipal League today accepts no city for final awards that its staff has not personally checked out. But the experience of the National Municipal League could not be drawn upon, principally because funds were scarce.

A second potential problem was that presenting cities would have to be left free to structure their own presentation. There could be no rigid set of minimum requirements; participants were given only a time and a description of the overall agenda. The presenters were paying their own way to come, and conference planners were in no position to make demands. Planners worried that presentations would leave little time for audience questions and comments. Additionally, many presenters might use presentation styles and visual media so similar (such as the multiple slide projector show) that there was a danger of too much of the same thing. It was clear that much of the give-and-take necessary for good information exchange would have to occur at informal meetings during the dinners, receptions, and breaks.

Another concern was that conference planners deliberately aimed at attracting at least half of the audience from among people who had not attended conferences on the cities before. In this day of special interests and ingrown professionalism, that was a risky objective. The program would have to have appeal to both the well-informed and the not-so-well-informed.

Fourth, the highlight of the conference was to be the "Composite City" exercise, which wasn't to be held until the morning of the third day. The process to be used was role playing with audience participation—something that would take a skilled chairperson and at least some preparation by the players on the facts of the case. All the players were extremely busy people and it was to prove impossible to get them all together until moments before the program. Role playing is considered an effective learning mechanism, but it is an unfamiliar concept to many people and it requires preparation to do it well.[1]

Despite the concerns, the Cities' Congress on Roads to Recovery proved as successful and exciting as the cities it was designed to feature. Conference attendance was good; 300 registrations pulled the budget to the break-even point, something few expected. Especially surprising was the registered attendance of participants from 35 cities not selected as presenters. Non-presenters included city officials, professional planners, and neighborhood and community leaders of many types.

The goal of half of the audience consisting of people who had not attended a "city" conference before was achieved, but not at the expense of a large attendance of urban "professionals."

Perhaps even more surprising than attendance was holding power. It was a three-day conference. Generally, there is a modest drop-off the second day of a conference—even at resort cities—and the third day is usually for the hardiest survivors only.[2] Conference planners found themselves overbooked for the last day's luncheon and busily "shoe-horned" a score of unexpected holdovers into a room they had once worried would be too empty.

Some of the process concerns about the sessions where presentations were made proved all too true. Nearly everyone had an audio-slide show, some equipment broke down, several presentations were too long, and some speakers rambled. In spite of that, conference participants stayed on. The presentations were credible to other conference attendees. It was evident that the frustrated questions of audience members found their way into hallway, dinner table, and bus ride conversations. Random questioning of participants showed they generally found their way to the person they wished information from, or more likely, they found another interesting conversation going on that made them forget their frustration of missing an earlier opportunity. The social events occurred exactly as planned and there was good informal mingling of participants throughout the three days.

The greatest surprise of all, however, came in the "Composite City" role play. In spite of the risks normally associated with that process, the role play proved to be one of the conference participants' favorite events and a useful and rewarding experience for the players.[3]

"Composite City" Idea

As the organizers of the Cities' Congress mapped its strategy, they contemplated a significant problem. Most conference participants probably would have been presenters at one of the eighteen cities' presentations. Most likely they would be busy people who would be inclined to head back home soon after their part was over. This steady fall-off of participants would almost certainly have the conference end with a few lonely local survivors—hardly suited for the strong upbeat finale conference planners valued.

In addition, the cases to be presented by the various cities at the Congress were so disparate that it would be difficult to communicate a sense of total dynamics involved in putting together the actors and actions needed for community revitalization.

The Congress planners decided to take a chance. If they invited a sampling of the presenters and a few highly respected names in the urban affairs field to put on something that was really attractive and useful to the audience, they might hold them for the end. They decided that the best thing to ask such people to do was to do what they do best — play out the role they play in their own community. The audience could act as critics.

An actual city case couldn't be used for the role-play script because it wouldn't be different from the earlier presentations. Conference planners were also reluctant to use an entirely fictitious scenario for the role play because it wouldn't be genuine enough for the "players" to do well. They decided to try it with a "composite city" — one that was a compilation of the kinds of circumstances that ignited the success stories to be featured in the earlier presentation. In effect, they wanted a large scale role-playing model — something not frequently done in the kind of setting being thought of. If could theoretically be very exciting — or, if the chemistry was wrong — a disaster.

The first draft of the "Composite City" case study did not fit the experience of some of the persons finally selected for various roles — such as mayor, developer, council president, neighborhood leader, and business executive. Hasty revision of some of the background "facts" put "Composite City" into shape and provided potential for weaving the several separate roles together into a constructive interaction that would make it believable.

Most important was to select a moderator who would be respected by all players and who would understand and respect the role-playing idea, and who knew the substance well enough to keep the program moving and on track. Ralph Widner, former Director of the Appalachian Regional Commission and former President of the Academy for Contemporary Problems, agreed to play that key role.

Role Playing as a Training Technique

The concept of role playing has its roots in turn-of-the-century psychiatry. J. L. Moreno, an Austrian, introduced the concept as "psychodrama"—a technique to assist in psychotherapy. In 1933, Moreno utilized psychodrama in a business training program conducted for R. H. Macy's.[4]

Role playing came into more popular use as a management training technique chiefly through the work of Norman R. F. Maier's marrying of psychodrama to the cast study technique, producing what he referred to as "structured role playing."[5] In general, structured role playing features a written case study and written roles. Maier himself suggests that actual situations from a subject company should not be used until experience is gained using more general case studies.[6]

Wolking and Weiner suggest that while structured role playing is differentiated from spontaneous role playing for analytical purposes, in practice the two techniques are often intermingled. In spontaneous role playing, the situation is drawn from the participants' imaginations as opposed to case studies. The basic objective of structured role playing typically focuses on making the individual more proficient in some area of his work- or job-related skills. The basic objective of spontaneous role playing is to help the individual understand himself and others better, as well as to explore new approaches in dealing with problems of human relationships.[7]

While role playing has become a rather well-known technique in the training field, it is a seldom-used technique in large group conferences. A review of the literature and three interviews with some well-known conference facilitators produced no recollection of its being used in a large conference such as the one suggested by Porter and his associates in Cleveland.[8] One exception was its use by the National League of Cities in the mid-seventies where city officials performed structured role playing in front of an audience of peers.[9]

A more exhaustive review of the literature might well find the use of role playing in front of large audiences more common in fields other than urban affairs or government administration. Clearly, in large conferences of the type held in Cleveland where the audience is extremely diverse and where the objective is group participation and idea exchange, the use of role playing was at least novel.

Acting Out the Scenario

The key role was to be played by Ralph Widner who would function as moderator for the session from his "role" as Chairman of the "Composite City" Eighties Council. The author played the role of Executive Director of the Eighties Council who would begin the session by outlining the "facts" in a visual presentation. All players and members of the audience had copies of the written case study and the visual charts that summarized key data. Other key players included: Theodore Dimauro, Mayor of Springfield, Massachusetts, as the Mayor; Ms. Sydney Fonnesbeck, Chairperson of the City Council of Salt Lake City, Utah, as Chairperson of the City Council; A. L. Taggart, President of the Near North Development Corporation of Indianapolis as Chairman of the Trustees of Good Hope Hospital; Donald E. Lasater, Chairman and CEO of Mercantile Trust Company of St. Louis as Chairman and CEO of the First National Bank; John P. Gaeth, retired President of Osborn Manufacturing Company of Cleveland as Chairman and CEO of Composite City Industries; Peter Cooke, Executive Director of Price/Prowswood Partnership of Salt Lake City as President of Prudential Land Development Corporation; and Frank Carrano, President of the New Haven, Connecticut, Central Labor Council as President of the Central Labor Council.

The group met together for the first time at breakfast on Friday morning, immediately prior to the session. Several of the case "facts" were discussed and clarified. An interesting debate centered on what would be an appropriate unemployment rate for an area like the one under discussion in "Composite City." The debate suggested that there continues to be poor reporting of actual unemployment in areas such as the one under discussion, causing people to have different impressions of what constitutes a critical unemployment problem. The debate was never clearly resolved.

The role play began with a review of the "facts" of the case in a visual presentation by the Executive Director of the "Composite City" Eighties Council. The setting was a meeting of the Council to discuss the problematic "South End." The audience was to be interactive with the role play — people would request to speak and enter into the discussion much as a local audience might at a real meeting of some city's leadership discussing a community concern.

During the case study discussion, a group suddenly entered the hall, playing out a citizens' demonstration protesting the "meeting" in "Composite City." Not called for in the case study, the demonstration was organized by the sponsors to add a note of realism. While there was risk that the demonstration could have precipitated a collapse of the order of the process, it came off extremely well and probably added to the positive spirit of the experiment.

As the role play proceeded, members of the audience joined in with many provocative and useful questions and comments. From beginning to end, the process seemed to evoke spirited interest by players and audience alike.

Key Points of Discussion

It is useful to review and reflect upon the key points of discussion and debate brought out during the role play. Five principal themes seemed to emerge:

1. There are few times in a community when all the actors needed to solve a major community problem are assembled together at the same time. Such events are critical to forming a critical mass for action.

2. Development today needs to be far more interactive with the residents of a target area than it was in past years.

3. Public officials have a special responsibility to be accountable to a number of interests for the bargains they strike with businesses, developers, or other community institutions.

4. There is a need for community stewardship that transcends political changes. Development projects take a long time to produce results worth judging.

5. There is a need for institutions involved in development to work at communication. Very often some parties with a real stake never fully understand what others have in mind.

As the discussion proceeded, it was clear that the case scenario had left out some actors who really needed to be involved in redevelopment plans. Leonard Ronis, President of the American Public Transit Association, appropriately pointed out that there was no transit plan referred to — something basic in considering how to connect people in a problem area with employment opportunity. Another person remarked on the absence of public school officials in the scenario. The need for neighborhood representation was brought out, or paid homage to, by virtually all participants — suggesting how fundamental that concept has now become. In fact, the issue of human scale and the neighborhood quality of life was frequently brought out in the discussions.

The quality of the discussions seemed to satisfy most participants that the role play had been worth waiting for. Nevertheless, while useful information was exchanged, the discussion left several important questions "hanging."

1. Assembling the right parties together at the same place and time may be the fundamental development management problem. How to do that appears to be more unguided happenstance than deliberate thoughtful intervention. How to make such events more deliberate was not dealt with.

2. A private-sector self-interest is fundamental to a long-term, public-private partnership arrangement. How government policy can contribute to creating that self-interest has been unclear.

3. The tool of tax-increment financing is emerging as a "solution" to reductions in federal redevelopment aid. In most communities, there is a poor track record for handling such a tool responsibly. Frequently the "cost" of abatement is borne by human capital agencies that depend on the property tax — which is the only tax abated. Public development departments and general government units are usually supported by income or sales taxes that are the primary beneficiaries of the development spurred by the abatement of the property tax. Competent handling of this tool seemed to be assumed by some and challenged by others with no real guidelines emerging.

Even though such issues were not considered in depth, participants leaving the event seemed to feel it had been far more useful than most sessions in other conferences they attended.

Lessons from "Composite City"

The apparent success of the "Composite City" role-play experiment surely suggests further use of the technique in similar conference situations. First, it successfully summarized and focused the discussions of the three-day Congress and clearly provided the "up-beat" ending needed.

The second accomplishment of the role-playing experiment was to provide a common factual base for the exchange of ideas. The two previous days of case studies tended to focus on what was unusual in Salt Lake City or Springfield, Massachusetts. "Composite City" forced the discussion around a common framework, and thus facilitated a more in-depth discussion of common experience than would likely have been achieved otherwise.

The third accomplishment of the role playing was a remarkably uninhibited conversation among participants. While the "facts" provided a common ground, it was not ground anyone really had to defend, so the mayor felt free to expose some of the weaknesses of mayors and likewise with the other players.

The result of the experiment is the exciting prospect of a broader use of role playing for learning and exchanging ideas in large conferences. The relative ease with which it was applied in Cleveland, and the usefulness attested to by attendees, suggests that it has real practicality for similar events. The skepticism and concern expressed initially by many of the urban scholars about the ability of the conference design to produce a real learning opportunity proved to be overly conservative. The best measure of the conference's success in producing a valuable exchange of ideas was that it kept most of the participants to the very end — something a celebration alone would have been unlikely to do.

The idea of a "fair"-type event proved to be workable overall. Two key factors in its success were very likely the opportunity for broad audience participation provided by the role playing and the substantial opportunity for informal exchange provided through the social events. The conference generally achieved its objectives in Cleveland, providing another positive event in a long-term effort to build confidence in the future of older cities.

II
But Are They Successes
of the Right Kind?

10

Becoming a Good and Competent Community

T. Michael Smith

Introduction

The word "recovery" stems from the Latin word *recuperare* which means to get back, to recuperate. It is often used in a medical connotation, to gain back one's health. The health of cities in history has ranged from a bad case of influenza to the deadly plague. There is little nostalgia in looking back on cities the way they used to be. The lesson of the Cities' Congress[1] was that in order for cities of today and the future to be healthy, they must take adaptive steps by learning from others to become incrementally better places to live.

The economic revival of downtown through the highly touted public-private partnership model at the Cities' Congress is far too limiting. This model must be viewed through a larger analytical community development model that I will outline in this chapter. The model will outline characteristics of what a "good" or "competent" community might possess and describe methodologies to lead us in that direction. The Cities' Congress allowed me the opportunity to assess how well cities are doing by solving their housing and economic development problems.

Briefly, the cities' strength was the ability to form associations to solve discrete tasks pragmatically. The weaknesses are that we still haven't learned to involve a broad enough cross section of the community to be involved democratically in deciding what the problems are, how to solve them, and to interrelate issues into a comprehensive understanding of community. The surprise was finding the diffusion of knowledge and skills of facilitation, leadership development, and education to the private, non-profit community, as well as the governmental sectors.

The thesis of this chapter is that the evolving "good" and "competent" community is directly related to the values we as individuals, and as a group, hold dear and the methods we use to develop the community. This is particularly important in our large urban centers in which the search for and development of community has not been well understood. Daniel Yankelovich in his recent book *New Rules* reports that ". . .in 1973, the 'Search for Community' trend [indicator]. . .stood at 32%, meaning that roughly one-third of Americans felt an intense need to compensate for the impersonal and threatening aspects of modern life by seeking mutual identification with others based on close ethnicities or ties of shared interests, needs, backgrounds, age, or values. By the beginning of the 1980s the number of Americans deeply involved in the 'Search for Community' has increased to 47% — to almost one-half of the population — a large and significant jump in a few short years."[2] I believe it has been enhanced because more and more people are coming together to work on projects such as those presented at the Cities' Congress.

Writing about participation in a democracy, John Dewey may have expressed it best when he said, "the keystone of democracy as a way of life may be expressed as the necessity for the participation of *every human being* [my emphasis] in formation of the values that regulate the living of men together."[3] The values are the point of origin and the point to which we return after each action to reflect upon the moral quality of what we have done.[4] These common values we hold about the quality of community desired dictate the methods we choose. In working to develop and create community we must be more explicit about where we are all going and how we are getting there.

Community development emerged out of the struggle for community in the 1940s, eclectically drawing upon the social sciences' theoretical and methodological contributions that would aid in understanding community and the processes of change, growth, and development. In this chapter community development will be defined from this discipline's point of view and more specifically as "a group of people in a community reaching a decision to initiate a social action process [i.e., planned intervention] to change their economic, social, cultural or environmental situation."[5]

The Community

Nostalgically resurrecting images of community "as it used to be" in the small rural village or the heydays of market cities is selective recall. In the two million years of human history, the city is only about 5,000 years old, representing less than 1 percent of the life of humanity.

> The growth of civilized traits has been very slow. Such attitudes as fair play, mutual confidence and good will may have been thousands of years in development. . .There was a high degree of social adjustment for the individual in the ancient village. . .But there were serious limitations to that old community culture. Good will did not extend to other communities; village life tended to be provincial; men were burdened by superstitions and taboos. . .the village was too small a unit to fulfill the destinies of human life and monopolize the whole of its members. . .Yet the old village culture produced some of the finest qualities the race has known. . .The age of force, of strategy, of conquest, of empire, and of feudalism swept over and submerged his ancient community. . .Men's minds were subjugated to indoctrination and propaganda. The common man became the tool of his master.[6]

The city at the close of the nineteenth century was, in the words of Andrew Greeley, "but one step removed from slavery; it was stagnant, limited and immobile. It exercised rigid controls over its members and there was within it much physical poverty and suffering. . .Suspicion and distrust were rampant in its highly stylized relationships. . ."[7]

Recovery of the city must mean more to its residents than a throwback to hard times for the majority of its members. Some things have been lost in the communal society but much has been gained in the newer contractual society of physical comforts, affluence, political freedom, and personal mobility. If community is to exist in modern society "it is a different kind of community [people are] trying to create than that which [their] ancestors left behind."[8] People have struggled throughout history for the establishment of a better life in community.

Large urban centers as we know them today are relatively new, as is the scholarship in attempting to understand urban living. The early urban community research suggests that urban neighbors were not likely to be close friends, relatives or co-workers. Rather they were characterized as being free but isolated by the impersonality and anomie of urban industrial life. The description of urban neighboring relationships by scholars confused the diffuse nature of informal ties with their absence. Warren concluded that "Scholars contended that primary relationships in the modern city had given way to weak, disorganized social ties bound up in formal, bureaucratically oriented relationships. Such relationships were often viewed as impersonal, transitory and segmental."[9]

Modern urban community researchers "now contend that intense, intimate social relationships still exist within community-based social networks."[10] Scholars who were comparing urban community life to the rural community ideal were scholars of their times. Our societal experience at urban communal living and the revisionist look at community in urban centers is another increment of human progress as well as scholarship.

Community is an intentional human intellectual endeavor as well as an emotional instinctual need of our very being. "The idea of community is precious to people although they often don't know how precious until it is lost; it must come from social arrangements that have endured long enough to enjoy some stability. Although difficult to define abstractly, the idea of community evokes in the individual the feeling that: Here is where I belong, these are my people, I care for them, they care for me, I am part of them, I know what they expect from me and I from them, they share my concerns, I know this place, I am on familiar ground, I am at home."[11]

When people refer to "being a part of the community" it is a more direct sharing in and helping of others. It is the much more active, instrumental, goal-oriented part of community life. Warren says it's the "resultant of shared behaviors and communications." But when people refer to "a sense of community," "it refers to the perceptions individuals hold about the *potential* [my emphasis] for active problem-coping resources" available to themselves and others.[12]

The irony of community in cities is people's freedom to be a part of community through their active involvement but at this historical moment, community's greatest meaning comes from the potential, the sense of community that people feel. The meaning of urban community living is still in process of being defined. As the problem-solving beings we are, action toward solutions is how we develop; and as "the nature of human community is problem-coping,"[13] it is our collaborative actions that knit us together in forming community. The paradox is moving from an ideal of a community that never really was, and from a notion of the community that might be, to the active cooperation of making community happen.

The major barrier to this active cooperation is "not only the specific problems of one type or another but also the general problem of inability of the community to organize its forces effectively to cope with its specific problems."[14] It is a dual problem of organizing the community for the full development of the individuals within it and solving discrete common problems.

As we embark upon this dual task, we need to make the implicit values that are important to us explicit to others. "Moral values [are] statements of how we ought to live in common with each other."[15] Personal meanings must be confirmed by others, otherwise they remain personal apprehensions. "It is therefore possible to say that values have a rational basis; they are *examined* values."[16] (Friedmann's emphasis.) Social scientists have shied away from moral assessments and people haven't had sufficient forums to articulate explicitly what they think ought to be.

The bold step has been taken by community sociologist Roland L. Warren and social psychologist Leonard S. Cottrell, Jr., in proposing characteristics of what a "good" and "competent" community might include. They both place a high value on their characteristics and ask that they be examined not as prescriptions but as suggestive measures to judge what kind of community we are working to create. These issues must be faced in order that those working to build better functioning communities are not working in the dark. It is a matter of having a holistic understanding about what kind of community we might be creating. Also, one needs some objectives that concrete practical effort may result in increased community competencies.

The characteristics of the "good" and "competent" community will emerge in a process of interaction. Some, however, may not be compatible with one another or appropriate for the stage of development in the community or region. But once the process begins to emerge, the results aren't predictable: Conflict and tension arise; time taken to do things expands exponentially; outcomes are different from initial expectations; unanticipated setbacks, and even embarrassment of special interests, occur. Therefore, Warren cautions that the characteristics must be looked at in the light of three questions: (1) How much of what we want is actually possible? (2) How much of what seems desirable do we actually want? (3) How much of a price are we willing to pay for it when other values are jeopardized by it? Seventeen characteristics described by Warren and Cottrell have been synthesized into twelve. They are described below.[17]

Characteristics a "Good" or "Competent" Community Might Possess[18]

Development of Primary Group Relationships. A community is a group of people who know one another well. This means the full pattern of functional social relationships which people may have with one another: nuclear or extended family, neighbors, clubs, churches, schools, business and service relationships. These relationships are developed on a face-to-face basis, in small groups, in naturalistic ways; they evolve slowly and last, all because of the relative permanence of the people.

Increase of Self and Other Awareness and Clarity of Situation Definitions. The degree to which communities can cope realistically with their problems is determined by the clarity with which each part of the community perceives its own identity and position on issues in relation to that of other parts of the community in a larger (community) context. Practice in down to earth, realistic, situational analysis of each concrete issue is the surest way of developing the capabilities called for.

Internal Communications. Individual skills of sending messages, receiving them and obtaining responses is essential to a viable interaction of community members with one another. An information collection and dissemination network is needed within the community or neighborhood, consisting of newspapers, local forums, discussion sessions. The networks will actually aid discussion and crystallization of opinion and should funnel the information, undistorted, to decision-making bodies within or outside the community.

Articulate Citizens. Each segment of the competent community and its citizen members has the ability to articulate views, attitudes, and intentions, and to express their perceptions of the relation of their position to that of the other citizens or segments of the community. Social interaction in small groups that relies upon all participants' knowledge and expertise to describe, analyze, solve problems, and link them to other problems or segments of the community nurtures the articulate community.

Participation. People commit themselves to a community, contribute to the definition of goals as well as the means for their implementation and enjoyment when they participate in a process of interaction which is both process- and product-oriented. All barriers and impediments must be removed so that all members of the community have the opportunity to participate.

Commitment to a Locality. When people see that what a community does and that what happens to it has a vital impact on their lives and values they cherish, when people find that they have a recognized significant role in the community, and when people see positive results from their efforts to participate, there is a committed community. To feel and to know that what one does makes a difference creates a committed people and in turn builds community.

Machinery for Facilitating Participation and Decision-Making. Processes of interaction for achieving consensus and decisions require rules and regularized modes of procedure that are known and accessible to all community members. Review, refinement, and revision of participatory mechanisms in communities are necessary to insure optimal and continuous communication and interaction.

Increased Autonomy. Communities, insofar as possible, should be masters of their own fates. It is necessary for a community to be aware of the context of relations in which it exists. Communities serious about their autonomy tend to resist policies made at national or at least extra-territorial levels for voluntary associations, businesses, service organizations or agencies, and churches which are local branches. Communities need to develop capacities to adapt to these larger societal mechanisms and relationships, to utilize the resources and supports and to reduce the threats to the life of the community from the larger system. The community must trust itself, more than well-intentioned outsiders.

Neighborhood Control. Equitable distribution of services and decision-making at the neighborhood level is necessary in urban contexts. Neighborhood control is part and parcel of community autonomy. Cities are proving more difficult to manage at centralized levels. The knowledge of what can be controlled at the neighborhood level versus what must be controlled centrally can only emerge from continuous testing.

Increased Power Distribution. Communities must be active participants in the decisions which most directly affect them. The extent and amount of power is developed over time. In any community, the refrain heard is that power must be distributed "more broadly than now."

Degree of Heterogeneity. The different life styles, subcultures, and values in a diversified, pluralistic society should be accepted and valued. Exposure, interaction, and time are essential to the development of a tolerant and pluralistic society. A point of consistent tension centers around the balance between heterogeneity and cohesion.

Conflict Containment. If all the above are in a state of development, conflict will naturally occur and intensify, and that is healthy. But procedures must be developed for working out accommodations that will keep conflict within bounds. Inventiveness and versatility are essential in utilizing existing and developing new procedures.

Methods of Community Development

Doing things together, people are reminded of their common interests and values.[19] It is from this practice and the activity that the meaning of community is derived and problems simultaneously solved. Warren says it's the dynamic "interaction of tasks work and process" that builds community;[20] Cottrell says it's the "inextricable relationships" of all the actions that creates community;[21] Friedmann says the "Good Society" is here and it's what is practiced *now* that brings it about;[22] Greeley says community "emerges slowly and gradually through constant hard work."[23]

When planning and development specialists attend to the problems of communities, they "will attend to the problem, not attend to the long run values and welfare of the whole community."[24] There are few more alluring myths in all history that problems can be set right in one mighty effort directed by a great organizing genius at the top. It was neither on the size nor on the complexity of urban problems that the Cities' Congress most intensely focused, but rather on the public-private partnership of business, industry, and government decision-makers marshalling their clout to overcome barriers and to rebuild inner cities. The essential weakness of the approach is its narrowness. Inner cities need a broader scope of methods to involve and activate many diverse segments of the community.

Community Development Methodologies

Jones, a community sociologist, synthesized community development methodologies in an attempt to improve our understanding of the orderly and effective arrangements of *how* we work toward the development of community. They were developed as tools to evaluate community improvement programs. The first five elements are listed in chronological order and the sixth is a facilitating mechanism to help nurture the preceding five. The first two are foundation methods, the essential first steps. The second two are the action methods, the techniques of how things get done. The last two are the connecting methods, the strategies that move things along and tie them together.

A word of caution: There are grave risks involved in utilizing the methods described below as a way to create good and competent communities. For example, as there is an increase in democratic decision-making (below), power will be distributed more broadly (above); this will cause great tension with existing power structures. But in a democratic society in which we espouse the philosophy of the full development of all of our citizens, taking the step to involve citizens more broadly in democratic decision-making is a high risk. This "must not be allowed to inhibit attempts to create competent communities if democracy itself is to survive."[25]

Broad Cross Section of Community Involvement. Anyone who has an interest, stake, or role in an issue or problem in the community must have the opportunity to participate. Moreover, there must be a structure which continuously reaches out by informing (people act on the things they know) and inviting diversified segments of the community to participate. Community problems and solutions are complex and they require variable organizational arrangements for people to participate. In democratic societies, all people have a fundamental right to try to influence the discussion of issues of public concern and to dissent from the majority opinion. It is the inclusion of the differing, even opposing, perspectives in the organizational structure that aids in building confidence in the outcomes of the organization's work. An assessment of the broad cross section is addressed by asking "Who's involved and who's not?"

Democratic Decision Making. "Ideally, democracy means individual participation in the decisions that affect one's life."[26] This definition is based on the assumption that the community knows the problems and issues confronting them. Without basic information, people exclude themselves or are excluded by others who withhold or manipulate information. The provision of information helps to assure early involvement, allows a balance of perspectives and power, and nurtures participants' continuous involvement. Discussions in groups must be free, open, and non-judgmental of persons involved. Every effort is made to strain toward a consensus of views, giving all participants the opportunity to articulate their views and contribute. Short of consensus, the fallback procedure for democratic decision-making is majority rule.

Group Building, Leadership Development, and Capacity Building. In community work, small groups are where people participate, act, and interact; where all people are viewed as contributors and capable of leadership; and where the most learning takes place (increase of knowledge, changed attitudes, and ultimately altered behaviors). People are pragmatically programmed learning organisms: They thrive on activity and remember what works for them in solving their problems. Group development depends on participation by all members in describing and defining problems, suggesting alternative solutions and actions for implementation. Giving people in groups the opportunity to do something on their own initiative as a contribution to the group is the foundation of leadership development. Essential to group and individual growth in knowledge and skills is the internal learning instrument of "each one teach one" and the external experts teaching group members. Through group activity, community and group norms merge: Refined and revised group development integrates the diverse interests and opinions and fosters the increased horizontal social relationships within the community. The measure to judge the extent of group building is how many people are involved, in what size groups, doing what kinds of things.

Problem Solving Process Followed. When people come together in the development process, it is generally to address a problem, and that necessitates some problem solving process be followed. The most common model followed to accomplish the task goals is to (1) define the problem or goal, (2) gather facts, (3) seek possible alternative solutions, (4) choose a course of action, (5) implement it,[27] and (6) evaluate the work and recycle the results. To determine whether some kind of systematic process is being followed, one needs to review the group's plan or guide for action.

Issues Linked in a Holistic Manner. Communities are complex organisms in which the parts contribute to the whole. To understand a community is to understand the horizontal interrelatedness of community segments to one another.[28] A community's problems must therefore be investigated broadly, allied influences recognized and assessed, and linkages made when and where appropriate. When "spin-offs" or unexpected outcomes occur, as they invariably do, it's likely that proper connections have not been made. The time that lapses between when a problem is initially defined and when a more holistic view of it is formulated begins to tell whether appropriate issue-linking has been done.

Facilitator, Educator, Coordinator Roles for Staff. A professional staff concentrates on the process as well as the product and allows the group and community to concentrate on the task goal. Staff roles are to foster the group's awareness and at times confront issues surrounding the processes delineated above that help to develop community while solving its problems. To judge the effectiveness of staff, one must determine who is doing what kind of work and whether the group's consciousness of community building processes is as deep as their understanding of the problem.

Analysis of Seven Cities

Having reviewed the characteristics of a "good" or "competent" community and the methods used to develop community,[29] we now turn to the application of these ideas. This section will compare the experiences of seven cities in applying these methods.

Seven cities from the Cities' Congress on Roads to Recovery presentations were selected to be reviewed: Akron, Ohio; Columbus, Ohio: New Haven, Connecticut; Oakland, California; Saint Louis, Missouri; Salt Lake City, Utah; and Washington, D.C. A reasonable mixture of cities was selected based on geographical distribution, population, size, and project diversity. What is reviewed here is based solely on what presenters provided or had to say (my personal notes, transcripts provided by Cleveland State University, and materials provided by the cities). There was no detailed investigation to determine the accuracy of what was reported. It was assumed that what was reported was a reasonable accounting of what took place, especially since each presentation had multiple presenters from different sectors of the partnerships.

This process analysis compared the intentional and incidental use of community development methods by the seven cities to try to understand how urban development strategies are nurturing or hindering the evolution of community in our larger cities. Information reviewed on strategies, techniques, and mechanisms was classified into one of the six community development methods and then weighted as strong, moderate, or weak. There is no other way to interpret this except as grading the cities. When I was in doubt,

I tried to be lenient in the cities' favor because of the lack of full information. This analysis helps in making judgments on which community development methods are most used by cities; whether these are the most important; what new things, if any, are revealed by this review; and what might be the one or two methods that cities could concentrate on to build "community" while they are solving problems.

Roland Warren, in his seminal book *The Community in America*[30] twenty years ago observed that task groups—such as the ones that presented at the Cities' Congress—would focus their work on the "action methods" (Group Building and Problem Solving Process) that produce task results, rather than on the "fundamental" and "connecting" methods that develop community. In the twenty years since Warren's work, we have observed some incremental improvements.

The Broad Cross Section of Community Involvement method requires an informative outreach that invites interested people, regardless of position, to participate in the variety of organizational structures used to define and solve a community problem.

Columbus, Salt Lake City, and Washington used this method. All three reported having, in one form or another, a public-private-neighborhood partnership. The clearest example of this is the Neighborhood Redevelopment Renaissance Project in Columbus. Beginning with the private initiative of the Battelle Memorial Institute, project staff informed all affected residents, organizations, and city agencies and invited their involvement without judgment of which ones were legitimate. Jubilee Housing in Washington crept along in implementing its project due to the extremely adverse circumstances encountered in the beginning (See Chapter 7 by Joel Lieske). As the project unfolded, all affected people or organizations were invited to participate. Salt Lake City had what appeared to be a strong public-private partnership for a downtown development project that was encroaching on nearby neighborhoods. After some initial confrontation, the neighborhood organizations became active participants. Local electoral politics allowed for a certain balancing of power and opening up of the organizational structure. The important thing, though, is that a lesson was learned and the system remained open.

Jubilee Housing built its organizational structures from the ground up while the Renaissance Project combined existing and new structures as mechanisms to encourage participation. Jubilee and Renaissance both have policy boards. Planning, organizing, and support committees were established to accommodate personal interests, skills, and tasks to be done at Jubilee. Once the project was underway, housing cooperatives, economic development corporations, and social service agencies were created and complemented by resource support committees. After five years of operation, a long-range planning process was begun with representative participants from all affected organizations.

Renaissance, on the other hand, began with a full year of planning as a way to involve people and chart the ten-year project. Multiple vehicles were used: task groups, committees, town meetings, individual interviews. Neighborhood development organizations and neighborhood associations have been effectively used or financed by Renaissance to implement parts of the plan. The city redevelopment and social service agencies have also been effective in carrying out the plan. It is also the only project reviewed in which 40 percent of its work was completed under the time scheduled: in six years.

Oakland initiated its economic development program as a perceived mandate from the electorate in the election of Mayor Lionel Wilson who had promised economic revitalization in his campaign. The city government defines a broad cross section of involvement to encompass a wide range of interests in economic development: neighborhood, commercial, industrial, downtown, and international. Programs and participants described did cover the range. They appeared open to new initiatives, making them flexible to constituencies. This multi-dimensional economic development program was unique in the presentations in that it was citywide in scope and covered most aspects of the field.

Downtown revitalization projects presented were limited to the public-private partnerships. The public sector saw its role as motivating the private leadership to commit itself to spend its resources on civic projects or large-scale projects that would create jobs downtown. Downtown development was seen as the province of downtown business people. The Priority Group in Akron, the Downtown Council in New Haven, and Civic Progress in St. Louis were the downtown business organizations created to respond to downtown development. St. Louis epitomizes the approach: Three existing organizations were merged to increase coordination and resources, the top thirty chief executive officers from downtown businesses were selected to meet monthly or more often in subcommittees, and each has to be able to commit his/her company to participation. Beyond activating business leaders, the city saw its role as "providing leadership in making the infrastructure happen" to meet the business development needs. In Akron, Mayor Roy Ray said, "This group [The Priority Group] takes sort of an overview of what is happening in the community. They are more or less a catalyst for making things happen in the private sector." In New Haven it was the same. Downtown redevelopment projects narrowed participation in partnerships dramatically.

When downtown interests are narrowly defined as the business leaders' province, then other techniques to entice citizens into downtown are needed. Publicity techniques used to improve downtown's marketability to the metropolitan area include the "shop downtown," "mall days," "New Haven, Look What We've Got"-type campaigns. Public relations boosterism programs produce short-term shallow results rather than a substantive commitment to shop or live downtown. "Commitment [to downtown]. . . is no easy undertaking that can be accomplished by. . .booster programs."[31]

The broadest possible definition of who participates is this method's greatest strength coupled with an attitude of openness that is inclusive when dissent and confrontation occur (which it always does). Narrow special interest group participation to plan and implement urban recovery projects is the weakness of this method.

The Democratic Decision Making method stresses public knowledge and early involvement in an issue or problem definition, with majority rule, utilized when consensus can't be reached. It is the nurturing of the attitude that, "What I say and do makes a difference."

Columbus's Renaissance Project with its year-long planning was highly visible, much discussed and written about. This enlightened initiative combined with the breadth of involvement was time-consuming (the prime criticism of democracy) but it appeared to reduce confrontation, with the project anticipated to be finished way ahead of time. Conflict arises, but it appears to be more content and less process focused—there is a common vision and language but different techniques.

Jubilee Housing in a northwest Washington neighborhood utilized a highly personal approach to contact all affected people one at a time, and then later moved to group meetings. This slower developmental approach played down public information, built credibility between the instigating middle-income white church members and the low-income black neighborhood residents. The information network relied upon was the neighborhood grapevine. The report demonstrated an openness and responsiveness to new initiatives. Community ownership emerged in establishing two businesses, a jobs placement program, a child care agency, and three cooperatively owned housing projects.

Salt Lake City's project unfolded a little differently. Two partners, one public and one private, were initially involved. Adjacent neighborhoods reacted negatively to the development plans, took public stands opposing the encroachment schemes and finally obtained a role in helping to redefine the problems and solutions of downtown development (meaning more than the commercial buildings in the central business district).

The decision-making gradient from majority rule to consensus moves from Salt Lake City to Columbus to Washington, which appeared to strain the most to obtain consensus.

The local press's role of keeping the public informed was underscored by Paul Poorman, editor of the *Akron Beacon Journal* and presenter at the Cities' Congress when he said, ". . .if you'll permit the analogy of a mirror —a mirror tells us unpleasant truths from time to time. . .we do not smash the mirror because it tells us these truths. As a matter of fact, we accept the mirror for what it is supposed to be, and I think that's the role of the newspaper."[32] In a sense, the press is a public monitor and evaluator of development programs. The Akron press is helping to keep the process democratic.

The electoral mandate of Oakland's administration has kept the entire process highly visible and under public scrutiny. The governmental knack of building compromise, combined with the enormous breadth of the city's economic development enterprise, has had a very positive democratizing effect.

The downtown business organizations in Akron, New Haven, and St. Louis by contrast have streamlined multiple organizations into one; assembled decision-makers (i.e., CEO's) who can make commitments; made decisions in executive sessions to implement redevelopment projects; and through promotional campaigns, sold them to the public. Aldrich Edwards, Executive Director, New Haven Downtown Council, records how the corporate process model works. "We have not concentrated on having the participation of every business in the community in our work. We have about 24 corporate institutional members. . .We have not been active in stimulating various committee meetings to discuss or deliberate what is best for the city. . .The meaningful area of project activity. . .is an interaction with the public and private sector to stimulate physical development in downtown. . .[and to]. . .stimulate developer interest in the downtown."[33] St. Louis, in its presentation, added an often-heard comment about dissenting opinion when one panel member said that it had "neutralized the opposition." Finally, Paul Poorman of Akron, criticizing closed door executive sessions, said that ". . .It's true, that some things grow in the dark. I was trying to figure out what they are, and mushrooms come to mind and so do silverfish, and so do real estate deals."[34]

Not wanting to be misunderstood at this point because of the negative connotation of the above narrative, I wish to point out that these cities have completed some very successful programs (revitalizing a theater district, new office and housing development, improving a river frontage, and reclaiming devastated areas as redeveloped industrial parks) and initiated spin-off activities such as downtown host, adopt-a-block, tutorial programs, and teen-age job fairs. The assessment here is to ascertain whether and how effectively democratic decision-making methods were utilized in developing community. The weakness is that the problems to be addressed are decided upon by a small segment of the community in contrast to the potential strength that comes from the early and continuous informing and involvement of all interested community segments resulting in compromise and consensus priorities. *The Group Building, Leadership Development, and Capacity Building* methodology provides the opportunity for individuals and groups to utilize personal skills and knowledge, and develop anew by learning from others, in order to solve common problems. As one of the two "action" methodologies, group building was widely engaged in among the seven cities, with groups being delegated to carry out important tasks.

Columbus and Washington developed or combined initiatives with the most groups. They actively sought out more people, assigned tasks for individual action, and in Washington's case, aggressively set out to teach group process, skills, and housing finance and management. Both cities relied heavily on the groups (whether neighborhood volunteers, or paid city or corporate staff) to do the work. The success of this method appears to have a direct relationship with the sixth method to be considered, the presence of a facilitating organization. (More on that later).

As a city initiator, Oakland worked mostly with existing groups, but when it was necessary, the city helped to establish an economic development corporation. To be sure, though, the leadership role at this phase is clearly in city government's hands—where they want it.

New Haven, as noted in the previous section, was anxious to do something: Procedures were streamlined for quick action on individual projects. When efficiency becomes the dominant priority, this method is frustrated. The strength of this method is in developing strong groups with the accompanying social ties, improving leadership abilities, and educating people—all time-consuming.

The Problem Solving Process methodology exemplifies American pragmatism: What's the problem? What's to be done about it? Do it!

The Renaissance Project as described earlier excelled here with its twelve-month planning effort and its annual review and revision of its comprehensive plan. In fact, the old argument of not involving too many people because the problem is too complex was in effect made null and void. One outcome of particular note were the negotiated contracts and agreements for implementation with participating resident groups and city agencies that cemented everyone together to do his or her share in redeveloping the neighborhood.

The Oakland economic development example is a good one in that breadth characterized the analysis, the decision-making, and the implementation. It is the breadth of the problem solving process that is particularly impressive here. Though the new administration had pre-defined the problem through the campaign, the process they followed was novel. This probably had to do with the responsiveness of the mayor to local neighborhoods as well as to industrialists.

The downtown development plans were done by consultants, reviewed, approved, and implemented, straight-forward and efficient. Done in this manner without the three previous methodologies, this type of efficiency model undermines community involvement and, subsequently, commitment to implement it. Political necessity and corporate efficiency combined in Akron and New Haven to expedite the process.

Jubilee Housing was confronted with a problem so complex and so far outside the frame of reference of most partners that existing assessments and known solutions weren't appropriate. In selecting the northwest Washington neighborhood which has a very low income, with hard-core unemployed residents and all the attendant social pathologies, Jubilee found it could not start out with a plan. Explorations of the neighborhood led them to the conclusion that *any* place was a good place to start. Housing was chosen, because to Jubilee, stable living quarters represented the basis of community building. One project after another built confidence, and after five years a planning process was started. Sometimes in the development process, the problem solving model must be tinkered with when circumstances almost defy reason. James Rouse in his Cities' Congress speech agreed when he said ". . .We have to invent new systems, structures, and relationships to solve these problems."³⁵ This was one of those cases!

The Issues Linked in a Holistic Manner method interrelates the segments of the community to the whole, placing the highest priority on the community to rely upon itself. The length of time necessary to accomplish this, however, is protracted.

Jubilee Housing was the most successful in linking issues holistically and laying primary responsibility internally on the community doing the work. This task has been nine years in the building so far. Columbus's Renaissance Project to renovate and develop housing did create mechanisms that connected community social service agencies and a referral office to make necessary linkages for citizens who needed assistance.

Oakland's single focus on economic development must begin to link economic development decisions to other community parts. City government, of course, does that, and Oakland's Cities' Congress presentation concentrated on economic revitalization efforts. It would be interesting to see how these discrete projects are connecting to other allied fields and issues.

Interrelatedness of urban problems often spills over political jurisdictions in a region. All center cities acknowledge regional linkages and symbiotic relationships with their suburban neighbors, but the truth is that the competition is fierce.

Akron took a unique approach by initiating a regional economic development plan: Agreement among the governmental units was reached, and each city competed to attract the industry that all had agreed was the most desirable for the region.

Downtown physical development projects were New Haven's prime concern. The presentation, for the most part, was concentrated on those projects. Closer scrutiny, however, revealed that the linkages that New Haven was weaving were incidental to their prime objective. In fact, all cities do create linkages almost unintentionally, and given enough time, awareness of these linkages begins to emerge. However, our knowledge of the ecology of urban systems must make interrelatedness a more intentional act.

The Facilitator, Educator, Coordinator Role for Staff method emphasizes the intermediary role of staff to concentrate on processes above as products, confront thorny realities (such as social and economic justice concerns of community segments), and keep the action moving.

Intermediary actions were best exemplified by Jubilee and Renaissance. These two organizations were broader in defining their role as staff to do outreach which informed both like-minded and dissident groups and individuals. When conflict arose with various interest groups, special attention was focused on resolving the impasse and reopening communication channels, thus retaining a diversity of opinion and groups in the partnership or project. In Columbus, for example, neighborhood residents raised serious objections to the project because of the displacement of residents and gentrification of the neighborhood. There were several concessions made to alleviate the problem: among them, a tenant purchase plan, and a $250,000 grant awarded to a neighborhood housing corporation to rehabilitate and market a substantial number of units as a part of the plan. Formal agreements were signed that tied the disputing entities together to complete the implementation of the plan. Interestingly in this case, the private developer was the facilitator.

The outreach to involve small business was added to subsequent phases of Akron's and New Haven's projects. The continual responsibility to be inclusive is vital in building community.

Catalyzing, expediting, and creating activity are a part, but not sufficient alone. In Akron, the mayor said he wanted to "marshal the clout" of the private sector, and New Haven said much the same. There the approach was essentially to reduce government's role to that of facilitator in the redevelopment of downtown, allowing private developers to do what they are the experts at doing. This "leave it to the experts" type of attitude is exclusive rather than inclusive. The norms of the community as a whole have to be considered if community is to evolve to higher forms of operation.

Individuals with big egos who need to take credit undermine the entire effort towards which a facilitating staff works; this is the essential weakness of this method. Bob Boulter of Jubilee Housing expressed the great strength of the method when he said, "The more people invest their time in a project, the greater their stake in seeing to the success of the project." The development of a city into a community must be based on this maxim.

Conclusions

The thesis of this chapter has been that the evolving "good" and "competent" community is directly related to the methods used to develop that community. Of course, it is obvious that people's notions of what the good community ought to be are varied: They are based on personal history, social class, ethnicity, location, or region. "Your Good Society will not be mine. It is only in its practice that we may join and merge the separate realities by which we live into a shared experience."[36] It is the practice which has been of concern here.

The methodologies used in public-private partnership models of downtown development as reviewed here are insufficient in "recovering" or developing communities. They have a few of the ingredients—but a few ingredients does not a good stew make. Downtowns are complex organisms and too interdependent on the metropolitan region to leave their development to limited segments of the community. The cities reviewed demonstrated that the public-private partnership model needs to be improved to include broader citizen involvement and to operate more democratically. The economic development of downtowns by the business association with participation by public authorities is an incremental step in the evolution of our communities, but not a particularly new idea. The partnership must, however, be incorporated into a broader community development effort if our cities are to change for the better. Let us distill what we have learned about the broader methods reviewed above.

I. American pragmatism and our penchant for groups are still strong active values among our citizens. The methodologies derived from these basic values that the seven cities excelled in were Group Building, Leadership Development, Capacity Building, and Problem Solving Processes. So deeply are these values ingrained in our personalities and in the evolution of our communities, that one hundred fifty years ago De Tocqueville said, "Americans of all ages, stations in life, and all types of dispositions are forever forming associations. . .If every case at the head of any undertaking, where in France you would find the government and in England some territorial magnate, in the United States you are sure to find an association."[37] Our maturing communities have improved over the past century and a half since De Tocqueville wrote. Continued education of citizens coupled with the refinement of techniques used in these two methods, will fertilize the blossoming of the community in America.

II. The surprise in the methods evaluation was the use of the Facilitator, Educator, Coordinator, and Role of Staff. It showed up very positively in four of the seven cities. In Warren's "great change" theory[38] of the American community, he says that, "one of the most notable changes is the gradual acceptance of governmental activity as a positive value in an increasing number of fields" and "The alternative position that 'government is best which governs least,' is a rapidly fading standard for contemporary judgment."[39] In the four cities, the intermediary had a vested interest in the outcome. The style of the special interest participant is the significant point here. The style of intervention was to facilitate, coordinate, and educate in a developmental manner for the divergent interest groups involved. What has to be added to Warren's 1963 assessment is that today we turn over to non-profit organizations, corporations, and churches many of the tasks we once wanted government to do. We are developing the type of skills and knowledge to intervene in ways that bring about the beloved community we want for ourselves.

III. Immediate improvement would occur if the "foundation methods" of a Broad Cross Section of Community Involvement and Democratic Decision-Making were more intensively used. The cities that did well in these methods established a cornerstone upon which the "action methods" —done well by communities for the most part—could be solidly built. "Traditional democratic theory [holds] that popular participation has been valued as an opportunity for individual self-development: responsibility for the governing of one's own conduct develops one's character, self-reliance, intelligence, moral judgement, in short one's dignity. . .The argument for citizen participation in public affairs is based not upon the policy outcomes it would produce but the belief that such involvement is *essential* [my emphasis] to the full development of human capacities."[40] Building on this foundation will decide the form "action methods" take and the context within which work is done and problems are solved. Community evolution is anchored here: As human capacities improve, the full development of community emerges.

IV. Time allows the divergent complexity that is community to evolve and grow into an identifiable whole. Linking small projects to larger systems, uniting dissenting factions, promoting diversity for the benefit of the integrity of the whole causes fear, apprehension, and concern at the very least and fear and conflict at the worst. "In contrast to a simple notion of a highly coordinated and explicitly organized set of services and helping, the reality of urban community life is one of pluralism and differentiation.

Often this complexity leads to terrible isolation. On occasion, all of the pieces fit together in a remarkable way to form very healthy communities and neighborhoods. More typical, however, the reality is one of incomplete and underutilized links between one kind of helping system and another."[41] The least understood and utilized method is the linking of issues in a Holistic Manner. Many more millennia and more intentional effort will be needed to create more remarkably ". . .healthy communities."

In conclusion, it is not the "recovery" of cities that we are dealing with, but the continuing struggle of evolving our communities to higher human forms. Our conceptions of the community are implicit in our values, beliefs, theories, and practices. These need to be made more explicit by a broader, more democratically inclusive style of community development in which more of our citizens have the opportunity to participate, contribute, and receive the full developmental benefits of involvement. I've advanced my notion of what the "good" and "competent" community might be by synthesizing Warren's and Cottrell's contemplations and how we might chart a path to achieve it utilizing Jones's excellent synthesis. Because of the respect I have for nature's wisdom of slowly correcting and improving life on this planet, I am not impatient for the results of our next steps as a community. I am very impatient, however, when community segments are excluded from development because they are poor, handicapped, black, female, elderly, or minorities or dissident voices of any type. *All* of us are needed to envision what our communities might be.

As we set about the task of realizing our hopes for our communities, we must be as efficient and effective as possible. The methods described here, if used, can enhance the development of community as we diligently work toward solving the important problems in our cities. After all, it took us two million years to evolve ourselves and our communities to their present status; to think one political administration or even the rest of this century are enough to develop our cities into the "good" or "competent" communities we envision is not realistic. Instead, we "must not be discouraged in the face of frustrations, misunderstandings, frictions, dissensions and obstacles." The community must be "perceived by an *unending series of beginnings*, [my emphasis] so the new community must not lose the courage to write off its losses, forget about its mistakes and start all over again."[42]

11

Redevelopment and Redistribution

June Manning Thomas

The Challenge

That urban redevelopment has, at times, directly harmed the poor is one of the darkest facts of redevelopment history. Commonly, the neighborhoods of the poor were the very areas cleared for redevelopment. In places ranging from Manhattantown in New York City to Yerba Buena in San Francisco, officials deemed low-income people's houses expendable, and flagrantly ignored requirements for relocation assistance and placement in safe and sanitary housing.[1] Protective legislation eliminated the worst abuses of the old urban renewal program, but new concerns have arisen concerning the detrimental effects of the return of the upper and middle class to the city upon low-income renters and home owners.[2]

In recent years, redevelopment projects have been less likely to directly harm the poor, but a second, related, problem has surfaced: the focus upon revitalization as a process for the benefit of middle and upper class citizens, with only indirect benefits for poorer members of urban society. The supposed rationale for such an emphasis is that all urban residents benefit from redevelopment projects, in the form of a healthier economy, stronger tax base, or heightened sense of community pride. Another rationale is that other programs, such as welfare and subsidized housing, focus on such problems, and that it is not the role of redevelopers to address issues of income maintenance.

The fact is, however, that the "other programs" have not been able to eliminate the problems of urban poverty. Furthermore, it is unclear how far indirect benefits of redevelopment projects flow; the contention that the effect is widespread has certainly not been proven by empirical research. The issue becomes one of increasing importance as federal financial support for urban redevelopment decreases.

The purpose of this chapter is to explore the state of human resources in contemporary urban America, and to reflect upon the lessons learned from the Cities' Congress concerning the impact of current redevelopment efforts upon urban residents, especially those of low income. Some conference speakers presented useful ideas for improving the status of low-income residents, and this chapter will examine these ideas and speculate upon their applicability elsewhere. On the whole, however, those in the forefront of redevelopment efforts were relatively uninvolved in the task of building human resources. Yet, in order to rebuild cities, we must focus not only upon physical structures—commercial and office buildings, housing complexes, and capital facilities—but also upon human resources, which should be developed to their fullest capacity. It is this task which offers the most difficult and potentially most rewarding challenge to urban visionaries. It is also this task, perhaps, which is least capable of being solved at the local level, and most dependent upon the uncertainties of federal aid.

Enormous problems exist among urban populations, and yet so do enormous possibilities. The problems are extensive, pervasive, and intractable. One author has said that the typical large industrial city has become a "sandbox" used to park the poor while the "adults get on with the serious things of life."[3] While the cities may not be "sandboxes," they certainly do retain an ever-enlarging portion of the poor. The exodus of the middle class has led to a more and more rigid polarization as suburban areas house the middle class, and the central cities, the poor. Unemployment, underemployment, and poverty combine with poor education, poor health, and racial discrimination to make it ever more difficult for central city youth to develop to their potential capacity as productive citizens. Meanwhile cities lose residents and tax dollars, and find the burden of caring for their remaining citizens increasingly difficult.

Polarization by Race and Income

In the 1960s, the National Advisory Commission on Civil Disorders charged that we were moving toward two nations in the United States, one black and one white.[4] That projection appears to have been accurate. The black population is heavily concentrated in central cities, which must also bear the burden of a relatively high rate of poverty. In this dual world, the suburbs serve as green havens for the white and the middle class.

The figures tell the story. In the nation as a whole, the percentage of families with incomes below poverty level has dropped in the past decades.

Only in central cities has the proportion of poor families increased in the past few years to levels above those of 1959 (see Table 1). The percent of families in poverty dropped markedly in nonmetropolitan areas, from 28.2 percent in 1959 to 15.2 percent in 1981, and fell as well in the suburbs (metropolitan areas outside the central city), from 9.6 percent to 7.7 percent, but rose in central cities, from 13.7 percent to 16.7 percent. Central city poverty had fallen to 9.8 percent in 1969, but has increased steadily since then. The burden of poverty, therefore, rests much more heavily upon central cities than upon suburban areas, and the situation appears to be worsening.

TABLE 1
Family Residence and Percent
Below Poverty Level by Race, Selected Years

	1981	*1979*	*1974*	*1969*	*1959*
All Races					
Total (% below poverty level)	12.5	9.1	8.8	9.7	17.7
Inside central cities	16.7	12.7	10.9	9.8	13.7
Outside central cities (suburbs)	7.7	5.4	5.5	5.3	9.6
Nonmetropolitan areas	15.2	10.8	11.0	14.8	28.2
White					
Total	9.5	6.8	6.8	7.7	14.8
Inside central cities	10.9	7.9	7.0	7.2	10.2
Outside central cities (suburbs)	6.5	4.6	4.8	4.6	8.3
Nonmetropolitan areas	12.4	8.9	9.0	12.0	24.3
Black					
Total	33.2	27.6	26.9	27.9	48.1
Inside central cities	33.3	28.5	25.5	21.5	34.3
Outside central cities (suburbs)	23.7	17.3	20.0	20.1	44.0
Nonmetropolitan areas	41.3	35.4	36.1	49.0	73.2

Source: U.S. Department of Commerce, Bureau of the Census, *Money, Income, and Poverty Status, 1980* and *Characteristics of Population Below Poverty Level, 1979 and 1981*. This data records poverty as defined in each specific year. The Census Bureau frequently changes the monetary value of the "poverty lines."

Poverty in general, it seemed, had reached a plateau during the decade from 1969 to 1979. However, 1981 data showed a marked increase in the poverty population, especially in central cities and nonmetropolitan areas, possibly because of the effects of the recession.

When examined by race, these trends become even more pronounced. Among both white and black families, the percent of central city families in poverty dipped in the early 1970s, only to rise in recent years. In 1981, one-third (33.3 percent) of black families in central cities fell below poverty level, compared to one-tenth (10.9 percent) of white families.[5] Also apparent in census data is a polarization between the races in terms of residence. In 1981, twenty-six percent of all families lived in central cities, as did twenty-two percent of white families. Yet over one-half, or fifty-five percent, of black families were central city dwellers. In contrast, forty-three percent of white families lived in suburban areas, but only twenty-one percent of black families.[6]

The effects of gentrification (the return of the upper and middle class to the city) on this phenomenon are negligible. To be sure, gentrification exists: The Urban Land Institute has estimated that three-fourths of all cities of more than 500,000 have become the scene of private-market renovation.[7] Congressional hearings documented the fact that professional couples of high education and high incomes have reclaimed low-income central city housing in a number of cities, often displacing previous residents in the process.[8] Case studies suggest that quite often the new residents, or "gentry," are white, while displaced residents are quite often black or members of other racial minorities. Nevertheless, recently released 1980 census figures show that this phenomenon is not extensive enough to halt the racial polarization of metropolitan areas. As Table 2 illustrates, in almost every one of ten cities known to be the site of gentrification activities, the percentage of white residents has continued to drop, while the percentage of black residents has continued to rise or has dropped very slightly. One major exception is the city of Washington, D.C., where gentrification has indeed been extensive enough to cause almost as great an increase in white residents as the black population has decreased.[9] Otherwise, apparently, white flight continues in spite of gentrification, and is joined, to be sure, by middle class black flight.

That the black middle class has begun to flee the central cities should surprise no one. Black middle class citizens have many of the same motivations as whites—they too desire suburban amenities such as good schools, new homes, and superior public services. Racial discrimination and exclusionary barriers to black suburbanization continue to hinder free mobility, and so residential patterns in suburban areas mimic the polarization of the metropolis, as suburbs tend to become segregated as well; nevertheless many blacks

TABLE 2
Racial Change in Ten Central Cities
(1970–1980, Percent Difference)

Sampled Central Cities	Census Tracts within 3 miles of Central Business District		Gentrifying Census Tracts	
	White	Black	White	Black
Atlanta, GA	-7.8%	+6.9%	-16.1%	+14.4%
Baltimore, MD	-3.6	+3.0	-4.6	+4.3
Columbus, OH	-2.4	+1.4	-1.5	+0.4
Dallas, TX	-20.8	+1.4	-36.9	+5.8
New Orleans, LA	-13.3	+12.7	-16.7	+15.3
Philadelphia, PA	-1.2	-3.0	+0.2	-5.5
Saint Paul, MN	-3.8	+2.0	-2.4	+0.2
San Francisco, CA	-8.1	-1.8	-7.7	-3.8
Seattle, WA	-2.8	-1.0	-3.4	-1.5
Washington, D.C.	+4.6	-5.6	+8.8	-12.3
Total (sample)[1]	-4.6	+0.3	-4.4	-1.1

Note: [1]Within all central cities of SMSAs, white residence fell by 8.6% and black residence rose by 2.1%
Source: Daphne Spain, "A Gentrification Scorecard," *American Demographics*, (November, 1981), p. 18.

have continued to move to suburban areas.[10] Of those blacks residing in suburbs during the period from 1975 to 1978, nineteen percent had moved from another suburb, and seventeen percent had moved from a central city. During the same period, only nine percent of black suburbanites moved from suburban areas to the central cities.[11] By 1981, although black mean family income was far less than white income in both central cities and suburbs, the mean income of black families in suburbia exceeded that of black families in central cities.[12] Table 1 shows that since 1969, the incidence of black poverty in central cities has arisen much more rapidly than the incidence of black poverty in suburbs. In 1969, about one-fifth of black families in both suburbs and central cities were poor. By 1981, 33.3 percent of black central city families fell below the poverty line, compared to 23.7

percent of suburban black families. Comparable figures for white families show a much less pronounced gap between poverty rates for white suburbanites (6.5 percent) and white central city residents (10.9 percent).

These numbers certainly show that all black poverty is not concentrated in central cities. If anything, they reinforce the impression that race is a critical factor in predicting differences in income and poverty rates among metropolitan citizens; suburban blacks have almost four times the rate of poverty of suburban whites. However, the statistics do seem to reflect a growing differentiation in economic status within the black population: Those who live within central cities fare worse than those who live in suburban areas. The metropolitan community is one polarized by both race and class.

Earning a Living

Of all the problems that plague urban populations, surely the most important revolve around the issue of employment. If people can obtain jobs that allow them to reach a moderate standard of living, they do not fall below the poverty level, nor are they as vulnerable to problems of poor health or inadequate housing. Employment is a basic necessity that, if supplied, reduces the negative effects of many other problems. Unfortunately, the very cities that have witnessed the flight of the middle class have also lost jobs by the thousands. More precisely, they have lost manufacturing jobs, which are the very kind that once supported working-class culture. As white-collar employment grows in importance, so does education, and yet the educational institutions of cities are part of the problem. Inner-city schools are not adequately preparing youth for the new world of work, or even, perhaps, for the *old* world of work.

These three problems are therefore intrinsically linked. While other issues are important, the status of employment, unemployment, and education determines in great part the nature of the task of building human resources.

For years central cities have battled to keep and attract new jobs. In many cities the battle has been a losing one. Central cities, no longer the unchallenged foci of industry and commerce, have had a rough transition into the "post-industrial" or "service" society. Capital investment has diffused to other parts of the metropolis, other regions, and other countries. Private-sector activities have changed "from production to administration, and to the service activities associated with administration."[13] For central cities, all of this has meant the transition from factories to office buildings. Urban renewal often increased the rate of this transition, both by razing small commercial and manufacturing firms, and by encouraging their replacement with office buildings.[14] The replacements, of course, hired white-collar rather than blue-collar employees.

The results of these changes are obvious even at the state level. Representatives from 13 states (only one of which was in the South) made presentations at the Cities' Congress. These states are not representative of all states, since the cities were chosen on the basis of having suffered population loss, but most of the states represented experienced loss of manufacturing employment during the 1970s, while only two of 14 southern states (plus the District of Columbia) suffered manufacturing loss during the same decade (see Table 3). Although service-sector employment increased in

TABLE 3
Employment Sector Changes, 1970–1980, Selected
States and Regions, 1970–1980 (Percent)

State or Region	Manufacturing Employment Change	Service Employment Change
California (W)	28.5	68.4
Conneticut (NE)	-3.8	51.0
Florida (S)	36.3	93.8
Indiana (MW)	-4.0	60.3
Maryland (NE)	-13.2	54.6
Massachusetts (NE)	1.9	46.1
Minnesota (MW)	19.1	73.2
Missouri (MW)	-4.2	52.9
New York (NE)	-17.0	24.3
Ohio (MW)	-11.0	48.6
Pennsylvania (NE)	-14.1	45.3
Wisconsin (MW)	12.9	67.0
Utah (W)	67.0	78.3
NE: Northeast	-10.0	39.6
MW: Midwest	-5.0	51.1
S: South	18.6	69.6
W: West	26.8	75.3

Source: Jacqueline Mazza and Bill Hogan, *The State of the Region, 1981: Economic Trends in the Northeast and Midwest* (Washington, D.C.: Northeast — Midwest Institute, 1981), pp. 76–79.

every state, over-all nonagricultural employment rose by 14.1 percent in the Northeast and Midwest, much less than the 44.0 percent increase in the South and West.[15]

Those working-class people in central cities in declining regions who at one point could count on stable factory jobs being accessible with no more than a high school diploma can no longer count on such jobs or on their stability. Those who cannot qualify for office or other growth-sector jobs join the ranks of the unemployed.

Unemployment rates are high throughout the country, but they are especially high in those metropolitan areas affected by a declining manufacturing sector. In 1981, the overall unemployment rate was 8.0 percent, but the rate in metropolitan poverty areas was 14.3 percent.[16] And the official unemployment rates do not show the true extent of the problem. Many people are defined as no longer in the labor force because they have given up looking for work. Others are in the labor force but work part-time involuntarily only because they can find no full-time job. The number of people out of work or working part-time involuntarily is much larger than the number of people officially unemployed.[17]

As with other problems, race matters. While the 1981 official unemployment rate is 6.4 percent for adult white males, it was 12.9 percent for adult black males, 12.8 percent for adult black females, and 40.2 percent for black teenagers. In metropolitan poverty areas, white males suffered a 10.9 percent unemployment rate, but that of adult black males was 16.3 percent, and that of black teenagers was 42.3 percent.[18]

The frightening thing about much central city unemployment is that it is chronic. Observers have suggested that we are raising a generation of youths who do not understand how to work, and will not understand because they will get no job in the near future. What this means is that many urban communities suffer from a state of economic depression, with no relief in sight.

Under the circumstances, the quality of the educational system is crucial. Urban residents sorely need a good education. In metropolitan areas as a whole, 71.3 percent of household heads have a high school diploma, as do 65.2 percent of central city household heads, but only 44.7 percent of those in metropolitan poverty areas have high school diplomas.[19] Central city schools have earned a well-publicized reputation as being among the worst in the nation. As test scores decline and social, behavioral, and racial problems soar, the ability of central city pupils to prepare for post-industrial society plummets.

The quality of schools, then, rates high upon the list of factors influencing a city's ability to recover. The middle class shuns inadequate school systems. Because it does, the quality of the systems declines even further as they become holding institutions for the children of poor families who cannot move.

Unemployment and poor educational systems are problems that can be solved, but they require a great deal of attention and effort. For this reason current attempts to redevelop American cities should include considerations of their effects upon chronically unemployed or working class residents, the school system, and the urban community at large.

Meeting the Challenge

Outlining the challenge is a simple task; determining successful ways to meet that challenge is vastly more difficult. One suggestion by James Rouse, developer extraordinaire, is to "stop thinking of the city as problems to be attacked."[20] Rouse, in a galvanizing keynote address to the Cities' Congress exhorted the audience to build images of what the city should be like, and then generate support for those images, as happened with Baltimore's successful riverfront development. An attractive idea: Build up to an image of the good city!

The only problem is that this approach works best for physical redevelopment; it is, in some sense, a visual tactic. Those who have typically become involved in redevelopment projects have tended to emphasize redevelopment as a physical renewal process. But as David Bergholz of the Allegheny Conference on Community Development (Pittsburgh) commented: Corporate leaders "like to build things"; but what do we do about the "social infrastructure" issues? A good question. Would these problems be solved by a riverfront development project? Would downtown office development improve the school system? Probably not. These "social" issues must be attacked as problems in their own right.

The first step, perhaps, is to understand that many "declining" cities possess great resources. Because of the nature of the economies of central cities, they often serve as headquarters for important companies and corporations. These powerful organizations and their personnel offer vast reservoirs of money and skills. In addition, those people directly in need of assistance because of income or residence also serve as resources, because of their direct involvement in urban problems and their stake in improving them.

The Cities' Congress presented examples of cities which have reached beyond the usual redevelopment participants, and which have attacked the problems of poor educational systems and chronic unemployment; but on the whole, if presenters are typical, we have a long way to go before these problems are solved. One of the first tasks is to understand the role of leadership and participation in the development process.

Leadership and Power

The question of leadership is an important one because it lies at the heart of the issue: For whose benefit will we redevelop the cities?

Many cities seem to follow the time-honored pattern of using a group to spearhead urban development that includes well-known civic and business leaders. The business leaders may be quite powerful, much more so than the ordinary membership of the traditional Chamber of Commerce. Rouse claimed that the power of such a group in Baltimore was critical for accomplishing redevelopment of the inner harbor. Other cities have regularly used such groups. Some have existed for decades.

The advantage of such organizations is that they create an immediate lobbying group for redevelopment, one with the clout to assure project implementation. Since the members may include the most powerful bankers and financiers in town, funding is practically assured. Since they may also include top executives of major corporations and foundations, the backing of the business community for sponsored projects is virtually automatic. Redevelopment backed by such a support system can greatly surpass (in size or possibility of implementation) proposed projects supported only by public officials and planners.

The strength of such organizations is also their weakness. Practically by definition, since such redevelopment groups are composed of persons of great power and influence, they exclude persons and groups without such power. The membership may, upon occasion, expand to include labor leaders, or leaders of major academic, health, or cultural institutions, but no others of lesser power. Hence, in Baltimore, only chief executive officers of major companies and institutions were invited to join the "Greater Baltimore Committee." In Cleveland, others involved in redevelopment efforts include the president of Cleveland State University and the president of Cleveland Clinic Foundation, a major medical complex. Milwaukee's organization, the Greater Milwaukee Committee, has existed for forty years with the staunch membership of major local businessmen. It also includes attorneys and labor leaders, but those labor leaders are heads of major labor councils. And Milwaukee has exceptionally broad membership. Even though these groups may be extremely effective in some cases, they have made decisions that proved to be in the best interests of their members rather than those of the city as a whole, or of low-income residents. A well-documented example: The corporate leaders of San Francisco Planning and

Urban Renewal Association sponsored the original plans, carried out by the San Francisco Redevelopment Authority, for the Yerba Buena redevelopment project. Firmly backed by those corporate leaders, the Redevelopment Authority planned to move out 4,000 area residents with little or no assistance in finding safe, comparably priced housing. Only strong, organized defensive action by residents forced the Redevelopment Authority to offer realistic housing assistance. (In large part because of these experiences, Congress subsequently mandated assistance in the Uniform Relocation Act.) In the meantime, the economic benefits of the project accrued to a small group of investors while the public gained the burden of paying for the convention and sports facilities for years to come. The original site of the project held 723 businesses and 7,600 jobs in 1963, and the work force consisted primarily of small proprietors and skilled, semiskilled and unskilled workers. The new Yerba Buena Center directly created only 3,600 jobs, with another 5,100 created indirectly, but located mostly outside of San Francisco. One author has estimated that over ninety percent of the new jobs were in office buildings and went to white-collar commuters. Other new businesses such as hotels and restaurants provided a number of jobs in the area, but previous research has documented the fact that such businesses hire minorities for the lowest level jobs—as maids, cooks, janitors—and favor whites for more visible, higher level jobs—as waiters, bartenders, etc.—thus perpetuating racial discrimination in employment.[21] Certainly the decisions made by elite redevelopment groups have spin-off benefits in terms of employment. The point is that these are indirect benefits that may or may not occur, depending upon the nature of the redevelopment project.

It is also important to recognize why leadership coalitions have tended to address physical rather than social or redistributive needs. To a large extent they are prone to the same inclinations as the rest of the populace—the desire, for example, for beauty in public places. Redevelopment projects that replace blight with physical beauty are naturally attractive, and such attractiveness is heightened by architects' renderings of new and rehabilitated buildings and public places. This love of visual change has also influenced the planning profession, ever since the days of the "White City" of Chicago's Columbian Exposition in 1893, and planners may influence redevelopment efforts into physical renewal channels. Employment programs and school innovation projects simply do not give one great aesthetic satisfaction.

Other reasons for physical renewal predilections are financial. Coalition leaders have often been investors. Physical development projects, such as central business district renewal or the construction of convention centers, appear to be sound investments for financial leaders of a city. The financial incentive factor is in fact a drawing card that policy-makers have used ever since the days of urban renewal. It is ironic that many of these projects have not made money. The faltering Renaissance Center in Detroit is a prime example, as are countless urban stadiums and convention centers. The fact is that such projects have often failed to make money because new construction is not sufficient to overcome the problems of large cities, many of which relate to poverty exacerbated by lack of accessible jobs and poor education.

Finally, even if leadership coalitions contain powerful members with strong desires to improve social ills, techniques for accomplishing such tasks are not well known.

At least three ways exist to improve upon the problems of this leadership coalition model, two of which were presented at the Congress.

One approach, which assumes that such leaders wish to assist with local social problems, is to apply corporate and institutional resources directly to the task of building human resources. This may involve appointing activist task forces or committees directly concerned with issues of human resources, such as health or education; or this may mean directly involving corporate executives, managers, and other personnel in efforts to improve social institutions, such as the schools. Cincinnati and Pittsburgh offer good models of approach. Their programs provide person-to-person assistance for students in ways that advance both their education and their employability. Another way to apply corporate resources is to encourage corporations and businesses to set up their own programs for racial minorities and low-income groups. While the most obvious area for these efforts would be job training, they might also include small-business assistance, or housing and neighborhood development programs.

A second way to expand the focus of redevelopment is to build and support indigenous leaders within communities of direct need. To a certain extent, this is the approach of the neighborhood organization movement. This may occur in modest forms, such as crime-preventive "neighborhood watch" programs, or in more aggressive forms, such as the organizations inspired by activist Saul Alinsky, or more recently, those formed by ACORN (Association of Community Organizations for Reform Now). Another way indigenous leaderships can be developed is to support cooperatives and other organizations that foster a sense of self-management. In Washington, D.C., Jubilee Housing, Inc. has managed to do just that by buying six apartment buildings, using foundation and church money to rehabilitate them, and gradually turning over their management to tenants by using a well-tuned system of tenant work committees to clean public spaces, collect the rent, and screen applicant tenants. In so doing, they have vastly improved the environment for numerous tenants, and in addition countered the pressures of gentrification, poverty, and crime.

The examples of such efforts are sparse. Cincinnati, Pittsburgh, and Washington are, of all cities involved in redevelopment efforts, among the very few to be directly concerned with building human resources. And the last example of an approach to broadening redevelopment participation is being implemented in even fewer cities.

Implementing this latter approach would make a redevelopment effort one that truly involved members of the groups that are most vulnerable to poor housing, poor education, poor employability. At various times in the past, public programs for redevelopment have attempted to require a mild form of such involvement—or participation—but in most cases this has been a weak, ineffective formality that has had little influence. Only in a few cases, such as the Model Cities program, where residents on Model Cities boards were actually given the power to determine program policy, have residents had any major influence at all, and that situation was not universal.[22] In recent years the federal government has retained some citizen participation requirements for programs such as Community Development Block Grants, but federal oversight has dropped rapidly, diminishing the role of citizens. Other programs, such as Urban Development Action Grants, never had much citizen input to begin with. If redevelopment is to become a public-private partnership, where the private sector plays a larger role, it becomes important that decisions not be left entirely to corporate representatives. The problem is not so much that such decisions would be wrong or evil, but that they may not be in the best interest of all sectors of urban society. Only by including the voice of all sectors can we insure that past mistakes are not repeated. At the very least, this means that civic organizations and redevelopment committees should broaden their membership to include the not-so-powerful, and the neighborhood, tenant, and church groups that represent the poor. All redevelopment efforts must be examined in terms of their effects on those of low and moderate income. When this is done, in spirit as well as appearance, assuredly redevelopment projects will not serve only the middle and upper class, or implement economic development to the exclusion of the chronically unemployed, or build beautiful downtowns to the exclusion of declining neighborhoods.

Education and Employment

Urban redevelopment efforts have often focused upon the problem of housing. Where federal support money (such as, in recent years, Section 8) has been available, redevelopment projects have primarily concerned themselves with low-income housing rather than social or human services. Yet, the comments of an administrator at Jubilee Housing are instructive. At the Cities' Congress, Robert Boulter noted that members of his church group approached its apartment house redevelopment projects with the idea that they could productively limit themselves to improving the terrible housing situation in the poorer sections of Washington's Adams–Morgan neighborhood. They soon found that it was impossible to focus narrowly only upon housing; the needs of the residents were much broader. They soon became involved in health services, a pre-school, and employment services. As Jubilee discovered, improved housing for people suffering from chronic joblessness and poor health was far from sufficient.

Of all the areas that could be covered, education and employment are two we can easily focus upon. The status of urban education is a problem that can be solved, or at least improved. The solutions may not be easy, and they may be multi-faceted, but they do exist. Likewise, the problems of unemployment and underemployment are not without potential solutions. The efforts of some cities illustrate ways that public and private resources can be used to help solve these problems.

For example, Pittsburgh's Allegheny Conference on Community Development is "a thirty-eight-year-old nonprofit organization that carries out the civic agenda of Pittsburgh's corporate leadership."[23] Like many of the organizations composed of corporate leaders, the Allegheny Conference actively participated in downtown renewal and economic development projects. In addition, since 1978 it has committed resources to the effort to improve the public school system of Pittsburgh. Its staff generated over one million dollars through its Education Fund, and assisted in a desegregation program. The Allegheny Conference also instituted a mini-grant program that provides money to teachers for innovative projects, and a Partnership-in-Education effort that links businesses with individual schools. Cincinnati has a similar program which Jay Chatterjee and Carol Davidow describe elsewhere in this book.

These kinds of activities are important steps in the direction of involving businesses and business personnel in the task of building human resources. Not only do they broaden the traditional definition of urban redevelopment, but they also provide substantive assistance for a problem that strongly affects the city and its ability to survive.

The problem of unemployment is no less crucial than that of poor education. As stated before, although it is often assumed that downtown redevelopment or economic development automatically increases jobs, it may only shift the location of jobs, or provide only professional and administrative jobs, or otherwise offer little assistance for widespread or chronic unemployment.

Recognizing this fact, Jubilee Housing in Washington, D.C., helped set up two institutions, Jubilee Jobs, an employment service, and the Washington Work Association. The Work Association established a local business, Five Loaves Bakery, that provides a neighborhood service and also hires local residents. It also has initiated smaller ventures, such as a commercial parking lot.

In Oakland, California, the city has established an Office of Economic Development and Employment which has sponsored employment training programs. Several businesses conduct special internal on-the-job training programs for which they receive reimbursements of up to fifty percent, and the city has established policies and goals for minority hiring and public projects.

It is interesting to note that, except for three or four examples, very little was mentioned at the Cities' Congress about improving the employment chances of the unemployed. When asked what the Allegheny Conference was doing in employment, which was listed among its concerns, David Bergholz commented that it had supported pre-employment and summer youth jobs programs, but had been "fairly unsuccessful. This is an area where most communities have had the most problems," he commented, and have not known how to solve them.

Conclusion

Issues such as poor public education and chronic unemployment have been with us for some time; surely they will not disappear overnight. The question is, are we redeveloping cities in such a way as to help solve such problems, or are we ignoring them?

The judgment must be that redevelopment is not, at present, synonymous with improving human resources nor has redevelopment greatly aided problems of redistribution. A few steps in the necessary direction have been taken by some organizations in some cities. Cities that have recognized the connection between the status of central city public education and redevelopment are headed in the right direction. When programs in such cities motivate students to see the linkage between skills learned in school and work-related skills, and when they actively promote improvements in educational attainments, they provide the kind of assistance that public education needs most. The experience of an organization such as Jubilee Housing, Inc., offers a striking example of the possibilities for self-management in multi-family housing, and reaffirms the truism that housing alone cannot minister to the needs of low-income urban residents. But more must be done. Until we develop the underused human resources that our cities offer, urban redevelopment cannot be successful; the linkage is intrinsic and inextricable. Only with a healthy, well-educated, employed population can cities improve to any significant degree.

Ever since the early 1960s, the American people have perceived the task of developing human resources as belonging to the public sector, not the private sector. Yet, under the current Reagan administration, it appears that the federal role in building human resources declines yearly, even daily. The issue is more than one of money; it is one of commitment. If the federal government perceives that it has a role to play in improving urban public education or in encouraging the employment of chronically unemployed youth, it sponsors and supports initiatives in those directions, even with budget cuts. If it does not, lack of money is a convenient excuse. Currently, it seems clear that the present administration begrudges the federal role in human services, and views such service areas as a useful source of money for the vastly expanding military sector.

It is difficult to imagine an existing city, in any region of the country, that has adequate resources to overcome the problems of income redistribution, chronic unemployment, and poor public education. Because of the peculiarities of municipal boundaries in the United States, most cities are left on their own in a political system characterized by the growing power and isolation of well-to-do suburbs. The only exceptions to this rule are those cities that have managed to continue to annex territories to which the middle class has flown, such as newer metropolitan areas of the South and West.[24] Cities in other circumstances are chronically short of resources. While the suggestions in this chapter would help in some way to prevent implementers of redevelopment projects from using what resources do exist without responding to the needs of the poor, the problems are too big to be solved at the local level, either by the public sector, by the private sector, or by the much heralded "public-private partnerships" which in most cases have used public money to help the private sector. It is true that the ideal situation would be to reduce city dependency upon the federal government, but it is also true that cities must cope with what are in effect national problems; the days of true independence are still far away. In the meantime, it is the responsibility of higher levels of government to assist in human resource development.

The Reagan administration has claimed that the level of government most responsible for these problems is the state government. Yet, the states are also unable to provide sufficient resources. It is for this reason that state governors first shied away from the movement toward "new federalism," claiming that the transfer of power and responsibility from the federal government to the states must also entail the transfer of money and resources.[25] Spatial considerations also limit the power of states: States which have historically conducted generous social service or redistributive school financing programs, for example, have been rewarded with high costs and taxes that drove away industries and other investors. The federal government is needed to overcome the spatial problems of redistribution.

Those who work to improve the redistributive record of redevelopment must also work to improve the federal commitment to assisting the human resource problems of American cities. Only with this two-pronged effort can cities truly recover.

12

Job Generation as a Road to Recovery

Robert Mier

Introduction

A city's recovery means:

- a regained ability to compete with its suburbs as a place to live;
- a regained favorable climate for investment and a consequent growth for jobs;
- as a product of the above two, a regained independence from external subsidies.

This definition of "recovery" included in the invitation to the Cities' Congress in Cleveland immediately focused attention on the importance of job generation. It was somewhat disappointing, then, to find very little discussion about jobs at the Congress. Most of the shared "success stories" focused on capital investment, usually in real estate, and assumed that jobs naturally follow from such investment.

The absence of "jobs stories" comparable to the "investment stories" raises a series of questions that guide the following reexamination of the Cities' Congress. Is it too early on the "road to recovery" to observe the new jobs being created? Is the generation of jobs even necessary for successful revitalization? Were there any patterns of "recovery" shared among the "success stories" that suggest a greater possibility that new jobs will be created?

Although 60 percent of the cases presented claimed specific job creation objectives, only 40 percent reported success in this area, and only 27 percent that the jobs were being captured by the low skilled and minorities. "Aldy"

Edwards, Executive Director of the New Haven Downtown Council, reported that adoption of an employment strategy reaching those segments of the population with serious unemployment problems was the "next step" in New Haven. David Bergholz, Deputy Director of the Allegheny Conference on Community Development in Pittsburgh, put it more bluntly:

> If you ask me candidly about where most communities have been least successful, it is around the issue of jobs. We aren't doing much beyond the usual things like summer youth employment.

Nevertheless, several approaches to job generation did emerge at the Congress, and I will examine them in a subsequent section. However, I first want to argue that generating new jobs is an essential component of recovery. I will then examine several approaches to job generation, including general service sector revitalization, high-tech manufacturing and research and development (R&D), public policy-induced job development, and self-help job development. In focusing on these approaches, I am attempting to be analytical rather than be reportorial—excellent summaries of the success stories have been presented earlier. I also will be trying to draw some generalizations from the presentations which I observed.

The final and concluding section of the paper will examine possible ingredients, hinted at during the Congress, that might stimulate recovery. I will argue that the latter two approaches—public policy-induced and self-help job development, probably in combination—represent the best local strategy for true recovery, a recovery that genuinely attacks social dependency.

Jobs for the Unemployed as an Essential Road to Recovery

The problem of "dependency" was a central theme of the Cities' Congress beginning with Porter's assertion that recovery was synonomous with "independence from external subsidies." As Porter candidly points out in his preface to this book, the concept of "dependency" is complex and fraught with ambiguity.[1] Nevertheless, the clear linkage between local-government fiscal stress and individual poverty emphasizes the need to focus recovery on those needing work. (After all, for every federal dollar spent in support of non-welfare related state and local government programs, more than four are spent in support of welfare.)[2] James Rouse passionately argued this in his keynote address.

Unemployment is a major social problem both with deep historical roots and with ties to the national and international economies. Nevertheless, as long as we are a society that recognizes a responsibility for those without work opportunities or unable to work, no city can afford to ignore employment problems. A city's self-sufficiency is integrally tied to that of its citizens.

If there is to be an effort to achieve greater self-sufficiency, is the stimulation of private investment sufficient? Many Congress participants believed so. "Sandy" Taggart, President of the Near North Development Corporation in Indianapolis, most clearly articulated it when explaining the logic of the recovery strategy for the North Meridan Corridor area of Indianapolis, he said:

> First, you've got to get the investment to create jobs. Then the jobs create a demand for better housing and retail services.

This reduction of the job problem to an investment problem was almost an article of faith at the Congress. However, this "supply side" conception ignores a myriad of problems that can get in the way of translating investment into job growth, including the technological reorganization of work, the need to retrain massive numbers of workers, and significant private investment in less productive enterprises that do not provide good quality work opportunities.[3]

An example of the complicated interplay of these effects often looks like this. In order to compete in the international economy, a local manufacturer must invest in new computerized numerical-control technology. An adverse effect of this is technological displacement of many skilled workers. In order to reemploy them, both retraining and job creation efforts are needed. The short-run effect is probably fewer jobs and greater "dependency," with the long-run impact a matter of speculation.

An effective road to recovery must not ignore these interactions. Because they are highly idiosyncratic, every investment opportunity must be probed for its employment impact. The implication of this, to be developed in more detail, is that local governments can influence investment decisions to enhance job opportunities for the needy.

Approaches to Job Generation

This section begins to look at some of the approaches to recovery being undertaken by cities represented at the Congress. To repeat, these include service sector, high-tech, public policy, and self-help approaches. The logic of distinguishing among them comes from the participants of the Congress themselves, and represents differences in emphasis and understandings of local development conditions more than uniquely different strategies. Thus, different approaches may overlap when viewed from the perspective of geography, sector of the economy, or key development factors. For example, high-tech development may affect the service sector and be public sector induced.

Service Sector Emphasis

Virtually every city presenting cases at the Congress reported significant developments in the service sector, usually in the central business district. Typically, the developments involve expansion of office and retail space, addition of hotels and convention facilities, and residential construction targeted to the professional class. Equally common was the presence of public money leveraging private investment. Examples include Oakland using an Urban Development Action Grant (UDAG) to finance a portion of a $48 million Hyatt Hotel, and Indianapolis using a $12.8 million UDAG for a variety of downtown development projects.

Nevertheless, little evidence of direct new job generation was presented in these success stories. This should not be surprising because such development often represents a job-holding action, yielding not net new jobs but rather an expansion of office and retail space and an upgrading of its quality.[5] In other words, the space per employee expands, but not the total number of employees. Such activity is important to job retention, but does not open job opportunities to the dependent populations.

Creation of construction jobs is often pointed to as a positive indirect benefit of downtown revitalization. However, with the exception of Oakland, no city reported efforts to open the building trades to minorities, women or low-income groups. Furthermore, few reported efforts to involve unions in the public-private partnership being formed to spawn recovery.[6] The Oakland exception, to be discussed in more detail below, consists of setting minority employment goals in any situation involving public financial support of private construction.

In sum, the revitalization of the downtown service sector probably received the most attention at the Congress. Although it did show the ability of cities to mobilize significant capital investment—particularly when public funds are used to leverage private investment—it also presented, of all the approaches, the *least* evidence of creating jobs for the "permanently" unemployed.

High-Tech Emphasis

Although there was little direct discussion of "high-tech" development at the Congress, it played an important role in the efforts of three cities: St. Louis, Indianapolis, and New Haven. The Washington University Medical Center Redevelopment Corporation in St. Louis was able to convince St. Louis–headquartered Monsanto Chemical Company to open a new research laboratory adjacent to the Medical Center. The key to Monsanto's decision appears to have been access, for research purposes, to Washington University Medical Center's fine medical library.

A comparable strategy is unfolding on the near north side of Indianapolis, where the city and the Near North Development Corporation are using Methodist Hospital as the "bait" to attract medically related manufacturing to an industrial park being developed adjacent to it. No industry has, as yet, been attracted. However, the site has been cleared, infrastructure installed, and the land cost "written down."

The third case of high-tech development is in New Haven, where Yale University has entered into a joint venture with Olin Corporation and the city of New Haven to begin development of an 80-acre research park on the site of a former Olin manufacturing facility adjacent to the University. Olin Corporation, a long-time resident of New Haven, will continue to operate R & D facilities on the site. Finally, the city promises considerable infrastructure improvements tailored to the needs of any prospective tenants.

Although none of the three cities promoted these "high-tech" developments as the central element of its recovery efforts, they are worth examining for two reasons. First, in each case they were presented as an approach offering great potential for new job creation. Secondly, throughout the nation, public attention is turning to "high-tech" development as a solution to the recession and heightened international competition.[7] It must be noted that only in the Washington University Monsanto case has any development moved to the implementation stage. Further, the jobs created there largely have been scientific and highly professional administrative jobs. In none of the three cases are sophisticated training programs being planned to attempt to open job opportunities to the local unemployed population because the likelihood of these programs being successful is minimal. Even efforts to upgrade skilled and semi-skilled workers dislocated by foreign competition have not been successful.[8] There is much less reason to be optimistic about the possibility of training the low-skilled for "high-tech" jobs.

Are the three cases of "high-tech" development useful approaches to providing meaningful employment opportunities, or are they examples of endeavors that have a high cost and have a low probability of payoff? In a speech to the Cities' Congress Planning Committee in April, 1982, Pat Choate cautioned that the technological transformation of production sweeping the world promises a significant net domestic job contraction in manufacturing with employment as a percentage of the labor force decreasing by an order of two or three.[9] In addition to high-tech production, the competition for new high-tech R & D facilities is becoming intense with virtually every major university or other research facility in the country developing adjoining research parks.[10] Furthermore, business location decisions are complex, multifaceted ones.[11] As James Rouse suggested in his keynote address to the Congress, it is highly unlikely that high-tech industrial parks will be adequate magnets to high-tech industry in isolation from a comprehensive effort to upgrade the quality of the urban environment including schools and social amenities. The sum of these negative effects doubtless would intimidate a bold gambler.

An important recent study by Bennett Harrison charts other pitfalls of a "high-tech" road to recovery and suggests an alternative path to industry redevelopment.[12] In discussions of high-tech development, Massachusetts, with its development along Route 128, is often cited as the prototype, along with California's "Silicon Valley." Harrison shows that in a recent two-year period, high-tech development in Massachusetts accounted for less than one out of four new jobs created, and high-tech R & D for less than 1 percent. This finding should be combined with David Birch's work showing that most job growth comes from expansion of existing industry. The sobering conclusion is that the economic development payoff from focusing so much attention on attracting new high-tech facilities appears slight.

The same issue may be examined in another way. Despite almost two decades of significant high-tech development, Harrison finds that the shoe industry in New England, after being ravaged by international competition, still employs one-third more people than all of the combined industries defined as high-tech. A major problem for New England is the technological transformation of the shoe industry. The problem involves a range of activities including adapting computer-assisted design to an industry with many small, individual manufacturers who lack the scale to adopt such new technology efficiently; developing vocational training focusing on the new design and manufacturing technologies; and promoting development efforts building on the skills of the workers who will be displaced by the new technology.

Although not discussed in "high-tech" terms, the best example at the Congress of investment-facilitating technology transformation is the Washington University Medical Center itself. Interestingly, the medical-services sector is generally excluded from lists of "high-tech" sectors even though it is a major consumer of new technology. As a consequence of WUMC's efforts, employment at the complex has expanded by several thousand. To me, this dramatically underscores the opportunities associated with high-technology catalyzed development once rigid and narrow approaches are abandoned.[13]

Public Policy Emphasis

St. Louis and Oakland represent interesting contrasts with respect to the role of local government in directly attacking the problem of unemployment. Former St. Louis Community Development Director John Roach attributed St. Louis's turnaround to a recognition that Community Development funds gave the city. a competitive edge against the suburbs which "could not be wasted funding poverty." This theme was reiterated by Lynton Edwards, Executive Director for Development, Mayor's Office, city of St. Louis, who described St. Louis's development strategy as based on the dual premises that " 'poverty' is a national, not a local, problem" and that " 'profits' is not a dirty word in St. Louis."

St. Louis, then, chooses not to attack dependency directly, believing instead that reduced dependency will follow from improved nationwide economic performance and an improved local private investment climate. This view, of course, is quite in consonance with the urban policy of the Reagan administration presented at the Congress by E. S. Savas, Assistant Secretary for Policy Development and Research of the Department of Housing and Urban Development. Following this thinking, St. Louis, for example, has invested its community development funds into public infrastructure improvements in places it believes likely to attract private investments, such as the one surrounding the Washington University Medical Center.

A critical question with regard to this public-private "partnership" is whether or not WUMC would have proceeded with its investment plans with less public investment in the area. In other words, in terms of a job-development payoff, could a lesser public role produce the same outcome, freeing public resources for investment elsewhere? Or, alternatively, could a more substantial social payoff have been derived from the public investment such as firm commitments to targeting employment opportunities for needy St. Louis residents?

The Oakland approach departs dramatically from that of St. Louis. Mayor Lionel Wilson told the Congress that employment, especially for minorities and youth, is the top priority in Oakland. Like other cities at the Congress, Oakland tackles the problem by entering into partnerships with the private sector. For example, thirty local corporations led by the Clorox Corporation, the Oakland Tribune, and the Kaiser Corporation, have joined to acquire a majority partnership in a new hotel development to be managed by the Hyatt Hotel chain. As was mentioned earlier, the city supported this development with an Urban Development Action Grant based loan covering 12.5 percent of the development costs. However, at this point, Oakland began to depart from the norm.

More than most other cities, Oakland seemed to have recognized what James Rouse stated to the Congress—that presently the urban real estate market is robust relative to that of the suburbs and that cities need not approach the bargaining table as weak partners.[15] They bargained for a return from their Hyatt investment which is being used to capitalize a revolving loan fund available only to neighborhood-oriented small businesses.[16]

Based on this early success at bargaining for profit sharing, the city has aggressively pursued its employment goals.

The city council has adopted a policy to promote minority and neighborhood organization equity participation in publicly assisted development projects. The policy states that any project receiving any form of public subsidy should strive for the following:

- 26 percent of all construction expenditures should go to minority firms.
- 50 percent of the construction workforce should be minorities.
- 40 percent of all professional work associated with the construction (architecture and engineering, legal, etc.) should be with minority firms.
- In situations where the city acquires the land and writes down its cost for the developers, the land is transferred through a minority- or neighborhood-based local development corporation (LDC) such as the Oakland Local Development Corporation. The LDC uses the land to capitalize at least a 40 percent share in a joint venture with a private developer.

The city of Oakland has had considerable success in realizing these goals. Office of Economic Development and Employment Director George Williams reports that the goals largely have been realized in the construction of a new convention center adjoining the Hyatt Hotel and in new office buildings occupied by the Transamerica Corporation, Clorox Corporation, and the Wells Fargo Bank. Mr. Williams characterizes the goal of an equity stake in the development property the toughest to achieve and one which provokes the "hardest bargaining." Nevertheless, some modest successes have been realized here. Minority firms own 6 percent of the Hyatt Hotel and 8 percent of the new $21 million Third Office Building in the Civic Center complex.

The city's confidence in its ability to achieve its goals hinges on efforts of the Oakland Economic Development Corporation, a quasi-public, nonprofit group, to continue to attract investment to Oakland, and on the OEDC's threefold thrust of training the disadvantaged, providing direct small business assistance, and using downtown development to generate capital for stimulating the neighborhood's economies. They believe that this comprehensive approach is essential to increasing the attractiveness of doing business with the city of Oakland. Otherwise, it would merely increase the development costs and presumably the amount of necessary public subsidy.

Finally, Mayor Wilson said that the city places considerable emphasis on

Oakland's neighborhood program for two reasons: to foster trust in the efficacy of public-private partnership, and to insure that the benefits of the development process accrue to the needy. Although there is no formal policy of increasing resident employment, the city has aggressively pursued such a goal. It has recently signed employment agreements with the Hyatt Corporation and with developers of the Third Office Building.

Several lessons emerge from this public-policy approach. First is the possibility of an authentic bargaining process taking place in which the public sector recognizes that it has something to give so that it shouldn't hesitate to get. Second is the possibility of directing the outcome of this bargaining process to upgrading local capacity, especially local ownership. Local control is viewed by Mayor Wilson as the best guarantor that the ultimate benefits of the development will reach Oakland's unemployed. Finally, as seen in both Oakland and St. Louis, public-sector professional staff are needed who understand business and development and are comfortable at the bargaining table.

Self-Help Emphasis

There were several development efforts presented at the Cities' Congress which included a neighborhood component. I have already described Oakland's neighborhood emphasis. An example of directly using the city's policy and program tools to promote neighborhood ownership is the development of a 13-acre industrial site. The city purchased the site for $1.2 million and is using a $1.5 million UDAG to finance site improvements. This $2.7 million public investment has been loaned to a neighborhood-owned, local development corporation (LDC) to underwrite a 50 percent equity share in the development. The other 50 percent share is held by a private developer, who is guaranting the $2.7 million loan in exchange for entitlement, for tax purposes, to depreciate the assets. This project is too early in the development cycle to generate any jobs. It promises financial independence for the neighborhood LDC and may create the conditions for further self-help development.

A second case is the Near North Development Corporation in Indianapolis. A non-profit entity initiated and subsidized by nearby Methodist Hospital, Near North is more directly concerned with neighborhood quality-of-life issues than with direct job generation. Accordingly, with assistance from the Planning Department at Ball State University, it has engaged in planning to promote housing and commercial revitalization.

The only case presented at the Congress of direct job generation efforts by a neighborhood organization representing the needy, or dependent, population was Jubilee Housing, Inc., in Washington, D.C., reported in detail earlier by Joel Lieske. (See Chapter 7.) Jubilee Housing efforts have been modest, but they represent part of a long community development tradition.[17] The multi-faceted neighborhood movement of the 1960s frequently turned to community control and autonomy as a solution to social distress and powerlessness.[18] Its major achievement lay in the creation of community development corporations sponsored by the Office of Economic Opportunity and the Ford Foundation.[19] Although the self-sufficiency movement struck a low profile throughout much of the 1970s, it by no means lost its intensity.[20] The economic development thrust of neighborhood efforts has been to intervene directly, either as partners or as activists, in as many "local" processes of job generation as possible to insure that jobs reach the current, often unemployed, residents of a given neighborhood, thus minimizing involuntary relocation and yielding some modicum of economic and social justice.[21] Their ultimate effectiveness is probably limited more by the sense of their "local" economic arena—a sense often sharpened in efforts at public-private partnership like those discussed at the Congress—than by their own inherent capacity. In Oakland, for example, there seems to be a broad public consensus that most job generation efforts at least partially "belong" to the local constituency, and that the meaning of "partially" ought to be determined in public-private negotiation.

Several themes seen earlier, as well as some new ones, emerge in the self-help approach. First is a willingness to enter into partnerships and to engage in bargaining with other actors in the development process. Second is an emphasis on local control of the development process through ownership, training, and management. Finally, there seems to be the possibility, exemplified by Near North and Jubilee, of trying to view development comprehensively and to engage in planning that goes beyond merely reacting to crises.

Conclusion

This review of the job-generating efforts and outcomes presented at the Cities Congress began with the observation that there was little to review and a question about whether the lack of success at creating jobs was important. I argued that a job-generation component of a recovery strategy, particularly one targeted to the unemployed, is important. Much of the Congress focused on innovative ways to stimulate capital investment. I argued that capital investment, though necessary, is by no means sufficient to guarantee recovery because the development process is not a simple one. As Peter Drucker and many others assert, a variety of policies are needed simply to target investment to more productive enterprises and to retrain the technologically "redundant" workers.[22]

The format of the Congress precluded probing too deeply into why there does not seem to be much job creation in current local economic recovery activity. In any case, David Bergholz's frank self-assessment, "[We] have been least successful . . . around the issue of jobs," serves as an adequate standpoint from which to begin to look for threads of promises rather than proven successes in the Congress stories. Several threads were present, and below I will sum them up. However, it is important to keep them in context, of which there are two dimensions that I believe are important. First, cities are intimately linked to the national and international economies, and will not be able to "go it alone." Secondly, they will continue to need external support from state and national governments. Few of the success stories at the Congress could have been told without the dependency of local governments on federal resources.

Although the Oakland case may come closest, no recovery model presented at the Congress in and of itself represented a clear path to eliminating dependency by generating jobs for the needy. However, a mixture of elements from various cases begins to present a picture of what that path might look like. The picture can be partially shaped if one thinks of Jubilee Housing as being located in Oakland.[23] Seven items seem to emerge:

1. Meaningful partnerships in development must be constructed involving not just the public sector, business, and civic leadership, as was so often seen at the Congress, but also labor and neighborhood leadership. The test of the "meaningful" nature of the partnerships might be the degree to which different actors actually enter into contractual arrangements.

2. Conscious and planned efforts to use every development project as an opportunity to upgrade the *human resources* of a community through on- and off-the-job education and training. Oakland's employment goals policy and the training it offers might be examples of this.

3. Encouragement of local *ownership*, especially that which is more participatory in nature such as cooperatives or community-owned development entities. Oakland promotes local ownership, but seems to stop short of promoting Jubilee Housing-type models.

4. Development and utilization of professional capacity to implement development efforts. The prevailing model of the Congress, as evidenced in St. Louis, was to turn the development over to the private sector. Jubilee Housing, supported by philanthropically sponsored technical assistance, shows the potential of neighborhood-based development entities that may be more responsive to the community.

5. A broad package of resources targeted to more comprehensively upgrading the *local quality of life*, including improving schools and rehabilitating public, physical infrastructure. James Rouse and Pat Choate stressed

the importance of this dimension, and almost every city at the Congress was struggling with the issues.

6. A *capital pool* to assist new business in capital formation, and existing business in technological transformation. Oakland's efforts to stimulate neighborhood-based, small business development is a partial example.[24]

7. A key to bringing the preceding six elements together and, particularly, to activating partnerships, is a *bargaining process* between all parties affected by the development process.[25] To exclude the community or neighborhoods and labor from the bargaining process during which significant development decisions are made curtails both and spirit of participation and probably innovation.[26] Few cities of the Congress, Oakland appearing to be one exception, seemed to view bargaining as compatible with the spirit of partnership. Further, there was no evidence that the bargaining process, where it did occur, was an open one.

These seven approaches begin to illustrate just how complex the process is of moving from increasing urban investment to generating jobs for the needy. This outline is not intended to represent a comprehensive theory of "recovery," but is rather a restatement of some things that seem to be working in a limited sense, and that should work better taken together. Clearly, these elements cannot exist in a vacuum apart from national and state level "recovery" efforts. Furthermore, there seemed to be enough evidence presented at the Congress that undertaking a few of them is not as effective as undertaking most of them. Without asserting the sufficiency of the seven-fold attack on dependency, I think it is reasonable to say that until all seven are present through public or private efforts—especially the concept of a bargaining process providing authentic participation—there is reason to be pessimistic about the roads to recovery discussed at the Congress. The challenge is to build a political consensus for an effective partnership in which all parties are treated as equals.

Postscript

After writing the preceding portion of this chapter, I began to work on the campaign of Harold Washington for mayor of Chicago, coordinating the formulation of his economic development platform. The platform which emerged incorporates and expands on the preceding seven-point program.[27] The program, as reflection on the seven points suggests, represents a substantial departure from the normal approaches to urban economic development. As such, it is already somewhat misunderstood and controversial.[28] My early experiences as the newly appointed Commissioner of Economic Development leave me confident that some lessons of the Cities' Congress will be well served, as the following example shows.

Chicago has long been embarked on a redevelopment plan for its Loop area. Shortly into the administration of Mayor Washington, redevelopment bids were accepted on a major block in the heart of the Loop. The winning bidder proposed a $400 million, 2.1 million square foot retail and office complex similar, except in scale, to developments presented at the Cities' Congress. The public investment in the project will be $20–30 million. The Washington administration brought the winning bidder back to the bargaining table to negotiate specific employment goals in a manner somewhat similar to Oakland's efforts and those advocated by James Rouse. Specific goals and an implementation program were agreed upon to maximize opportunities for Chicago residents who are women or minorities in five specific areas: construction jobs, construction sub-contracting, jobs with the development organizations, jobs with the development tenants, and retail entrepreneurial opportunities. None of this would have been achieved under a more traditional approach to development.

13

Recovery of Cities:
An Alternate View

Norman Krumholz

Failures of the Cities' Congress

The Cities' Congress on Roads to Recovery put the spotlight on sixteen cities and twenty-one "success stories"—all of which were said to have helped their respective cities move away from dependency toward recovery. Recovery was defined as "the city's regained ability to compete with the suburbs as a place to live: a regained favorable climate for investment and a consequent growth of jobs; and as a product of these two, a regained independence from external subsidies."

As originally conceived, the policies of recovery also included a component which emphasized equity and the need to suburbanize the urban poor and make jobs available to them. As the architect of the Congress has written, "standing alone. . .a policy of making inner cities competitive with the strongest suburbs is neither adequate nor just. It must be accompanied by a complementary policy, a policy that enables those whose residence in the inner city prevents their being self-reliant to relocate outside cities for convenient access to jobs which they can fill."[1]

This equity aspect, especially the decentralization and employment of the inner-city poor, did not receive emphasis at the Congress; instead, the Congress devoted itself to sharing success stories, lifting the morale of those in attendance, and advising participants to form or strengthen local public-private partnerships in order to accomplish the recovery of their cities.

Federal aid was seen as demeaning, often wrong-headed, and faintly unfashionable. The message was clear: "We politicians, businessmen, and

173

civic leaders can accomplish the recovery of our cities by ourselves through improved local leadership and the medium of public-private partnerships.

Would that it could be so, but it cannot work. Success stories like those recounted at the Congress can, and have for the past thirty years, worked to enhance and expand the institutional, cultural, and downtown areas of many cities. Sometimes these projects added new taxes to the dwindling coffers of their cities. But these projects have done little or nothing for the poverty, joblessness, and declining neighborhoods of poor and working-class central-city residents.

Six of the cities confidently presenting their success stories at the congress—St. Louis, Cleveland, Pittsburgh, New Haven, Cincinnati, and Baltimore—constitute fully one-third of the eighteen cities in America suffering most acutely from urban hardship conditions.[2] Conditions in none of these cities are getting better. By any reasonable measure of the prosperity of place—level of population, concentration of low-income families, relative income, employment, economic investment—the more distressed cities were weaker by the beginning of the 1980s than they were ten years earlier.

Perhaps it is time to face the fact that efforts aimed solely at new physical development—no matter how innovative, costly or well-designed—cannot deal in a coherent way with the array of social and economic problems that constitute distress in American cities.

This chapter asks if the Congress broadened our understanding of distress or redevelopment, added to our knowledge of public-private partnerships, or showed us how distressed cities can function without federal aid. It concludes that the Congress did none of these. A more useful approach to city recovery would have emphasized the essentiality of continued federal support while also pointing out some actions that hard-pressed cities might take in behalf of their own resident population. Such a program is suggested in the last part of this chapter.

Did the Congress contribute to our understanding of urban distress or redevelopment? Most of the success stories described projects that varied little from the urban renewal programs of the fifties. In many respects the Congress, with its sustained boosterism, seemed to celebrate urban renewal, unaware that the phrase became an epithet in central city neighborhoods twenty years ago. The renewal format of most of the success stories is well-established and simple. It begins with the definition of a problem: the city's tax base is lagging; a neighborhood is a "slum;" an industry needs room for expansion; or an area is considered aesthetically unattractive or threatening to a nearby hospital or university. In response to the problem, a plan for relief is prepared, nominally by the city but often actually carried forward by private consultants financed by private interests. The city then certifies the area as "blighted," provides subsidies and public powers like eminent domain, finds a private developer, and executes the plan. The outcome of the process is a new building or a group of new buildings, a redesigned site, and frequently the replacement of the former resident population with new tenants of higher income and lighter coloration.

The urban renewal worked, at least in terms of commercial buildings and improvements. It also raised the aesthetic attractiveness of areas in downtown and in institutional centers. Cleveland's Erieview, Philadelphia's Penn Center, Pittsburgh's Golden Triangle, Denver's Mile High Center, San Francisco's Embarcadero Center, Boston's Government Center, Bunker Hill in Los Angeles and other developments attest to how well it worked.

But while urban renewal succeeded in rebuilding small parts of some cities, it had little success achieving its other goals. For example, renewal failed to relocate the displaced poor into standard, low-cost homes, generate new increases in city jobs, stabilize the declining revenue base of many cities, or halt the exodus of middle-class whites into the suburbs. When Scott Greer opened his 1965 book on renewal by stating, "At a cost of more than $3 billion, the Urban Renewal Administration (URA) has succeeded in reducing the supply of low-income housing in American cities," there was no serious challenge.[3] Renewal may be a great success in some respects, while creating inequities and other problems more vexing than those originally solved. Examples to illustrate this point abound.

> Let me give you an example of an opportunity we have taken in St. Louis. The development I have been responsible for is called Mansion House. It is right downtown. . .on the river. . .next to that magnificent Saarinen Arch. Five years ago where Mansion House is, there was the worst slum area in the city of St. Louis. After nine o'clock at night. . .you didn't dare walk around down there because you took your life in your hands. Today, Mansion House is built. It is three, magnificent, thirty-nine-story towers and a great complex of commercial and other facilities. It is highly successful. . . .It is the pivot point in the rebirth of downtown St. Louis.

The speaker went on to praise the development, the financiers, and the cooperation with other public and private participants who contributed to the Mansion House success.

The speaker, who was also the project's developer, might have made the identical presentation in 1982 at the Congress, but the Mansion House presentation was made in 1969.[4]

Others viewed the Mansion House project in a different light. In 1975, a Ph.D. candidate named Robert E. Olson wrote about it in his dissertation on the Missouri Urban Redevelopment Corporation Law:

> Mansion House was the second application of the URC in downtown St. Louis . . . .The total building cost [was] $52 million. The development was partially financed by a FHA-insured $36 million loan, and the original equity capital was

supplied by nationally prominent businessmen. . . .The project was not successful. . .vacancies have ranged about 50 percent. . . .The original private investors
have been able to use the complex as an enormous tax shelter, allowing them to
avoid paying $26 million in personal income taxes to date. The mortgage pay-
ments are not current, and the ultimate loser is the Federal Government which in-
sured the original $36 million loan. In addition the City of St. Louis has abated
property taxes mounting to $400,000 a year for ten years of the property's exis-
tence.[5]

The same difference in interpretation could be applied to most of the success stories told at the Congress. Representatives from St. Louis's Washington University Medical Center told of the Medical Center's determination
to remain in the city. Once this decision was made, hospital officials developed a plan to "stabilize the surrounding neighborhood and protect the investment." Using Missouri State Law 353, which provides the power of
eminent domain for private redevelopment corporations as well as 25 years
of reduced taxes, the project moved ahead. The redevelopment is now 70
percent completed. Its 185 acres include new office buildings, new medical
facilities, amenities and site improvements, and a substantial number of rehabilitated homes which house higher-income residents than before—truly
a successful effort for Washington University Medical Center as well as the
cooperating banks, consultants, and developers.

But others have a different view. Robert E. Olson says St. Louis taxpayers are needlessly subsidizing major redevelopment projects like the
Medical Center. The price tag for all Law 353 projects in St. Louis over the
next 25 years, says Olson, may be as high as $141 million. Olson notes that
Kansas City does not grant such tax advantages, but even so, 1.4 million
square feet of new office space is now under construction in that city.

St. Louis Alderman Bruce T. Sommer supports this critical view. He
points out that as of January, 1977, tax abatement has taken property
assessed at over $50 million off the tax rolls. Included in this amount is the
Washington University complex and a downtown complex being developed
by Mercantile Trust Company. Sommer contends that the abatement was
unnecessary in both projects. Specifically, he contends that the bank's new
$30 million, 35-story office tower would have been built without the tax
abatement it received since Missouri is a non-branch-banking state, and the
bank could not leave downtown St. Louis in any event. Donald E. Lasater,
the bank's chief executive officer, agrees, stating: "Yes, we probably would
have put up a new office building without tax abatement, but due to the risk
factor it might not have been as large as the $30 million, 35-story tower we
built."[6]

Supporters of tax abatement claim that the increase in taxes on earnings
resulting from the new jobs created by new development offset any abated
taxes. But critics contend that there are few permanent new jobs produced

since many projects do not expand economic activity but simply shift it from old buildings to new ones. They also point out that the schools get nothing from earning taxes. From 1971 to 1976 the schools, which get 57 percent of all property tax receipts, lost $700,000 to $900,000 a year through declining taxes on real estate. Over that same period, downtown St. Louis property value declined more than $5 million, and the drop for the city as a whole was $14.3 million. Not surprisingly, St. Louis's schools are close to financial collapse.

Critics also wonder what the future holds for those parts of St. Louis where the potential for private profit-making or the need for institutional preservation is not as pronounced as it is in those areas covered by the Law 353 Redevelopment Corporations—at least 47 of which have already been approved. They wonder if adequate public funds are available for normal maintenance and services in poor and working class neighborhoods, or if they are being drained away by powerful redevelopment corporations operating in areas of strong profit potential. They also question what happens to businesses and families displaced from Law 353 projects who are not eligible for relocation assistance, since Law 353 displacees are not covered by the requirements of the federal Uniform Relocation Act. Looking at income and family dependency data, observers ask what happens to the health and housing needs of the 14.4 percent of the St. Louis population in poverty, or of the 67,000 people receiving Aid to Dependent Children who cannot bargain for their needs against the needs of the redevelopment corporations. They wonder how the public interest is served when the city trades uncollected property taxes—which provide social and educational services for lower-income people—for physical development—which provides benefits for higher-income people. In the meantime, the listener to the St. Louis success story would get no clue that St. Louis has one of the highest welfare rolls in the nation or that it tops the nation's urban hardship index.

Columbus's success story told at the Congress raised many of the same questions. In Columbus, the Battelle Corporation, the world's largest private non-profit corporation, bought much of an adjacent neighborhood for an expansion which was subsequently made unnecessary by changed plans. The neighborhood, which had become the home of many low- and moderate-income families, was rehabilitated by the Olentangy Management Company, Battelle's real estate subsidiary. It has now become a fashionable restoration area for upper-income homeownership, and has "created a higher economic return than originally envisioned"—a successful accomplishment for Battelle, Olentangy, and the planners, architects, and bureaucrats involved in the process, but perhaps somewhat less successful for the now-displaced low-income renters.

There are plenty of similar success stories. Boston's Hub has been "turned around" from a blighted, low-income district to one featuring high-priced offices, condominiums, and shops. But the low-income and ethnic enclaves, once the charm of Boston, have been displaced. Revitalization is making it all but impossible for the poor and working class to live in the city. Racial tensions are high. The Hub may be revitalized, but are the problems created worse than those solved?

Renaissance Center is a $350 million symbol of born-again Detroit, represented by half a dozen skyscrapers, a riverfront mall, and a collection of fashionable restaurants. Ren Cen was put together by the broadest public-private-union coalition. But in 1981 Ren Cen lost $33.4 million. More importantly, while Ren Cen was "saving" Detroit, the city lost over 70 percent of its factory jobs, and has "60 percent of its people on some sort of transfer payments."[7]

Virtually every city engaged in urban renewal over the past thirty years can tell a similar story. Massive construction projects, both public and private, have been built; yet, in spite of them (perhaps because of them), the life situation of low- and moderate-income residents continues to worsen. The success stories told with such pride at the Congress were mostly current variations on a much older theme. It was no surprise that the owners of downtown real estate and the trustees of powerful institutions could use the means at hand to protect and enhance their properties.[8] Nor was it surprising that the coalition of groups that have a big stake in producing growth and physical structures—property owners, developers, banks, unions, architects, planners, contractors, politicians—the brick-and-mortar lobby—would hail each other's work, or that the media would find it exciting and positive copy.

Unbalanced Partnerships

At least one important change, however, has occurred since our earlier efforts in urban renewal. Distressed cities are now willing to absorb more project risks and costs than formerly. Today, cities provide more extravagant and imaginative inducements than those offered by Title I, and inducements include local as well as federal subsidies.

Milwaukee's Grand Avenue Mall is a good example. The city hired the Rouse Company's American City Corporation for $100,000 to study the project. American City suggested as a minimum that the public underwrite $30 million of the project's financing. Accordingly, the city produced a $12.6 million Urban Development Action Grant (UDAG). Since the UDAG program is designed to provide modest public funding in order to leverage private investment at a ratio of about seven to one, Milwaukee presented as its "private" investment a new Hyatt Hotel and a new federal office building. How did a federal building become a private investment? It was declared a private investment through the ingenious device of having a private developer build and lease it back to the federal government. Milwaukee also committed $20 million in tax increment financing to the deal and agreed to acquire and demolish old buildings, relocate tenants, replace utility lines, and build two new parking garages and an $11 million public concourse.

Detroit provides another example of creative public-private financing in its 350-unit Trolley Square housing project. The city purchased the land, discounted its value, and sold it back to the developer; it leased the air rights at favorable rates; it provided one parking space per apartment and agreed to pay all operating costs; it provided 14 years of tax abatement; it sold bonds to provide low-interest construction financing; it provided expensive public improvements; it processed a UDAG loan to build the project's foundations and a parking garage; and it helped get the developer permanent financing at 7½ percent interest with FHA insuring the mortgage. As of 1984, the developer claimed to be taking a loss despite monthly rents running from $400 to $1,000.

The primary beneficiaries of these public subsidies are large corporations, developers, and institutions. In the process, the tax burden is shifted from capital to consumers, and from large corporations to small businesses and homeowners. But more crucial than the question of who gets the subsidies are questions like these: How many jobs do these projects actually produce? Are they permanent or temporary? Who gets the jobs, city residents or suburbanites, the technically skilled or the unskilled? On these matters crucial to the needs of city residents, the record is usually silent.

Ironically, while large corporations and institutions justify these public subsidies as necessary to generate new jobs, studies show that the generators of most jobs tend to be small concerns. As one careful analysis concludes, "Of all the net new jobs created in our sample of 5.6 million businesses between 1969 and 1976, two-thirds were created by firms with twenty or fewer employees."[9]

A nagging doubt arises. Does the publicly subsidized splendor of downtown and the institutional parts of our cities really have much to do with a city's recovery? The answer must be no. The recovery of cities is far more than brick-and-mortar projects. The city is people, and unless most of them are employed, self-respecting, and respected, the new towers of downtown are a mockery and a delusion.

Consider Cleveland, a community which presented as its success story at the Congress, its recovery from the disarray of municipal default in 1978 to fiscal respectability and a more stable, respected national position. This improved the climate for investment, and $750 million in new development was underway. Cleveland, it was declared, was America's come-back city. It was an impressive success story, but it is unlikely that such stories will make much difference to the powerful social and economic trends which have gripped the city in a downtown spiral for the past thirty years. (In the two years from June 1982 when the Recovery Conference was held to June 1984, six tax issues were submitted to Cleveland's voters. Following the failure in February 1984 of the attempt to raise the city's income tax from 2 percent to 2½ percent, 600 city employees were furloughed.)

For a less boosterish but more detailed look at Cleveland's future, a team at the Brookings Institution has produced a quantitative examination of the effects that alternative revitalization policies might have on Cleveland's population, employment, housing stock, and transportation between 1980 and 1990.[10] If present trends are projected, the group predicts a 17 percent loss of jobs, an 18 percent loss of people, and a 30 percent increase in the average tax burden of the typical Cleveland household. By mathematical simulation, the group then applied to the city five alternative revitalization packages in jobs, housing, transit improvements, suburban growth restrictions, and fiscal equalization and simulated a 1990 future based on these improvements both as individual packages and as one cumulative package. It was found that even if all five revitalization packages were applied simultaneously—a most unlikely prospect as the authors point out—decline would not be reversed, only its rate would be slowed.

Against these harsh realities, "promotional" campaigns and "success stories" have a hollow ring. It would seem more useful and reasonable, instead of congratulating ourselves on the imminent prospect of recovery, if we planned our strategies more carefully toward coping with stasis, no-growth, or decline.[11] It would also be more in line with the responsibilities of local government toward its resident population if we set as our first objective the need to improve the employment prospects, and the relative and absolute real income of the low- and moderate-income residents of the central city. At a minimum, this suggests as the highest priority, not subsidized downtown development, but a city manpower strategy designed to put its people to work.

Let us turn from redevelopment issues to public-private partnerships. An important aspect of the Congress was its emphasis on public-private partnerships where they already exist, and the calling of such partnerships into being where they do not exist.

Public-private partnerships were recommended as a new approach to helping local governments deal with Reaganomic cutbacks in federal programs, resistance to local tax increases, the current recession, and other dismal aspects of the urban crisis. The concept is simple: Representatives of business and government meet together, share ideas, identify problems, and pursue community objectives for mutual benefit. New attitudes of trust and co-operation are developed among the partners which facilitate a common vision and program. New leadership styles based on achieving positive changes in civic affairs are then to replace the older leadership styles associated with urban decline.

There are a wide number of forms these public-private partnerships may take. For example, the city may use its legal and administrative powers to spur private job training efforts; it may, as we have seen, provide business with special tax breaks, eminent domain powers, and other fiscal and regulatory incentives to promote development; it may privatize public services by contracting with neighborhood organizations or private corporations.[12]

The concept implies that business and government are equals, and that they can trade off inducements in a cross-commitment strategy for mutual benefit. Actually, in our system, business and government are far from equals: Business has a disproportionate share of the power. Further, as cities and state governments slide deeper into crisis, they will be less and less likely to deal with business as equals and more likely to pile on public inducements in the hope of encouraging business to invest so that employment and growth can be maintained. If anything is clear from the Congress's success stories, it is that communities in greatest difficulty provide the greatest inducements to private developments, and they do not have to be bribed, pressured, or duped to do so.

In our market-oriented private enterprise system, decisions on what will be produced, where it will be produced, where corporate headquarters will be located, what production technologies will be used, how manpower will be allocated—all momentous decisions with great public impact—are decided by businessmen, not government officials. These decisions are of enormous consequence for all American society, since they impact on jobs, growth, the standard of living, and the economic security of the individual worker; yet, we find it appropriate that corporate executives make them using broad personal discretion. If a major conglomerate decides to "milk" one of its corporations to feed another with a higher rate of return and ultimately closes down the former, it is considered regrettable but uncontrollable. If Pittsburgh-based U.S. Steel disinvests in its steel producing facilities while spending $6.5 billion to acquire Marathon Oil, the nation's 17th largest oil company, the mayor and people of Pittsburgh can only cross their fingers and hope for the best.[13] Indeed, if any corporation decides to move its headquarters from Snowbelt to Sunbelt or Singapore, there is nothing public leaders can do. Yet, if a corporation indicates its need for tax breaks or a major improvement, public officials can usually be convinced to provide the necessary help.

None of this is new. Public-private partnerships are as old as the Republic. Alexander Hamilton laid out his recommendations in favor of direct fiscal grants to business in this way:

> This has been found to be one of the most efficacious means of encouraging manufactures, and is, in some views, the best. . . .It is a species of encouragement more positive and direct than any other, and for that reason, has a more immediate tendency to stimulate and uphold new enterprises, increasing the chance for profit, and diminishing the risk of loss. . . .[14]

Since Hamilton's day, government has provided business with subsidies on water, rail, and highway transportation; favorable tariff and trade policies; funds for research and development; tax abatements and low interest loans; and in times not-so-recently-gone-by, with the U.S. Marines to protect foreign investment. Today, giant corporations, like Lockheed, the Pennsylvania Railroad, and Chrysler, can be sure that the public will bail them out if they fall on hard times. To say that public-private partnerships are a new idea in contemporary America is to overlook this rich history. After all, both the redevelopment of the central city through urban renewal and the massive post-World War II construction of housing in the suburbs depended on public-private partnerships including publicly supported mortgage financing, public sewer and water grants, and public road programs.

There is little evidence that government at any level is disquieted by this situation. Government is naturally anxious that business perform well. After all, if business doesn't invest, the economic distress which may result can bring down the government. At every level, government tailors its tax and subsidy policies to stimulate business investment. Government must be ever mindful that in our system, although it may forbid or prohibit certain activities, it can not command business investment. It must induce rather than command. Business, then, enjoys a unique position of power and privilege which substantially exceeds that of government.

That position is further fortified by other realities. Capital and private management in our system are becoming increasingly centralized; government, on the other hand, is becoming more fragmented. Personnel shortcomings also tend to weaken the local government in its "partnership" with business. In such areas as economic development, local governments are notoriously poorly staffed—so much so, that they cannot critically evaluate the profit and investment claims of their private "partners."

Rather than public-private partnerships among equals, the success stories presented at the Congress suggested that public officials discerned the content of the public interest simply by asking the private developers, or institutional clients what they wanted done and then helping them do it "so the numbers would come out." This is hardly the role presented in recognized texts on public administration where "public conditioned expertness is the ability to resist the pressure for a decision in favor of a particular party or interest. . . ."[15]

What of the future of public-private partnerships? It may be much like the past, especially in cities and regions suffering substantial economic decline. There we can expect more public-private partnerships like the 1975 Volkswagon assembly plant deal in which the citizens of Pennsylvania supplied an estimated $210 million in public subsidies to attract a Volkswagon Rabbit plant which paid less in property taxes in 1980 than the price of one Rabbit; or Detroit's Poletown deal in which a viable, working class neighborhood of 464 acres was cleared, and $225 million in public subsidies provided to keep General Motors and its 4,000 jobs in town; or the many cases in Any City U.S.A. where private corporations need only breathe the threat of departure to have the city rush to the rescue with a full range of subsidies and legal, fiscal, and administrative powers. As time goes on, the pivotal role of the private sector will be more and more visible as will be its veto power over many public decisions. Public-private partnerships seem to be moving toward an oligarchy, jointly administered by public and private sector representatives, to satisfy the requirements of the physical development process.

A number of factors may modify this future. For one thing, in cities like St. Louis, the many redevelopment corporations empowered to put deals together are sure to come into conflict over alternative development plans.[16] Political conflicts may then slow the process. More crucially, a declining number of fiscal inducements from the federal government, produced, ironically, by the notion expressed at the Congress that public-private partnerships will make such subsidies less necessary, may impede cooperation. In that event, cities will have fewer fiscal inducements to bargain away. Time will tell whether cities will be able to attract private investment with such reduced means.

The Dependency of Some Cities is Permanent

This raises the question of whether troubled cities can go it alone without federal aid. Many Congress participants seemed to believe that the troubled cities should be weaned from this dependence. Speakers suggested the city dependency was inappropriate and demeaning and that it was somehow due to municipal mismanagement, incompetence, or an inadequate supply of public-private cooperation. No doubt some cities (like some corporations) could do a better job with their resources, but cities also suffer from factors indigenous to the system over which they have little control.

One of these factors is the way metropolitan development takes place in the United States. Our metropolitan development system is based on the practice of public and private institutions which control local housing, building and zoning codes, mortgage financing, real estate customs, the siting of public housing, and the dual housing market. It produces good housing, safe neighborhoods, satisfactory schools, and viable public institutions for most middle-class and upper-income urban households. These households in our older metropolitan areas increasingly live in the suburbs. At the same time, the system consigns through the trickle-down process a disproportionately high proportion of low-income urban households— especially   low-income   minority   households—to   the   oldest,   most deteriorated neighborhoods of the central city. These neighborhoods are characterized by overcrowding, poorly maintained buildings, high crime rates, and inadequate public services. This phenomenon is not the result of neutral market forces; it is the outgrowth of our development system.

As Anthony Downs has noted, "American urban development occurs in a systematic, highly predictable manner. . . .It leads to precisely the results desired by those who dominate it."[17] Cast into local terms in Cleveland, it is no accident that the city of Cleveland contains the 26 poorest neighborhoods in Cuyahoga County. Nor is it an accident that the city is home for 97 percent of all public housing in the county. The central city not only has the oldest infrastructure and capital plant, but it also has few high-income residents and many high-cost residents. This is the basic cause of the fiscal crisis in many central cities. It results, not from any lack of city managerial or administrative capacity, but from characteristics which are deeply rooted in the American development process and which act to the disadvantage of the central city. The inequities which arise from this system can only be addressed by federal power and money.

A second reason why federal funding will continue to be important to hard-pressed central cities is the likelihood of rising public-labor costs.[18] Cities concentrate their expenditures in services and manpower, such as police, firemen, teachers, health, housing and sanitation operatives, and so on. There is little expectation of increased productivity in these services— first, because increasing productivity in these services is complex and difficult; second, because most citizens would be opposed to many such increases. We don't want teachers with too many pupils, or nurses with too many patients, or police with too many neighborhoods to cover anymore than we'd like the Cleveland Orchestra to play a 40-minute symphony in 20 minutes. It is difficult if not impossible to substitute capital for labor in these public services. By contrast, capital investment and economies of scale in private sector production activities may produce a rise in output justifying an increase in wages. Despite these important dissimilarities, municipal pay scales are set according to equivalent work in private sector production. Any rise in wages in private sector production is soon translated into a rise in the public sector. These growing costs have little to do with city mismanagement, corruption or inefficiency; rather, some observers consider them inevitable.

Given the political power of public employees and the fact that public employees vote in local elections and have an interest in increasing public spending, it seems reasonable to assume that governmental wages will not necessarily fall if wages in the private sector drop. In that event, self-help offers no way out for our cities, and federal help will be needed to avert a deepening crisis.

Finally, the very scale of federal expenditures in central cities over the last three decades raises questions of local ability to provide essential services in the event of substantial withdrawal of federal funds.

In fiscal 1979 the federal government proposed spending $91.7 billion in all central cities. About 62 percent of these funds were programmed for retirement or social security assistance, and $28.7 billion was directed toward income maintenance, health care, food stamps, and unemployment compensation. Additional funds were pledged to various EDA and HUD programs whose purpose was physical improvement and housing.[19] This large-scale federal urban program represented a realistic response to the realities and needs of urban distress.

Although President Reagan has moved to cut assistance to central cities, it is hard to imagine central-city survival without substantial federal aid. Central-city governments ceased long ago to be fiscally self-supporting. In 1975, all cities in the U.S. received 39.4 percent of their revenues from intergovernmental transfers, and cities of over 500,000 received 45.8 percent. Intergovernmental transfers provided the average big city with almost as much revenue as did all their local taxation.

Speakers at the Congress argued that this dependency is unseemly, and long-term population and representational trends are weakening the political strength of central cities. Some of this has the ring of truth, but given their structural problems and conditions of support, it is absurd to presume that distressed central city governments can soon—or ever—become self-sufficient. Perhaps the most damaging aspect of the Congress was the tacit support it provided the Reagan Administration's program of benign neglect for cities in distress.

This is not to say that central city governments should not do more for themselves. Cities should drive harder bargains in development deals; they should become more entrepreneurial on their own; and they should develop a manpower strategy aimed at maximizing employment opportunities for indigenous, low-skilled, and unemployed workers—particularly minority youth. But continued support to distressed cities seems essential. They cannot cure their fiscal dependence by an act of will.

Thus far, we have been trying to resolve the problems of troubled cities with general, trickle-down programs. An alternative approach would begin with targeted programs focusing narrowly on root causes. America's cities are dissimilar and the problems they face vary in intensity. Urban distress is far from universal. It occurs in certain cities and in certain areas within these cities. It is linked with concentrations of poverty and with unemployment and racial discrimination.[20]

Redevelopment activities of the past did little to address these problems directly. Cities have not been run rationally to concentrate their policies and their resources on the welfare of their resident population. Adopting such a course mandates that city political leaders do things in a different way, which might involve them in a collision course with businesses, public bureaucracies, and other institutions that find it more profitable to milk the city than to make it a going concern.

Recovery will involve both federal and local governments in continuing efforts to improve life for low-income city residents. Specifically, the most important obligations of the federal government are to provide jobs, raise the real income of the central city poor, and to end racial discrimination in housing. The city's priorities should be aimed at sharpening the city's own entreprenuerial and bargaining skills, developing local manpower strategies, and improving the social and morale needs of citizens by helping neighborhood-based community organizations.

In adopting the first of these federal objectives it should be clear that the need is to create jobs for low-income city residents, not necessarily to create jobs in the city. Indeed, it is likely that the best employment opportunities for many inner-city blacks lie in the blue collar manufacturing sector which is increasingly located in the suburbs. If job creation programs are focused on central city areas rather than on low-income central city residents, adequate employment may never be generated. After all, there were and are powerful economic reasons for job movement away from the central city, and massive subsidies would be required to reverse that trend, if it can be done at all.

Another important consideration regarding job creation has to do with whether such programs will actually reach the unemployed urban poor and whether the employment created will be permanent or temporary. Subsidizing the private sector in order to increase investment in central city locations does not necessarily assure employment opportunities for the urban poor.

Planners in many cities can give examples of projects that were high in public cost and low in new job opportunities for the urban poor.

In Cleveland, for example, in the late 1970s, the city provided $740,000 in public subsidies plus over $500,000 in relocation payments to an inner-city industrial park which promised to provide "hundreds" of new jobs for the nearby residents of two large public housing projects. A new bakery and a mattress factory were built and two other plants were helped to improve and expand their locations, but only eight new jobs (three of which were short-term) were actually filled by neighborhood residents.[21]

Capital subsidies are not the answer to the problem of unemployment and sub-employment in the ghetto. Labor subsidies would do much more to solve the problem. Rather than subsidizing expensive (and not very efficient) filtering-down schemes of the sort just described, a simple wage-subsidy program would be more logical and cost-effective. Employers hiring a worker who had been certified unemployed for a given period of time would receive an hourly cash subsidy with the amount decreasing over time as the worker's productivity increased with training and experience.

But full employment would do little to eliminate poverty among those millions of households without a member in the labor force or those families whose full-time earnings fall below the poverty level. For those households, a national family assistance plan or income-maintenance program would be effective.

Obviously, both job development and income-maintenance programs will require major federal participation. Since the beneficiaries will constitute a small minority of the U.S. population (concentrating on the most distressed part of the total population in the most distressed cities), it can be argued that such programs will not be politically popular. That is true; they are simply necessary.

The second federal objective is the end of racial segregation in housing. In 1970 the American population was more racially segregated than it was in 1960, and the 1980 census confirms that segregation has again increased in the last decade. Racial segregation is not only in conflict with basic American ideals of freedom and equality, but it also threatens our efforts in schooling, employment, and development programs. Policies to increase minority job opportunities and incomes or improve education cannot be fully effective so long as minority residential choices continue to be restricted.

Up to the present, our efforts to overcome racial segregation in housing have met with hostility. Typically, these efforts have been weak and uncoordinated. They have depended much more heavily on moral suasion and legal "sticks" rather than on "carrots." Perhaps it is time to face the probability that no solution to decentralizing and thus weakening the problems of the ghetto is possible without support from the white middle-class. How might we seek and obtain such support?

We might simply try to "buy" a political constituency for the issue, a strategy that has a well-documented history in our country. Since we want open housing, it may be time to try an economic rewards policy in order to end racial segregation. That policy should be developed with one overriding characteristic—all parties to the action should be left better off than before. Advantages should accrue both to black households moving out of the ghetto into integrated areas and to white families already living in the receiving communities. Since the objective of racial integration is desirable for our entire society, it is appropriate that the federal government play a lead role in the process.

Where Cities Can Do More

But continued federal participation is not enough. City governments must also do more for their troubled resident populations. As we have seen, since the beginning of the urban renewal program, city officials have accepted the notion that the city and its people would automatically benefit from any development, and that public subsidies were therefore appropriate. But the use of federal and local subsidies to stimulate new development has not been carefully tied to the welfare of city residents, especially to those most in need. New development is not an end in itself. It is valuable only to the extent that it provides jobs for present or future city residents—especially city residents who are unemployed—and a net tax increase to the city coffers. This implies that cities must sharpen their bargaining skills.

First, cities must learn to be less profligate in giving away the local tax base through tax abatements and exemptions designed to attract businesses. There is no evidence that the $1 billion given away annually by states and cities to lure businesses has any real effect. The inducements are so widespread they tend to cancel each other out, succeeding only in raising the rate of return on private capital. If city subsidies are deemed absolutely essential, they should be carefully programmed to retain existing businesses and to start up new businesses—particularly those that offer jobs to indigenous, low-skilled, unemployed workers. As a prior condition for the use of public powers or subsidies, the city should seek guarantees on the number of new jobs generated, the number which will be filled by CETA-eligible residents, and the net revenue increase that will be generated. Performance guarantees should be written into all agreements, with sanctions provided if the guarantees are not fulfilled.

Some of this hard bargaining is apparently underway. The Oakland story at the Congress included a construction-contracting set-aside for the city's minority firms and minority workers. Hartford has pursued vigorous affirmative hiring actions on behalf of its minority population and has also insisted that the city be given an equity share in certain hotel and office developments. Santa Monica has imposed a moratorium on land development while it works out arrangements for sharing the speculative profits of new developments. Flint shares the profits of a new hotel with neighborhood groups. San Antonio insists that its CETA-eligibles get first crack at all new jobs and controls all leases in a new hotel in the interest of resident minority workers. In all these examples local officials are trying to adapt the local economy to public purpose.

A city's manpower strategy—its most important obligation—should include assistance for neighborhood-based economic development activities. Neighborhood organizations, with their great knowledge of street level activities, could help provide a crucial interface between neighborhood needs and manpower resources. Individual operations might be on a small scale, but the payoff in terms of jobs developed and useful work accomplished relative to money invested is likely to be very high. Consider two small-scale Cleveland case studies—one in housing, the other in energy.

The Tremont-West Development Corporation is a democratically elected, non-profit neighborhood organization operating in a low-income racially mixed area. Its 1983 budget was $72,000, with funds being drawn from the Community Development Block Grant and local foundations. Since its inception in 1979, TWDC has renovated 42 formerly vacant and vandalized homes which have been resold to low-income families. The rehabilitation is done by a crew of eight formerly unemployed neighborhood residents who now also do private work in carpentry, roofing, painting, and weatherization. TWDC has also organized the weatherization of 32 homes in a four-block area as a low-cost group insulation project, is planning to turn 25 units of public housing which were marked for demolition into Cleveland's first low-income co-op, and has set up the city's first land trust for neighborhood recreation.

The same process involving multiple benefits is clear in the Broadway neighborhood which administers a home weatherization and insulation program. The program provides work careers for low-skilled residents who do the energy audits and insulation work while helping homeowners reduce energy costs. In 1982, the program performed 104 energy audits and completed 60 weatherization and insulation jobs at an average cost of $340. Gas savings on homes receiving attic and wall insulation averaged 41 percent. All insulation work is done by four full-time employees who were unemployed neighborhood residents.

In both Tremont and Broadway, neighborhood people are working for each other; rehabilitation and energy conservation dollars remain in the neighborhood; property is improved; and work skills are sharpened. Seed grants and loans to such programs are provided, not as charity, but to help the groups move forward under their own power. These efforts do not result in cataclysmic or dramatic renewal, but the economic development that does take place raises the resident's sense of control over his own environment. At this level of modest success, social cohesion and mobilization of resources is attained along with positive values that include respect for oneself and one's neighbor and respect for the importance of work.

To a large extent, the troubled cities—with the continuing assistance of a concerned federal government—have the power to transform themselves and "recover," but only by working directly toward a more viable local economy and toward a resident population which is employed, responsible and self-respecting. This means the cities must develop a more focused entreprenuerial capacity designed to serve the interests of the most disadvantaged of their people. When we begin to view governmental power and fiscal incentives as part of a grand strategy for dealing with the fundamental and basic problems of poverty, unemployment, and racial discrimination, our concern with the recovery of cities will be properly concentrated.

14

The Reagan Revolution and Beyond

Larry C. Ledebur

Introduction

The Cities' Congress on Roads to Recovery has dramatically documented the growing recognition of the need for and potential of public-private collaboration in responding to the problems of the nation's cities. While public-private partnerships are not new, recent sweeping changes in federal domestic policy have created a new impetus for establishing new working relationships and innovative institutions for revitalizing urban areas. As a consequence of this reorientation of federal policies, cities confront the challenge to become increasingly self-reliant in meeting their needs by mobilizing local leadership, ingenuity, and resources.

Greater local self-sufficiency is one of the three primary pillars of the Reagan domestic program. The task of this paper is to place the Cities' Congress on Roads to Recovery within the context of changing domestic policies and the challenge they pose to cities. Many of the President's domestic policies are controversial. The rapidity with which they were instituted often preclude careful tracing of their underlying rationales and, to a lesser degree, the political orientation driving them. This paper attempts to trace the major strands of these reoriented policies and objectively present their supporting logic.

The Reagan Revolution

The election of Ronald Reagan as President brought about the most fundamental changes in the direction of federal domestic policy since the New Deal and the ascendancy of Keynesian economic policies in the 1960s.

Whether the 1980 elections represented a "watershed" in U.S. political history or a mere temporary disjuncture born of the frustrations of the electorate with the adverse drift of events in the 1970s is unclear. Regardless of the pervasiveness of this political philosophy or the duration of the Republican Administration, the dramatic reorientation of domestic policy pursued by the President will affect the course of events over the next decade and beyond.

The arch of the Reagan Revolution rests on three basic pillars, each necessary to support the edifice: (1) the program for national economic recovery, (2) a dramatic realignment of the nation's intergovernmental system, a "New Federalism", and (3) a return to greater local responsibility, self-reliance and initiative in meeting local needs and aspirations. This third pillar of greater local self-reliance and initiative, as well as the critical need for innovative approaches to this end such as public-private partnerships does not stand independently. It exists and must be understood in the context of the conditions and events that set the stage for the Reagan Revolution and the remaining pillars of the President's national economic recovery program and the proposed New Federalism.

Prelude: The Crisis Decade of the 1970s

In the first 25 years after World War II, the United States prospered. The last decade of this quarter-century, the 1960s, witnessed the most sustained economic growth uninterrupted by fluctuations in the business cycle in the history of any industrial nation. In this period, the nation rose to ascendancy in the international economy as the war-torn countries of Western Europe struggled to rebuild their shattered economies.

As the country prospered, it increasingly turned its attention to social issues. The federal government and the courts came to be viewed as agents of social change. Redistributive equity became a national priority. Dramatic inroads on economic deprivation occurred through the War on Poverty. Significant gains in civil rights were achieved through the judiciary, legislation, and federal programs. Spurred by the documentation of rural poverty, Congress mandated the Appalachian Regional Commission and the predecessor to the Economic Development Administration. In response to the urban riots of the late 1960s, major urban programs were initiated to address the problems of the nation's cities. Throughout this period, national surveys documented a growing sense of optimism and well-being—the conviction of most Americans that they and their children would be better off in the future.

Events of the 1970s shattered this national mood of optimism and well-being, and laid the foundation for the Reagan Presidency. The decade was widely perceived as a period of industrial malaise with the United States entering the 1980s with a troubled national economy. Most frequently cited as causes of alarm were declining rates of national economic growth, the national productivity slowdown,[1] seemingly intractable inflation,[2] decreasing competitiveness of U.S. products in domestic and international markets in industries where the nation's dominance had been unchallenged in the post-war period, and the decline of major industry sectors such as steel, automobiles, and shipping. Widespread discussions of the adverse trends emerging in the 1970s led to the observation that the "world's largest economy is also one of its sickest."[3]

Prudence dictates caution in attributing the malaise of the latter part of the 1970s to any single cause or set of causes. Several factors, however, indisputably contributed. One observer argues that the long trend for good performance of the economy ended when three major sets of problems that had been "brewing for years matured, converged, and blew up in our faces; the problem of inflation, the energy problem and its consequences, and finally the problem of a government increasingly incapable of controlling its budget or of dealing with any large problem incisively because its own swollen political agenda kept getting in the way."[4]

Concurrently, the scope of the federal government and the scale of its intervention in the economy and intrusion into the lives of individuals became contentious political issues. Two observers argue that a corollary to redistributive policies in the 1960s and the crisis management decade of the 1970s was a virtual explosion in the size and scope of government.[5] As documentation they cite the seven percentage point increase in government's share of gross national product between 1960 and 1980 and other forms of government intrusion such as regulations, mandates, directives, and court decisions that proliferated over this period.

These domestic issues, compounded by the perceived impotence of the U.S. in international affairs highlighted by the Iranian hostage crisis, set the stage and formed the backdrop for the 1980 Presidential campaign. National polls found the electorate bewildered, angry, and receptive to the Reagan message that the source of the nation's domestic problems was "big taxes" and "big government" undermining the vitality of the free enterprise system and the independence, ingenuity, and self-initiative of local governments and individuals.

The Reagan Response

In the State-of-the-Union address, the newly elected President pledged to put the nation on a fundamentally different course leading to renewed economic growth, diminished inflation, low unemployment, increased defense capacity, and a sharply reduced federal role in domestic affairs. Over the course of the first two years of the new administration, the three pillars of the Reagan program leading to this fundamentally different course were set forth: (1) the economic recovery program, (2) a new federalism, and (3) local initiative and self-reliance.

Economic Recovery Program

Shortly after assuming office, President Reagan proposed a far-reaching program for economic recovery focused on "supply-side incentives" for increased rates of savings and industrial investment. The major components of this program, subsequently labeled "Reagonomics" in the press, were as follows:

Tax Reduction. Prefacing the largest tax cut in the nation's history, the President in the 1981 State-of-the-Union address stated, "the taxing power of government must be used to provide revenues for legitimate government purposes. It must not be used to regulate the economy or bring about social change." This philosophy was implemented in the 1981 Economic Recovery Tax Act (ERTA).

Deregulation. The premises of the President's program are (1) that the regulatory burden imposed on the private sector dampens productivity and contributes to the poor performance of the economy, and (2) that social regulation, in many cases, represents an unwarranted intrusion in the affairs of private citizens and state and local governments. The policy of deregulation has been implemented through appointments of federal officials committed to deregulation, budgetary, and personnel cutbacks in regulatory agencies, relaxation of enforcement, and increased White House supervision of the regulatory process.

Monetarism. A major tenet of Reaganomics is that strict control of the money supply is necessary to reduce inflation. Through restrictive monetary policies, the Federal Reserve System, an independent arm of the federal government, has dramatically reduced the rate of inflation from previous "double digit" levels.

Federal Spending. The Economic Recovery Program was designed to achieve substantial reductions in government outlays while increasing defense related expenditures and balancing the federal budget. The 1982 budget was approximately $60 billion less than that proposed by President Carter, reflecting economies achieved through cutbacks in domestic programs while providing the first phase of the defense build-up. The massive tax cut legislated in ERTA and the sluggish response of the economy to this "supply-side" stimulus has precluded the goal of a balanced budget.[6]

The New Federalism

One year after implementing the Economic Recovery Program, President Reagan proposed a historic reordering of the nation's federal system of government, a "new federalism." As initially proposed, this realignment of the intergovernmental system would have devolved more than 40 federal education, transportation, community development, and social service programs to the states. The objectives of the new federalism were set forth by the President as follows:

1. Restore the balance of responsibilities within the federal system and reduce decision, management and fiscal overload on the federal government.

2. Provide a clean separation of domestic welfare responsibilities between the federal and state/local sectors.

3. Abolish the existing, unworkable federal/state grant-in-aid system which tends to transform non-federal units to subordinate middle-management extensions of the "Washington bureaucracy."[7]

The President's decision to attempt the reordering of responsibilities within the intergovernmental system at this juncture in the nation's history is premised on the belief that over the past 30 years, reapportionment, governmental reform and modernization, and extensive operation responsibilities for domestic welfare programs have dramatically strengthened state and local capacities for full and responsible partnership in the U.S. governmental system.[8] While less explicit, the new federalism must be viewed as an integral step in the President's effort to significantly diminish the scale of federal government and its role in state and local affairs.

In the year since its initial proposal, the New Federalism remains mired in controversy and negotiations with state governors who maintain the federal government should retain responsibility for basic welfare services, in particular, Aid for Dependent Children and medical insurance for the elderly. In addition, states, struggling with their own deepening fiscal crises, are witnessing erosion of their fiscal capacity to assume new program responsibilities in the continuing national recession.

The President's formulation of intergovernmental reform is guided by his enduring goal of contracting the scale of federal government in domestic affairs. Other formulations have as their explicit objective the rationalization of an overburdened and archaic intergovernmental system.[9] The need for reform is clear. Since the Great Depression, responsibility for many of the programs to be returned to states under the New Federalism had been assumed by the federal government because of inadequate state resources, expertise, institutional structures, and, in many cases, the lack of state commitment to the social objectives of the programs. Accompanying this centralization of policy and programs has been the shift from the historically predominant intergovernmental relationship of the federal government to the 50 states to one in which the federal government presently attempts to relate directly to and monitor the approximately 70,000 subnational jurisdictions that are in direct receipt of federal assistance through 580 grant programs.[10] This centralization of program responsibility and the accompanying shift in the relationship of the federal government to subnational jurisdictions has resulted in a severely congested and overburdened intergovernmental system.[11]

Economic Development in a Reordered Federal System

In perhaps no other area of federal policy are the implications of the changes currently being implemented more profound than for economic development. Over the last two decades, the federal government has played a major and often dominant role in local economic development, a position assumed through the sheer magnitude of government funds and the categorical nature of federal programs. In most cases, these federal development programs by-passed state governments, dealing directly with local jurisdictions, a process contributing greatly to frayed relationships between states and their cities.

This federal presence is now diminishing. Budgetary constraints, changes in federal economic development programs, and the orientation to providing the now more limited federal assistance through block grants to states are reducing the federal role and the contribution of federal resources to meet local development needs. Under the proposed New Federalism primary responsibility for urban and rural economic development would be invested in state governments, and, through them, in local governments.

The foundation for this transfer of responsibility for economic development was established by the controversial report of the President's Commission for a National Agenda for the Eighties.[12] The source of the controversy was the basic thesis of the Commission's Urban Report that the economic fortunes of cities must be allowed to fluctuate in response to the changing imperatives of the national economy. The welfare of cities, it was argued, is intricately linked to the vitality of the national economy, and their longer-term interests are better served by federal policies that promote the growth of the national economy than by place-specific urban development policies that attempt to counter the consequences of economic change —in short, the best urban policy is a national growth policy. The strength of cities, according to the Commission, is their ability to adapt to, rather than to resist, the industrial transformations occuring in their economies.[13]

Flowing from this general thesis was the recommendation that "space-oriented, spatially sensitive" national urban policies be replaced with "spatially neutral, national social and economic policies" that emphasize the growth of the national economy and the welfare of people rather than the welfare of specific places. An explicit Commission recommendation, significantly more radical than the urban policy thesis, yet largely overlooked in the ensuing controversy, was that "a national social policy should be based on key cornerstones, including a guaranteed jobs program for those who can work and a guaranteed cash assistance program for the working poor and those who cannot work."

Although not a creature of the Reagan presidency, the Commission's basic urban policy recommendations are echoed in, and at the core of, the administration's policies. The 1982 Urban Policy Report, the first of the Congressionally mandated assessments of urban America issued by the Reagan administration, states:

> The most basic responsibility of the Federal Government is to provide and maintain the framework within which our free enterprise system can flourish to the benefit of all: protecting individual rights, enforcing contracts, and preserving the value of currency. The background for the administration's urban policy is the economic recovery program. . .which seeks to restore economic vitality to American industry and to create productive jobs for workers. Inasmuch as the U.S. economy is predominantly an urban one, all urban areas—and the people living there—will benefit from a healthier national economy that leads to an adequate tax base.[4]

Urban Policy Under the New Federalism

The clearest statement of the administration's urban policy is the first draft of the Urban Policy report that was subsequently "sanitized" in response to outcry from the nation's mayors and many congressional representatives. The thesis developed in this and the final report is that cities must adapt to the changing requirements of the national economy. The diversity of circumstances, problems, and resources among cities is so great that no nationally administered urban policy can be sufficiently responsive to local conditions and needs. Past urban policies, it was argued, "attempted to shift the responsibility for the fate of cities and many of their citizens to the federal government—a responsibility which is well beyond the capability of a national government, as the results have shown. By abandoning the large-scale panaceas of the past and instead focusing on more local solutions in the future, this administration is pointing the way to new opportunities for cities and city dwellers across the land [pp. 14–15]."

The basic principles that guide this administration's ongoing formulation or urban policy are (pp. 12–14):

1. It is the responsibility of the national government to provide and maintain the basic framework within which our democratic form of government and free enterprise system can flourish to the benefit of all—the protection of individual rights and equality of opportunity.

2. The private—that is, non-governmental—institutions of our society will have a greater opportunity to play their essential roles in promoting the general welfare. It is not the command decisions of government, but the myriad decisions of families, citizen groups, businesses, and associations, each in pursuit of their individual goals, that primarily determine the patterns of urban development and the nature and quality of urban life.

3. Government intervention is required in the following circumstances: to assure the provision of public goods, such as police protection; where the benefits of an activity would otherwise accrue to one party while the costs would be borne by another; to prevent exploitation where natural monopolies exist; and to help those who cannot help themselves.

4. Government programs whose unintended effect is to undermine personal ambition and prolong unwarranted dependence should be revised so as to avoid these undesirable outcomes and to encourage self and family support, while their intended function of providing for those who cannot help themselves is retained.

5. To assure proper democratic accountability and responsiveness to citizens, government activities should be arranged and paid for by the smallest jurisdiction that encompasses most of the beneficiaries of those activities.

6. Federal government programs whose benefits are local rather than national will be turned over to the states and localities, along with appropriate revenue sources.

7. Where federal aid for local functions is continued temporarily, it will be delivered through block grants wherever possible, with minimum federal regulation and maximum local flexibility.

8. Programs that have regional or interstate benefits can be handled by interstate cooperation and joint ventures of the affected jurisdictions; they do not necessarily require a role for the federal government, other than relaxation of any regulations which unnecessarily interfere with local cooperative efforts.

9. The fiscal viability of cities depends first and foremost on their ability to perform a useful role in their regional economy, and secondly on their state governments, which establish boundaries, boundary-change and annexation procedures, taxing authority, debt limits, and the forms and processes of sub-state governance. The administration will encourage states and localities to take the initiative in identifying local needs, determining what, if any, government action is appropriate, establishing priorities among these needs, and acting on them.

10. Local leaders both inside and outside of government hold the key to developing a strategy for their city that capitalizes on the city's comparative advantages and makes it more self-reliant. The federal government will permit the comparative advantages of each city to be asserted fully, and unless a clear and direct national purpose is served, the government will not intervene in ways whose ultimate effect is to favor one city over another. However, areas of distressed cities may be recognized as a special case. The federal government will help them, for example, by joining state and local governments in designating experimental Enterprise Zones in a number of such cities.

11. Important local resources that should not be overlooked by local leaders and which constitute powerful assets and allies in revitalizing urban areas are the city's neighborhoods and the city's private sector, both corporate and voluntary. The administration is drawing attention to the vast potential for civic revival offered by these institutions.

These 11 guiding principles, the last two in particular, frame the third pillar bearing the weight of the Reagan "Revolution"—simply put, *self-reliance under local leadership*. The administration argues in the Urban Policy Report that "responsibility for the success of local institutions, both private and public, must rest primarily with those institutions [p. 3]." "Greater self-reliance is essential to the long-run good health of our cities. Efficient and responsive local efforts will occur only if cities squarely shoulder the primary responsibility to shape their individual fates [p. 9]."

The first pillar supporting the foundation of the Reagan "Revolution" is the national economic recovery program. The second is the "New Federalism." Inevitably, the ability of state and local governments to assume the expanded responsibilities proposed under this restructuring of the intergovernmental system and to achieve greater self-reliance under local leadership must rest with the success of the economic recovery program in stimulating economic growth. If this pillar crumbles, states and their local governments will face further erosion of their fiscal capacity to meet existing obligations, assume increased responsibilities, and participate as full and equal partners in local initiatives to achieve local self-reliance in meeting local needs.

The Challenge of Local Self-Reliance

The New Federalism and reorientation of federal urban policy poses a major challenge for cities to become increasingly self-reliant in responding to local needs. That cities can respond to this challenge through innovative approaches and organizations was extensively documented by case examples of the Cities' Congress on Roads to Recovery that are discussed throughout this volume.

After a two-year study, the Committee for Economic Development, an organization of corporate chief executive officers, concluded:

> External forces should be neither ignored nor underestimated. But whatever conditions prevail, local communities will have both substantial latitude to determine and principal responsibility for their own future. The evidence of recent decades demonstrates that communities which actively mobilize their public and private resources can deal effectively with difficult problems and create new opportunities.[15]

Responding to the need for greater self-sufficiency and reliance in efforts to promote the social and economic revitalization of the nation's cities will measure the will of all urban constituencies, both public and private. The critical test of cities will be their ability to innovate in institutions and processes that engender collaborative approaches to urban problems and opportunities. This is the urban challenge of the 1980s.

Public-Private Partnerships: The Critical Catalyst

Urban change and its increasing rapidity has challenged the social and economic vitality of the nation's cities throughout the post-World War II period. Problems of cities, that many have come to view as intractable, are the inevitable consequences of social and economic change. National preoccupation with urban problems, however, has obscured recognition of emerging opportunities for the revitalization of our cities and reshaping the urban environment to enhance the quality of life afforded its residents.[16]

The pace of change, driven by the ongoing transformation of the national and international economies, new technologies, and increasing regional competition, in all probability, will accelerate throughout the last two decades of this century. The current industrial restructuring of cities is a process of adaptation of urban economies responding to these national and international transformations. These adaptations, although they are creating serious economic dislocations, are essential to the economic future of cities and to national economic growth and efficiency. Efforts to impede or reverse these industrial adaptations are short-sighted, eroding the longer term competitiveness of urban economies. Effective approaches to urban development must build upon and facilitate these industrial transformations.

As a consequence of the changes occurring in urban areas throughout this century, the public and private sectors are becoming increasingly interdependent. The tradition that assumes a clear distinction between the public and private sectors in urban areas is no longer valid, if it ever was, and the old rules and traditions defining separate functions do not work to the best advantage of either. A new highly interdependent set of relationships has emerged. The decisions and actions of local governments and businesses directly and indirectly affect the other. Because of the interdependencies, it is unlikely that urban problems will be self-correcting or adjustments to economic change will be automatic. Nor can either sector independently undertake effective measures to respond the problems of change.

This interdependence of urban interests is compounded by radical changes in urban political systems. In most U.S. cities business and professional interests historically exerted powerful, if not predominant, political influence in local government. Over the years, however, both community goals and the focus of political influence have shifted in many, if not most, cities. Beginning in the last century, ethnic coalitions and labor organizations emerged as major political forces. And in this century, especially since World War II, numerous groups, including minorities, environmental associations, neighborhood and civic coalitions, and consumer organizations have exercised profound influences on local politics. Over the last two decades, these organizations and coalitions have developed the ability to use the legal system, federal consultative hearing procedures, and confrontational techniques to pursue their goals.

The fragmentation of political influence, growing throughout the century, inevitably has resulted in diverse and conflicting goals, strongly held and vigorously contested, particularly where there are significant distributional consequences of proposed actions. The complex web of interdependencies in the urban environment narrowly circumscribes the range of actions that can be undertaken independently without affecting directly or indirectly the welfare of vested interests or organized groups that have the ability, at a minimum, to delay, and in many cases, block implementation of proposed projects.

An unfortunate corollary to this increased political pluralism in the postwar period, aggravated by the large-scale intervention of the federal government, was a growing reluctance of many business leaders to become deeply involved in their communities. The stridency of local politics and the frustrations of working with the federal government and multiple local jurisdictions caused many businesses to disengage from full partnerships in the lives of their communities and, in some cases, to opt for the expediency of relocation to the suburbs or new cities that they perceived to have better business climates.

The Need for Partnership

Neither the public nor the private sectors, acting alone, has the necessary resources or expertise to sustain and enhance the vitality of the nation's cities. Effective action requires collaborative efforts of local governments and the business community. This challenge for greater self-reliance provides a unique opportunity in the nation's history for restructuring the relationships between the private and public sectors and demonstrating that local governance and local resources can sustain the vitality of our cities more effectively than more remote levels of government.

All too often, however, relationships between the public and private sectors in urban areas have been adversarial rather than cooperative and have posed major impediments to collaborative efforts. There is encouraging evidence, however, that the qualitative dimensions of the relationships between local governments and the private sector are improving. Increasingly, business leaders are recognizing that the success and profitability of their enterprises depend, in no small way, on the environment of the cities in which they operate, that relocation is an increasingly expensive luxury often trading one set of problems for another, and, therefore, that the welfare of their communities must become a part of their corporate "bottom-line."

In turn, public officials and urban electorates are coming to understand that the welfare of their cities is integrally related to the health of their business community and that their capacity to enhance the quality of urban life depends on the interest and involvement of the local business sector and the resources it commands. The experience of the last two decades amply demonstrates that efforts of local governments to revitalize their cities without the commitment and cooperation of their business community are self-defeating.

The dramatic curtailment of federal involvement in urban areas and heightened awareness of the mutual interpendence of all urban constituencies creates a new opportunity for forging new working relationships and bringing the business community back into a full and productive partnership with local governments and neighborhoods. As demonstrated by the Cities' Congress on Roads to Recovery, many urban areas are now forging new relationships between local governments, neighborhoods, and business and are working cooperatively through innovative approaches and organizations to create more viable communities.

The Concept of Partnership

Although often presented as a new approach, public-private partnerships have a legacy in advocacy and practice. Throughout the nation's history until roughly the mid-1960s, citizens, local governments, and businesses worked cooperatively to meet community needs, a working relationship that began to erode with the assumption of greater responsibilities by the federal government and local political fragmentation. In 1978 President Carter announced a "new urban policy," entitled "A New Partnership to Conserve America's Communities." More recently, President Reagan established a Task Force on Private-Sector Initiatives endorsing joint public and private efforts to meet local needs.

As the concept of partnership becomes popularized, there is a risk that this promising approach to revitalizing our cities can become primarily a public relations device or a political exhortation to business leadership as did "corporate social responsibility" in the 1960s and 1970s. More critical, perhaps, is the risk of creating unrealistic expectations for the potential achievements of partnerships that, if not fulfilled, will lead to acrimony and public disenchantment.

It is important, therefore, to reach beyond the rhetoric and "romanticizing" of partnerships to a more realistic understanding of collaborative approaches to urban needs and the role and contributions of the public and private sectors. In a pioneering 1978 study of coordinated economic development, the National Council on Urban Economic Development defined the collaborative process as follows:

> Collaboration on a joint public/private development project involves the timely sharing of resources and expertise and the coordination of activities. In essence, it is a negotiated business deal in which trade-offs are made, and risks, benefits, and profits are shared. It is a multi-faceted process structured to fill gaps in the local business climate, such as unavailability of capital, problems with land assemblage, high taxes, and potential weak demand for the project. The process is also

designed to reconcile the city government's activities with the private investor's needs for timely action and a long-term stable commitment.[17]

Building on this definition, the Committee for Economic Development stated in its recent study, *Public-Private Partnerships: An Opportunity for Urban Communities*:

> The linchpins of public-private partnerships are negotiation and cooperation. Collaborative approaches evolve through several discernible stages: goal setting, project formulation, establishment of resource commitments and responsibilities, with implementation proceeding through coordinated but independent actions. In other cases, implementation is undertaken jointly.
>
> Partnerships are voluntary associations for the mutual benefits of public and private participants. Collaboration does not require that any participant go against their essential interests; rather, cooperation permits each sector to achieve their shared goals more efficiently and effectively.
>
> Risks and liabilities must be shared among public and private participants, just as benefits are. Partnerships, almost by definition, require equitable commitment of capacity and investment. Public and private investment are necessary to underwrite many development projects and are a means of pooling risks and limiting the liability of individual participants.[18]

The cornerstones of partnerships emerge from the definitions. First, partnerships are "cooperative" and entail mutuality of goals and benefits. Partnerships, rather than corporate philanthropy, are for-profit operations and investments—in essence, negotiated business deals with the public sector.

Second, partnerships are associations for the mutual benefits of participants. Thus, collaborative arrangements do not contravene the interests of either the public or private sector. They serve mutual and common goals, or subsets of goals, or at a minimum, these associations serve the separate goals of each participant.

Third, there is a shared commitment of investment, risk, and liability in partnerships. Public and private investment is often required to underwrite the scale of many projects and provide a means for pooling risks and limiting the liability of individual participants.

Fourth, the hallmark of public-private partnerships is negotiation. Project goals must be negotiated among participants, as must investments, project design and management. Negotiation involves willingness to compromise, to seek resolutions that ensure basic and essential objectives, but a willingness to trade off what might be considered optimal conditions to achieve agreement. In an increasingly complex and interdependent urban system, the future cannot simply be planned, it must be negotiated.

Moving beyond the rhetoric and political appeal of public-private partnerships to the more realistic view that they are negotiated business arrangements involving trade-offs and joint investments, risk, and liabilities represents an essential step in considering the potential of collaborative arrangements to contribute to the goals of cities. The decision to become involved in collaborative efforts should be based on careful appraisal of the type of problems for which joint efforts represent effective approaches and a recognition of the resources and expertise necessary for cooperative partnerships.

The potential for cooperation between local governments and business arises from the sometimes discrete, sometimes overlapping objectives of each sector.

Private Domain: Business pursues its internal non-public objectives, seeking to maximize its internal long-run rate of return on investment through its for-profit operations. This, however, is not a discrete domain of the private sector. Economic development is an objective of local governments concerned with stimulating employment, strengthening the tax base, influencing patterns of development, controlling possible disamenities of private development, as well as sustaining political support of their constituencies.

Public Domain: This is the traditional sphere of responsibility of local governments in which they seek to provide for public goods and services, enhancing the general community welfare, and sustaining and building political support. This domain, however, is not wholly government. Business also seeks to improve the functioning and efficiency of local governments and is concerned about government attitudes toward and perceptions of the local business community. Independently, businesses seek their objectives in this area through political support of particular candidates or issues, lobbying efforts, philanthropy, etc.

Public-Private Domain: Both business and government seek a set of objectives that are neither fully private nor public, but a complex mix of each. In pursuing public-private objectives, the private sector seeks to improve the quality of their community both for its residents and as a place for doing business. Concurrently, business strives for improved relations with the community as well as its more traditional objective of maximizing profit. These objectives of the private sector are pursued by measures such as adjusting business decisions for their community impacts, business urban ventures and philanthropic activities. In this sphere, government expands its traditional objectives to considerations of community welfare, the quality of life, and community and economic development. Local governments pursue these objectives through measures to improve the local business climate, inducements to private sector development, and quasi-private community and economic development corporations.

Local governments and businesses will interact and have legitimate interests in each of three domains. In each, both sectors can pursue their objectives independently, interacting with one another primarily through established and conventional modes. In the primarily private domain, local governments and their business communities can engage in joint ventures to assist business development. In the primarily public domain, cooperation can take the form of business assistance to local governments through loaned executives, services, and equipment, and through city promotional activities. Cooperation in both the primarily private and essentially public domain generally take the form of one sector providing assistance to the other. The motivation for providing the assistance is that improved performance of one contributes to the ability of the other to achieve its primary objectives. Business, as well as the wider community, benefits from greater government efficiency. Local governments and their constituencies benefit from growing vital economic bases.

Public-private partnerships are designed to achieve mixed public and private objectives. Opportunities for partnership exist where coordinated, joint government-business ventures can jointly achieve objectives of participating principals. For example, a partnership can provide a competitive rate of return to business participants, significant public relations benefits and achieve their public objectives. In turn, these joint enterprises can promote local community and economic development, improve public services and infrastructure, and enhance the political standing of public officials.

Decisions to engage in public-private partnerships must be based on clear delineations of the objectives of both sectors to be served by the undertaking. A basis for partnership exists when each sector can achieve its objectives more effectively by acting in concert than through independent initiatives.

Barriers to Cooperation

The success of cities and their institutions will ultimately be judged by the quality of life afforded their citizens. The current dimensions of urban problems create a clear need for urban institutions to move beyond established ways of pursuing this goal. Innovative approaches are needed for reaching consensus on urban objectives and mobilizing the manifold resources of the city to sustain and enhance the social and economic vitality of the city.

Public-private partnerships, leveraging and coordinating the resources and capabilities of both sectors, will be necessary to respond to the complexity and scale of today's city and the changes presently occurring in its industrial base. In a survey of 564 corporations, most executives agreed that the development of their cities will require joint efforts by business leaders and local governments.[19] Despite this consensus, few of the firms surveyed had been involved in cooperative ventures with their city governments or neighborhoods. This suggests that barriers to cooperation exist that impede the formulation and implementation of joint efforts.

In their study of public-private partnerships, the Committee for Economic Development examined the preconditions upon which cooperation in cities must build:[20]

1. A civic culture that fosters a sense of community and encourages citizen participation rooted in practical concern for the community.

2. A commonly accepted vision of the community that recognizes its strengths and weaknesses and involves key groups in the process of identifying what the community can become.

3. Building-block civic organizations that blend the self-interests of members with the broader interests of the community and translate those mutually held goals into effective action.

4. A network among key groups that encourages communications and facilitates the mediation of differences.

5. Leadership and the ability to nurture "civic entrepreneurs," that is, leaders whose knowledge, imagination and energy are directed toward enterprises that benefit the community.

6. Continuity of policy, including the ability to adapt to changing circumstances, that fosters confidence in sustained enterprise.

These preconditions are the "civic foundations" for public-private partnership. Where they are not found, cooperative efforts are likely to be limited, fragile and confront commonly found barriers of mistrust and misunderstanding among sectors.

Studies of corporate attitudes have found that business leadership tends to view local government as lacking in flexibility in its mode of operation and having an inadequate grasp of the ways in which corporations can make decisions and the criteria they use. A necessary basis for successful negotiation to establish cooperative development projects is a realistic understanding of the objectives and motivations of the private and public sector representatives and the factors that determine their latitude for decisions and actions.

Public bureaucracies are devices for making decisions according to rules. Their scope for discretion is extremely limited. Greater latitude and flexibility is vested in elected officials for whom the basic test of political leadership is their ability to retain the support of the electorate that brought them to office. Public decision-making, therefore, inevitably involves reference to established rules and procedures and introduction of political judgments.

Local political leadership, moreover, must guard against being perceived as co-opted and controlled by business interests. This risk will vary from city to city depending on the historical relationships between the public and private sectors and the perception of business in the wider community. This risk is real in negotiations with business for partnerships which will involve a variety of balance sheet considerations that cannot be matched by the more intangible public sector considerations of benefits and costs of proposed actions. The risk implicit in these situations is that the appropriate range of public objectives will be narrowed and local government officials will be tempted to adopt a "balance sheet" mentality inappropriate to public sector considerations.

While progress can clearly be made in making local governments more efficient, flexible, and responsive to the private sector, public decision processes, by their very nature will appear to business as overly politicized, vacillating and inconclusive. As a consequence, business executives, accustomed to working with different decision rules and procedures, will find more extensive interactions with public officials to be time consuming and frustrating.

Improving the potential for partnerships will often require that business achieve a greater understanding of local government decision-making processes, the constraints under which these proceed, and the need to weigh political tradeoffs among multiple and often competing objectives and constituencies. Business must recognize the political need of local government and elected officials to be, and no less important, to be perceived to be, independent, equal partners in cooperative projects, serving primarily as representatives of wider community interests.

In turn, local government officials must gain a better appreciation of business decision-making and the way local governments are viewed by business. The basic objective of business leadership must be the success of the enterprise for which they are accountable. The unique potential of partnerships is as an approach through which business contributes to public objectives by actions consistent with their profit orientation, an approach in sharp contrast to public pressures for "corporate social responsibility."

Nor should business objectives be narrowly construed as profit-seeking. Business seeks public acceptance. Responsible business leaders are concerned about the quality of the environment in which they, their families, and employees live and work, and recognize that the welfare of the city affects the success of their enterprise. Business, thus, will often view public-private partnerships in a broader context than the financial opportunities they present. Nonetheless, their concern for profit cannot be discounted, nor should it be.

15

The New Era in
Public-Private Partnerships

Robert C. Holland

Starting this essay with the term "The New Era" may well stir in readers' minds visions of over-optimistic, platitudinous notions, full of either local boosterism, campaign rhetoric, or both. On the contrary, I strike just one note of optimism: the benefits to be gained from the realism that is being injected into the roles of the public and private sectors in urban economic development.

A hard-taught evolution is taking place in our understanding of urban development—why we want it, how much we want of it, and how to go about getting it. Most of the options that have appealed to various citizens for achieving these goals have been tried and found wanting. Government officials have tried the tactic of pounding on the business community. Public policymakers have also tried the grand strategy of using government taxing and spending power to pursue their dreams of a good society. But the first technique has proved futile, and the second has demonstrated a chronic tendency toward overextension that turns counterproductive.

Private citizens or firms, for their part, have tried paternalistic or philanthropic efforts to adopt a city and fix it the way they saw best. A great many other businesses have also tried simply benign neglect, paying whatever taxes they have to and leaving it to others to try to make a city better. But in present-day communities, citizens (and that includes employees and customers) typically will not accept either of these approaches—at least not from their substantial businesses. Complaints from voters, politicians, shareholders, customers, employees, and their surrounding neighborhoods shake that kind of *status quo*.

The latest, and in some quarters the sharpest, jolt to previous thinking has come from the curtailment of federal fund flows into urban-related programs. I see no prospect for that curtailment to be significantly reversed, for it seems to me that it rests on a broad and deep taxpayer consensus that transcends political party or sectoral interest.

In this evolving atmosphere, it seems to me that the technique of local public-private partnership aimed at community improvement is the best alternative option left—and it is probably the only option that is capable of being expanded a great deal in the contemporary environment. What do I mean by public-private partnership? The definition I like best comes from an extensive study that the Committee for Economic Development recently completed, entitled *Public-Private Partnership: An Opportunity for Urban Communities*:

> Public-private partnership means cooperation among individuals and organizations in the public and private sectors for mutual benefit. Such cooperation has two dimensions: the policy dimension, in which the goals of the community are articulated, and the operational dimension, in which those goals are pursued. The purpose of public-private partnership is to link these dimensions in such a way that the participants contribute to the benefit of the broader community while promoting their own individual or organizational interests.

Cooperative action for *mutual* benefit—that, it seems to me, is the enduring motivational key to success in this field. Some fine examples may be found in Cleveland—something few people would have thought possible a few years ago. I am particularly taken with the vision of the city projected by a new organization, Cleveland Tomorrow. The vision of a resurgent city adapting to a changing economics base is drawn from a careful study, and the group of industrialists who are working to implement it have the stature to make it a practical vision. It strikes me as a careful, rational analysis of Cleveland's key industrial problems, and it presents a well-targeted set of functional programs that could help deal with those problems.

Beyond it, what is the next big step to progress? I endorse the stirring call that James Rouse made to the Cities' Congress for the development of an even broader and longer-range vision of what any city ought to become, embracing the whole metropolitan area. I am talking not just about a collection of wishful dreams, but a coordinated vision of achieveable goals, knit together, in which all segments of a city's society can see what they have to gain from such a future, come to endorse it, and be willing to support the sometimes hard public and private actions it might take to get there. We need to look beyond the frustrations of today, beyond the recessions and their discouragements, to what can and ought to be years down the road.

What I am calling for is thoroughly consistent with the more limited goals of such groups as Cleveland Tomorrow. The action programs advocated by

Cleveland Tomorrow strike me as essential early steps toward reaching that future. So why bother with the vision? Because developing that future vision can also make it easier to get there. It can encourage all the community's many decisionmakers to push more in the same direction, instead of galloping off in all directions.

The gains from this kind of new-era vision of what a city can and ought to become, are manifold. Let me point to what I think are its two most underemphasized benefits. One is the resultant lowering of *investment risk* for the firms investing in the area. The provision of an atmosphere in which future uncertainty is reduced and surrounding prospects brightened is an incalculable benefit to these firms, and indirectly to their employees and customers. That kind of atmosphere can be created by a careful and stable working together of the public and private sectors, at every level at which their actions affect the community.

For government officials, well-executed public-private cooperation in developing a community vision can reduce their *political risk*. The development of a high degree of private sector consensus concerning the directions in which the community should go can make a government policymaker's job easier operationally and less subject to termination politically.

In a world where most of us are risk-averse these days, these risk-reducing dimensions of public-private cooperation action enable some communities not as inhibited as other communities to advance fairly quickly in ways that out-compete the laggards.

Along with risk reduction, public-private partnerships, well designed and well executed, have a remarkable ability to increase benefits. They have a well-nigh unique ability to enhance community environment, jobs, and incomes. They can add significantly to the best that either the private sector or the public sector can do by itself in these directions. The truth of that conclusion was repeatedly demonstrated in the success stories told at the Cities' Congress. And the intriguing fact is that all the necessary ingredients for a good public-private sector partnerships are *home-grown*. It is up to the *local leaders* of *each* of the major parts of the community to put those ingredients together. No community I know of is doing so badly that it cannot be helped—and none is doing so well that it cannot be improved—by more vigorous efforts by its various leaders to make its public-private partnership grow and prosper.

16

Goals, Processes and Leadership

Paul R. Porter and David C. Sweet

Some Aspects of Progress

The earliest known remains of *Homo sapiens sapiens*, the singular sub-species that displaced *Homo sapiens neanderthalensis* and commonly known as the human race, are about 42,000 years old. Agriculture has been practiced for about 12,000 years, and for nearly half of its duration there have been cities. They have sprung from fortunately situated villages, flourished, and disappeared, to be succeeded by other cities repeating the cycle.[1] Given the problems of some of today's cities, it is tempting to assert that internal troubles caused the demise of cities that no longer exist. Such may indeed be true, but it cannot be proved. Other causes, better known to history, were probably sufficient.

The essential functions of cities have not changed greatly in some 50 centuries. As Lewis Mumford has written, cities already had a mature form at the dawn of history. Ancient Ur and Babylon, Periclean Athens, Rome of the Empire, Ch'ang-an of the Sui dynasty, medieval Paris, and 18th-century London: each was a large concentration of people (although the number might vary greatly) in a small geographic area which served simultaneously as a center of commerce, non-agricultural production, administration, learning, and specialization of skills. The same may be said of American cities of the late 20th century. (One prominent feature of ancient and medieval cities was lost with the rise of the nation-state: walls no longer encompass a city as a defense against foes.)

The continuity of most functions notwithstanding, urban settlements that have evolved in the past two centuries are as different from their predecessors as they were from villages, or villages were from the presumed cave dwellings of Altamira. Unlike any previous condition of the human race, a majority of people (in industrial nations) live in urban settlements, and so rapidly have they drawn people from the countryside and so unsettling is the change to accustomed ways that even the word city has acquired a contemporary meaning quite different from its historic one. Until only a few decades ago, it meant the whole of an urban settlement. But with the urban population growing faster than cities could (or wished to) extend their legal boundaries, the contemporary meaning has come to be restricted to the settlement's core. (It is the restrictive meaning that is used throughout this book except when the historic one is obvious.)

The cluster of technologies that grew from the inventions of the dynamo, the electric light, the telephone, the high-rise building, and the automobile made urban living more appealing; and kindred technologies on the farm made it unavoidable for many who went from a rural poverty to an urban one. Thus by promise and by necessity, the city—in its historic meaning— became the larger part of society in the very decades that fabulous progress in the conquest of disease was fast increasing total population.

There is no law of nature that the blessings of invention and discovery will neatly mesh or have no flaws. It should not be surprising, then, that so big an event as the transformation of the historic city into the contemporary metropolis has been accompanied by a record of blessings working at cross purposes and submerging old problems into new ones. Cities of the late 20th century are indeed having a rough passage in a time of considerable turbulence, and the phenomenon is not peculiarly American. A casual tourist can observe traffic congestion in Rome and Paris as bad as in any American city. A rusty blanket of smog often hangs over Athens; air pollution is doing irreparable damage to the marble treasures on the Acropolis. Inner London, Manchester, and Glasgow have lost population at a rate like that of St. Louis, Cleveland, and Buffalo.[2] Recent but substantial minorities— South Asians and Caribbean blacks in Great Britain, Algerians in France, Turks in West Germany—congregate in decaying neighborhoods of these nations' cities. Nasty confrontations have flared in London, Liverpool, and Marseilles. In Europe, as here, basic industries have been shaken by competition from Japan and some Third World countries. Unemployment in the metal-working industries of the British West Midlands is more severe than in the auto and steel centers of the United States.[3] The 24-member Organization for Economic Cooperation and Development, a heritage of the Marshall Plan, has recently created an urban affairs department to help its members better comprehend their problems.[4]

The urban condition has been worse. What is today the grim side was not long ago the squalid. Charles Dickens and Victor Hugo in novels and William Hogarth in drawings portrayed a brutish condition that was probably normal for a large proportion of city residents since cities began. With a camera Jacob Riis recorded with stark realism the poverty, misery, and filth that were common to residents of New York City slums in the late 19th century. Aptly, he titled his book *How the Other Half Lives*.[5]

Sanitation is a reliable guide to the immense progress that has been made in making urban living healthier and more pleasant. Elizabeth Barlow reminds us that it has not been long since "hogs were the sanitationmen of the day, collecting garbage from gutters, and steaming manure smells rather than carbon monoxide filled the air." As late as 1940 when the first U.S. census of housing was taken, 42.5 percent of all year-round housing units in the United States lacked some or all household plumbing (piped hot and cold water, bath and toilet). The percentage was reduced to 15.7 percent in 1960, 6.9 percent in 1970 and 2.0 percent in 1980; the urban component was 0.56 percent.[6]

Have We Peaked in National Well-Being?

Past progress in itself is not persuasive evidence that the recovery of troubled cities is feasible. No trend is a straight line for long. It levels off, zig-zags, or unmistakably curves upward or downward. Some scholarly observers believe we have peaked in national well-being: that "post-affluent America" is a condition that we have already entered.[7]

They have some statistical support. Table 1 in June Thomas's chapter shows no progress during the 1970s in reducing the percentage of families living below the officially defined poverty level and a recent increase. The income gap between whites and blacks that had been gratifyingly narrowing has widened again. The auto industry is in severe trouble. By 1982, 22.6 percent of the automobiles purchased in the United States were made in Japan. Layoffs of workers in U.S. auto plants exceeded 200,000; another 600,000 were idled in plants supplying parts and materials. Unemployment in Detroit reached 19.7 percent; a third of its residents were on welfare.[8] The sober *Wall Street Journal* recently reported "a continued rapid deindustrialization, not only in steel, but also in machine tools, foundries, rubber, mining, and industrial equipment."[9]

Clearly, important changes are occurring in the structure of American industry, and they will increase the difficulties of some cities. Forecasts that the national well-being will be less in the future than in the past could prove to be true. If true, a lower level would at least retard the recovery of most or all cities. Yet, a prudent view of the future is that its most predictable trait is an indifference to prophecy.

Efforts by governments and institutions when well-planned and well-organized have in past times beneficially influenced unfolding events, and we may assume that they will do so again. As a guide to the most desirable efforts in creating a better future for troubled American cities, it will be useful to attempt an objective review of the success stories told at the Cities' Congress and their appraisal in the preceding chapters. Presenting the conclusions before the analysis, it seems fair to say:

1. The success stories do not represent undertakings fundamental enough to reverse the decline in the cities where they occurred.

2. This conclusion in no way disparages the value of the successes. None was intended to serve the recovery idea described in the book. Each was designed to serve a specific purpose for only a part of a city or one aspect of the city's well-being. Enough of that objective was accomplished or was being accomplished for the effort to be termed a success.

3. Each of the reported successes was a contribution to the recovery of the city in which it occurred even though not motivated by a recovery concept. Lessons drawn from them can contribute to the development of a strategy for achieving the generalized goals.

4. They confirmed the importance of the recovery goals, i.e., that cities should become competitive with suburbs as a place to live, attract investment to create sufficient jobs for their residents, and in this manner free themselves from a permanent dependency. They also illustrated that recovery goals are inevitably long-term in character (requiring probably a generation or more to be fully attained, although substantial progress could be made sooner).

5. Some things that affect the condition of cities are outside the competence of government. Their correction will require leadership by institutions that can evoke loyalties more intimate than are given to agencies of government.

6. Nonetheless, a major role by governments, including the federal government, is indispensable to the recovery of cities.

7. The most distinctly upbeat side of cities is an effective and growing collaboration between governments and private institutions.

Creators of "The Good and Competent Community"

The central principle of public-private partnerships is that each party brings to it something of importance that the other party cannot. There can be as few as two parties—one public, one private—but those that are significant to the issues discussed in this book have involved a larger number of both public and private parties. Many entail complex negotiations before a workable relationship is established. Major redevelopment projects reported to the Cities' Congress by Robert Shetterly of Oakland, Carlo Marchetti of Springfield, Massachusetts, and Delano Erickson of St. Paul included participation by the respective local governments, the federal government as the source of crucial UDAG loans, and international as well as domestic investors.

Public-private partnerships are not new, as several chapter authors have observed. Krumholz cites a plea by Alexander Hamilton for federal government support of new manufacturing industries. (See Chapter 13.) Hamilton was the intellectual father of the Bank of the United States, and while it lasted, it was an example of the one-on-one relationship consistent with Hamilton's advocacy of a powerful centralized government. Madison, who with Hamilton and Jay, was a co-author of the Federalist Papers, held a view of society that is more relevant to today's multi-party creations with which we are concerned. Society, he argued, consists of a "multiplicity of interests" or "factions," and to enable each to be protected, the new government should rest upon a separation of powers that would ensure that "ambition must be made to counteract ambition," resulting in a "constitutional equilibrium."[10] Madison, of course, was not intentionally giving a prescription for contemporary public-private partnerships. His purpose was to win support for a government yet to be created, but his realistic view of society as a multiplicity of interests that needed to be reconciled in an equilibrium determined his concept of the new government. It is also a justification for multi-party partnerships that ideally will, in Mier's words, be achieved by "a bargaining process between all parties affected by the development process."

Not many of the partnerships in the success stories can be said to be a product of bargaining between all affected parties. On the private side, developers, bankers, manufacturers, architects, and medical centers were, as a rule, more actively represented than labor unions or neighborhood organizations. There are several plausible explanations for the circumstance. Their economic interests are more concrete, they have greater resources, and they are more sophisticated.

Business Contributions

The business contributions to the partnerships have often been imaginative and public-spirited as well as substantial. To foster and recognize such contributions, the College of Urban Affairs with the support of the George S. Dively Foundation has established the George S. Dively Award for Corporate Contributions in Urban Development. The award concept grew out of conversations between David C. Sweet and George S. Dively, chairman emeritus of the Harris Corporation, aimed at recognizing the role that many private corporations have played in urban development initiatives to achieve a community goal. The award sought to focus national attention on outstanding efforts in this area by giving $25,000 to a selected corporation to be used for five graduate fellowships in urban development at universities designated by the recipient.

In its first year the College received sixty-seven nominations. They were reviewed and screened by a panel of local urban development experts, and the top eight nominations were reviewed by a distinguished panel of judges.[11] They selected the Ralston Purina Company from St. Louis as the 1984 award winner, citing it as "an outstanding example of corporate leadership in urban development [by] a substantial and long-term commitment of both corporate leadership and corporate resources to the redevelopment of the LaSalle Park project." In an acceptance speech at a Cleveland City Club luncheon, John P. Baird, senior vice president and general counsel of Ralston Purina, observed that the award would encourage further needed involvement by corporations, and through its fellowship stipends to graduate students in urban development, ensure broader study and research.

Holland has soundly observed that the partnerships have a "policy dimension, in which the goals of the community are articulated, and the operational dimension, in which these goals are pursued." In communities where labor is known to have been an active participant, it is mainly in the organizations that are concerned with policy, such as the Greater Milwaukee Committee, the Greater Cleveland Growth Association, the Allegheny Conference, and similar bodies in St. Louis and Oakland. Lane Kirkland, president of the AFL-CIO, sent two senior representatives to the Cities' Congress, and labor representatives also attended from Chicago, Cleveland and New Haven—all concerned with policy rather than specific projects.

In contrast, so far as the Cities' Congress was representative, neighborhood organizations appear to have a negligible hand in policy, but are frequently able to affect redevelopments in their neighborhoods. Only Cleveland and Columbus were represented in the Congress by neighborhood spokespeople, although more would have attended had there been a source to pay their expenses. A significant and probably growing influence may be observed in two comments by chapter authors:

Bertsch writing about the Renaissance project in Columbus, "The poor today, unlike a few decades ago, have power. They have spokespeople. . . . They could not be ignored and were successful in helping the project."

Lasater, "Community organizations representing a neighborhood's residents must be listened to with respect and their cooperation sought."

A. L. (Sandy) Taggart, who was the head of a family-owned regional bakery before becoming president of Indianapolis's Near North Development Corporation, described its relationship to neighborhood groups this way: "You've got to have a relationship in which you don't demean what they bring to the table. You aren't reticent about what you bring."

Newspaper publishers have a prominent role in the goal setting of some cities. Four who spoke at the Cities' Congress were Thomas Vail, publisher and editor of Cleveland's *Plain Dealer*, Paul Poorman, editor and vice-president of the *Akron Beacon Journal*, Wendell Ashton, publisher of Salt Lake City's *Deseret News*, and David Starr, publisher of Springfield's morning, afternoon and Sunday newspapers. Starr was the initiator of below-market-rate development loans by the city's banks and the Massachusetts Mutual Insurance Company and is a member of a Springfield central committee that breakfasts weekly with the mayor.

Resourceful and committed leadership from heads of local government is indispensable to the public side of the partnerships. It was evident from those who spoke at the Cities' Congress: Mayors George Voinovich of Cleveland, Roy Ray of Akron, David Mann of Cincinnati, Lionel Wilson of Oakland and Theodore Dimauro of Springfield, Deputy Mayor John Kraus of Indianapolis, and Council President Sydney Fonnesbeck of Salt Lake City.

All "factions" (to use Madison's word) are not consistently nor equally represented in the diverse partnerships responsible for the success stories, but a broadening of participation does occur. And from the processes of adjusting separate "ambitions" to a larger mutual interest, it is possible to observe the emergence of new goals and new leaders for the "good and competent community" envisioned by Smith. As Madison did in the nation, some rise from their group interest to local statesmanship.

The Health of Neighborhoods

Goetze, judging what is required to make weakened neighborhoods healthy, has introduced the medical concept of homeostasis—a balance of "many forces joining to maintain an organism's equilibrium," among which he includes a motivation of residents "towards increased self-reliance." The homeostasis analogy is appealing as a description of neighborhood health. Progress toward homeostasis may be observed in neighborhoods examined by him, Bertsch, Lieske, and Krumholz, as well as in British neighborhoods improved by an "Envelope Scheme" described later. In each case the initiative came from outside—from sources as diverse as a gas company, an insurance company, a research institute, a medical center, a church, a university-sponsored neighborhood development center, and in the British instance, a local government. Each entailed an improvement in housing and a parallel involvement of residents in mutual efforts to improve their immediate environment. A potential for recovery existed, but in the weakened condition of these neighborhoods, an external agent was needed to activate it. It is a reasonable conclusion that in many neighborhoods health will be restored only with the aid of an external agent.

Goetze's homeostasis analogy is relevant also to the process of continuous renewal of a neighborhood's population. Fewer than half of the American people (49 percent) lived in the same home in 1980 that they had occupied in 1975. Only 33 percent had lived in the same place for as long as 10 years.[12] The turnover is normally highest in neighborhoods where most residents are renters. Rouse calculated in 1955 that a 10-year program to replace the worst one-quarter of the housing of Washington, D.C. would increase the annual turnover rate by only 3 percent.[13] A stream of new residents is crucial. In Goetze's words, "When neighborhoods become unattractive to new residents, existing residents spread out to fill vacancies."

While new residents are essential to a neighborhood's health, the housing renovation needed to attract them may threaten the displacement of existing residents through the process known as gentrification. The gentrification threat may be exaggerated. A senior HUD official concluded in 1979 after an extensive review of known studies: "Very little reliable information exists. The work that has been done can be characterized fairly as impressionistic and generally devoid of carefully constructed research designs."[14] Nonetheless, when displacement does occur, it is a serious matter for the people removed from their homes. The problem will grow when redevelopment becomes more widespread.

Few people today will defend the large-scale displacements that characterized some of the urban-renewal projects in the 1950s and 1960s. An acceptable redevelopment policy requires that the people who will be affected shall be heard and that ways be found to enable residents to remain in their neighborhood if that is their choice. Where the problem has arisen in the redevelopments reported to the Cities' Congress, satisfactory relocation arrangements for displaced residents to remain in the neighborhood appear to have been made in the Washington University Medical Center redevelopment and in the Battelle redevelopment.

And the Wealth of a Nation

It seems unlikely that cities that have heavily lost residents will regain a substantial number. It is doubtful that it would be to their advantage to try.

Many population losers were once too crowded. Heavy losers, however, cannot continue to lose heavily without creating excessive burdens for the residents who remain. People who leave for a suburban residence do not take with them a share of the city's debt or pension obligations. The per capita share of those who remain is thus increased and must be reflected in higher taxes, reduced services, or both. Every departing taxpayer, whether residential or commercial, adds a mite or more to an incentive for others to leave. As an institution, a city has an obligation to its residents, its service suppliers, and job providers to arrest heavy population losses, to stabilize at least, and in some cases, to grow again. Concisely stated, the city's obligation is to make itself competitive with suburbs as a place to live.

When cities compete poorly, a move-up process produces a social cost in the weakest neighborhoods.[15] Expanding suburbs draw residents from the city's stronger neighborhoods, and vacancies in these are soon filled by people from weaker ones. In the weakest of all, some houses remain vacant, and with the departure of customers, stores are vacated, too. Houses or stores left vacant for long threaten the survival of the neighborhood around them. They become an eyesore, a target for arson, and an incentive for remaining residents to leave when they can afford it.

While a move-up process unaccompanied by a flow of new residents transmits a social cost downward to the weakest neighborhoods, a consequent idling or destruction of capital in them transmits an economic cost upward to the city and with diminishing force, to the region and the nation. As long as the number of households continues to increase (as it still does in all metropolitan regions—even those that are losing population), the demand for new housing will continue to rise. A replacement of housing that has been demolished or that remains vacant will increase the demand in excess of the rate of household growth.

A suburban replacement of city housing that has been discarded prematurely has an inflationary effect. Savings are diverted to housing from other needs. A corresponding suburban replication of underused city infrastructure increases the capital needs of public utilities and suburban governments. Their borrowings inflate interest rates in some unknown degree, and home buyers who borrow are penalized by a city's declining competitiveness as a place to live. This conclusion, it should be said, rests on deductive logic. We are not aware of empirical studies that attempt to measure the inflationary effect. But if the effect is more than slight, it is a reason for home buyers, private business, and the federal government, as well as city governments, to promote the conservation and use of existing housing stock.

The Public Interest in Conserving What We Have

"A decent home and a suitable living environment for every American family"—the proclaimed goal of the Housing Act of 1949—continues to be elusive. Burnham wrote in his ambitious plan for Chicago early in the century:

> Chicago has not yet reached the point where it will be necessary for the municipality to provide at its own expense, as does the city of London, for the rehousing of people forced out of congested quarters, but unless the matter shall be taken in hand at once, such a course will be required in common justice to men and women so degraded by long life in the slums that they have lost all power of caring for themselves.[16]

The public housing that Burnham foresaw as a prospect was begun modestly in the New Deal years and more ambitiously after the Housing Act of 1949. When Rouse wrote *No Slums in Ten Years* in 1955,[17] replacing a quarter of the housing stock of the nation's capital with new public housing was still thought to be possible and desirable. It was in that year and the next that the ill-fated 33 high-rise buildings of the Pruitt-Igoe project were opened in St. Louis. They covered 57 acres and housed at one time 10,000 people.[18] But it was in New York, with Robert Moses as the driving force, that public housing was built on a grand scale; it became the home for more than a half million people.[19]

Seventeen years after Pruitt-Igoe was opened, conditions in it were so bad that only 20 percent of the units were occupied. Soon after, the buildings were demolished. No other large public-housing project fared so badly. But the public housing route to a decent home has lost its appeal. The Council on Development Choices for the 1980s, a group of distinguished citizens including governors and mayors, mobilized more than 1,000 people to help prepare its report on *The Affordable Community*. The report lists 29 proposals for creating "an adequate supply of affordable housing," but public housing is not one of them. The report did not even bother to oppose it.[20] In Great Britain, public housing (known there as council housing) has been more successful, although some of its high-rise projects, especially in Glasgow, have been strongly criticized.[21] Until recently, about 35 percent of all British housing units consisted of council housing. But in that country, too, the public-housing approach may be at an end. Prodded by the Thatcher government, local governments have sold about 500,000 units to tenants. The sales are popular with the new owners and with municipalities hard pressed for funds.

The shrinking of city populations partially explains the declining demand for public housing and other forms of subsidized new construction. But also there has been a major shift in opinion: Some of the housing that was demolished in land clearance for urban renewal was recognized to be worth saving. The Cinderella projects of the Brooklyn Union Gas were among the pioneers of successful rehabilitation. Jubilee Housing has shown what can be done with group sweat equity, and Lincoln Life with introducing home ownership along with rehabilitation. Lasater has shown what a resourceful bank can do in adapting different methods to the particularities of neighborhoods. Renaissance in Columbus and the Medical Center redevelopment in St. Louis have successfully combined rehabilitation and new construction in large-scale projects. Krumholz has recounted a quasi-bootstrap success (which he also inspired) in Cleveland's Tremont-West.

Resourceful as these successful efforts have been, they are not enough. Neglect by many owners—occupants and landlords—is wasting the capital investment of earlier generations. Cleveland, like many other cities, has tried to stimulate owners to act with low-interest loans from Community Development Block Grant funds. But owners are loath to spend the money if inaction by others continues to degrade the neighborhood. Short of wholesale redevelopment by an institution, a bold entrepreneur, or a band of gentrifiers, rehabilitation flounders in many neighborhoods for lack of concerted action. A recent British innovation obtains it.

Known as the Envelope Scheme (envelope connoting inclusiveness), it was described in a film and talk at the Anglo-American Colloquium on Urban Policy.[22] In selected neighborhoods in Birmingham, England, where it was introduced in 1978, the city government at its own expense renovates the exteriors of all houses in a block at the same time. They are given new roofs, gutters, waterspouts, doors, and windows, and a painting of woodwork and a mending of brickwork. Before the renovation, advice of the affected parties is obtained in block meetings. The average cost is about $6,000 per house.[23]

The local Conservative Party embraced the Envelope Scheme when it came to power in 1981. Don Lewis, chairman of the city's housing committee, claimed the following benefits of the program in his presentation to the colloquium: (1) *all* homes in a block must be brought up to an acceptable standard if neighborhood deterioration is to be reversed, and experience had shown that the only way to obtain the participation of all was for the city to assume the cost of the exterior renovation; (2) the cost to the city was less in the long run than the cost of continued neglect; (3) major savings in the cost of renovation were achieved by having the most experienced contractors do a whole block at a time. In the case of houses too far gone to be worth rehabilitating, the city acquires them through eminent domain, has them replaced with new houses in the same architectural style, and sold. The central government has reimbursed the city for 75 percent of the cost. At the time of the colloquium, about 2,500 homes had been renovated. In many cases owners of the benefitted homes had followed with interior renovation through sweat equity or building-society loans previously unavailable.[24] The Thatcher government has announced that it will give financial support to the introduction of the Envelope Scheme in other cities.

The decision of a conservative government to pay the costs of wholesale exterior renovations of privately owned homes expresses an inherent public interest in the proper maintenance of private property if neglect of the property causes damage to the property of others.

In this country, as in Great Britain, a parallel public interest in the use of private property has long been manifested in zoning practices. A similar public interest is recognized in the centuries-old practice of eminent domain. The obstacle to some adaptation of this British innovation to American cities is thus not the principle itself but the method. While a direct transfer of it to the United States is probably not practical, the British experience is a standing invitation to American pragmatism and inventiveness to find acceptable ways to prevent neglect of maintenance by some property owners from injuring both the public interest and the values and prospects of other property owners.

Attracting New Enterprises and Jobs

When David Bergholz of Pittsburgh told the Cities' Congress that "where communities have been the least successful, it is around the issue of jobs," he identified the major problem where local self-reliance has the least to offer. In the private economy, a community's level of employment is determined principally by demand in distant markets and by competitive suppliers outside the community—increasingly from abroad. When a steel mill closed in Youngstown, there was little that the community could do to generate alternative jobs.

Communities are not completely helpless, however, in fostering job opportunities for their residents. New technologies and changing consumer preferences will continue to doom many jobs which once looked promising to their holders. Some other kinds of losses, however, can be averted by community actions. Mier has suggested some.

Keeping the durable jobs from being taken away is an important end in itself and may be the means of attracting others. If the hospitals associated with the Washington University Medical Center had moved to suburbs in the early 1970s, as two other hospitals had already done, St. Louis would have lost 10,000 jobs. The move would have been a convenience for doctors living in the suburbs, but the new location would have been beyond the practical travel range of many low-paid employees. According to people familiar with the decision to remain in the city, it was a close call. An important factor in the decision was the availability of a partial tax abatement that could be conveyed to purchasers of redeveloped housing and commercial properties. The city also agreed to make street improvements which amounted to about $2 million.

Were the jobs worth the price? Not everyone has thought so.[25] But most of the city's's residents have apparently approved because they have continued to elect mayors and council members who have repeated the tax-abatement incentive in numerous other projects. One reason for the approval is that some 5,000 additional jobs have been drawn to the redevelopment area. Some were drawn from elsewhere in the city, but about 3,500 appear to have been a net gain. An imaginative offer of access to the center's medical library lured a Monsanto toxicology laboratory to the city.

Another success in *preserving* jobs was told in a recent issue of *Reader's Digest*.[26] The success was a cooperative effort of the management of an ailing Ford transmission plant in Detroit's industrial suburb of Livonia and Local 182 of the United Auto Workers (UAW). The stimulus was Japanese competition.

Two men, according to the magazine, were principally responsible for keeping the 68-acre Livonia plant from closing permanently. One was its new manager, Marvin Craig, who had begun his career in the industry as an assembly-line worker in the same plant. The other was Robert (Red) Little, president of the UAW local. Both knew that the plant had been badly run. Craig persuaded the chairman of the board and Little, his members, to start involving the workers in improving efficiency. Eighty employee-involvement committees with more than 700 members met weekly to hear ideas on how to produce a better product at less cost. In 1982 Ford paid employees at the Livonia plant $600,000 in cash for ideas that saved the company $3.7 million. With 91 percent of the union members voting in favor, negotiated changes in work rules were introduced which were estimated to cut labor costs by 25 percent. Together, management and the union found ways to upgrade existing equipment enough to reduce a projected investment cost for a new front-wheel overdrive transmission from $1.5 billion to $1 billion. Then the Livonia plant bid for the contract to make the new transmission. Their competitor was the Japanese Toyo Kogyo in which Ford held a 25 percent interest. The Livonia plant underbid the Japanese and obtained the contract.

While the story has intrinsic interest as an example of labor-management cooperation to save threatened jobs, it is not our main reason for telling it. We do not wish to suggest that foreign competition will be so successfully overcome if workers and managements in other plants simply duplicate the

Livonia story. Our principal reason for telling it is to illustrate two other points we wish to make.

The first is that while most jobs in the Livonia plant were saved, the process of saving them also meant losing some. The save-some-lose-some pattern is reaching, in varying ways, throughout the auto and steel industries and others as well. How many workers will be made redundant by the process is still unknown, but it is clearly evident that many laid-off workers, like others from plants permanently closed, will never return to the shrunken payrolls of their industry. Retraining will help some find other jobs in the same community, but it is not a cure-all. Other displaced workers will migrate. Still others, because of age or other limitations, will remain unemployed.

It will be unfortunate both for them and their community if they come to be treated simply as a burden. They are also an unused resource, and as a resource they could be gainfully employed in restoring neglected housing and infrastructure. Their true wage cost would be a net figure after subtraction of predictable costs of unemployment insurance, welfare and neglect to property. The calculation of the costs will not be simple. Neither will their financing. But both could be done. The resort to public works to reduce exceptional unemployment has a long and generally respectable record in American history.[27] While the instrument is subject to improvement, it is an appropriate one to use in cities where unemployment levels remain high.

Some Things Government Cannot Do

The second point about the Livonia story is that the jobs that were saved were saved by the management and the union; no other help was needed and government participation would have been distracting. There may be occasions when the government, at the city, state or federal level, may be able to facilitate management-labor cooperation if requested by the other parties, but intervention in the bargaining process would be undesirable.[28]

In another realm, Thomas notes the limitations of both commercial redevelopment and government programs for benefitting poorer members of the community. She writes: "The fact is, however, that the 'other programs' [welfare and subsidized housing] have not been able to eliminate the problems of urban poverty." She presents provocative data on changes in the percentage of families whose income is below the officially defined poverty level. For all races, the percentage declined sharply during the 1960s, was at a plateau in the 1970s and rose in 1981. Not only was the percentage much higher for blacks than whites, but as other scholars have noted, the gap between the average income of whites and blacks has widened.

While the recent increase in the percentage of families below the poverty level may be provisionally explained as an effect of a recession, the provocative question is: What accounts for the plateau? There may be multiple causes, but probably one is the spectacular increase in the number of single-parent families, as some prominent black leaders believe.

Bayard Rustin, organizer of the 1963 March on Washington for Jobs and Freedom, attributes part of the cause of black poverty to "the collapse of black-family structures—a result as well as a cause of the black plight—and the alarming increase in the number of unwed black mothers, most of whom live in poverty."[29] William Raspberry, a widely respected columnist, writes:

> The main reason the gap between black and white family income is widening again, after a long period of catch-up, is that a growing percentage of our families are headed by single females. Family break-up is part of that, but not all. Fifty-five percent of our babies are born out of wedlock, many of them to adolescent mothers. Legislation can't fix that. We'll have to do it ourselves.[30]

It is not believable that the situation that Rustin and Raspberry note will continue indefinitely, but the change will come with the aid of private institutions that can inspire behavior and evoke a loyalty beyond the capacity of goverment. "Ourselves" as the remedial agent can mean such organizations as the NAACP, which announced in October, 1983, that it will make a major study of the connection between black poverty and family structure. A remedial agent might also mean churches. Lieske has shown a significant potential in religious motivation concerning urban problems.

A Vision as Large as a City

Three non-academic contributors to this book—Rouse, Lasater, and Holland—have each asserted the need for a vision of what a city might be. Like Burnham, they recognize the truth in, "Make no little plans, they have no magic to stir men's blood."

The most important question concerning the success stories appraised in preceding chapters is, What lies beyond? There will be others like them, some inspired by their example and others originating independently. But unless they inspire and shape a larger vision than animated them, their true value will be realized by no more than half.

The needed larger vision is a vision of all of the city: not only its houses, workplaces, shops, schools, transportation, parks, and arts, but how they function at their best to enrich the lives of all who live or work within it. "Enormous problems exist," writes Thomas, "and yet so do enormous possibilities." The problems are well known, the possibilities much less so. A vision will make them known.

A vision of what a city might be should be supported by an inventory of the city's human and physical resources, and it should give guidance on how they may be fully employed.

A vision should include the support of a city's grown-ups for the city's children. It should project, in ways like those described by Chatterjee and Davidow, the preparation for citizenship and self-reliance, and it should inspire, in ways not yet known, a saving of children from premature parenthood.

A vision should portray the health of neighborhoods and how they both nourish and are nourished by a vigorous downtown. A city cannot withdraw into its neighborhoods nor abandon its renewal.[31]

A vision can inspire hope and confidence if it is common property because all elements of the community helped to create it. Suggestions made by Kunde might be enlivening ways of bringing in all elements.

More than any other large city, Dallas has systematically sought to define its goals and to do it through a process of widespread participation. The concept of community-formulated goals for a "city of excellence" was introduced in 1964 by a new mayor, Erik Jonsson. He persuaded 26 local citizens to devise "a goal setting and achievement process." From their recommendations came a permanent organization known as Goals for Dallas, Inc. It is an independent, non-political and non-profit corporation with an executive staff, financed by over 160 individuals, businesses, and foundations and governed by a 45-member board of trustees. The organization estimates that since its beginning, more than 100,000 Dallas residents have participated in meetings to formulate and pursue its goals.[32]

Cycle II of the process was begun in 1977. It embraces 205 stated goals under the supervision of 17 committees concerning citizen involvement, continuing education, cultural activities, the design of the city, economy, elementary and secondary education, energy, environment, government, health, higher education, housing, human services, public safety, quality of the citizenry, recreation and leisure time, and transportation.

A few of the 205 goals are development of neighborhood organizations and groups; a new central library downtown; a dialogue between the arts and mass media; an effective growth-management strategy; development of minority businesses; basic academic skills for all students; a Dallas energy policy; correction of the malodorous environment; recognition by citizens that the central business district and its perimeter are critical to the life of the city; elimination of long waits by patients at Parkland hospital; greater attention to alcohol and drug abuse; a comprehensive housing plan; elimination of redlining; effectiveness and fairness in the criminal court system; a stronger family unit; a major sports complex in the Dallas area; a comprehensive regional transportation strategy; and improved taxi service.

Each goal and its status are described in a 364-page book, *Goals for Dallas—The Possible Dreams*, and matrix charts identify the local organs of government and private institutions that have accepted responsibility for seeking achievement. A set of 205 goals obviously includes quite a few small ones. The organization's leadership has astutely recognized the importance of making it possible for any citizen to identify with at least one goal. In 1983 the organization concluded that 201 of the 205 had been partly or fully realized. A new set will be undertaken in 1984. It seems plausible that Goals for Dallas has been a significant factor in the city's rise to economic and cultural eminence.

The Idea of Recovery Compacts

Two trends of fundamental importance were noted in the Preface: (1) a shrinking of the population and political influence of cities, and (2) a growing popular opposition to federally directed urban policies. Either can change, but it seems probable that redistricting after the censuses of 1990 and 2000 will further reduce the political influence of cities. The second trend, being political in character, is more subject to reversal, but there is plausibility in Ledebur's appraisal that "the dramatic reorientation of domestic policy by the President [Reagan] will affect the course of events over the next decade and beyond." The continuance of either trend would make it prudent for cities to seek a recovery of the nature discussed in the Preface.

An attempt to be specific about a process that may be expected to require a generation or more would be irrelevant. Many unpredictable things will happen in that time; diversity, not uniformity, will be the rule; and more wisdom will come from doing than from speculation. However, it is not inappropriate to venture an expression of general principles that can be a guide. We offer these:

1. Recovery can only come incrementally, or as said earlier, from a hundred successes on a dozen fronts.

2. Given the present condition of cities, external aid will be required in a long transitional period. It should have a dual purpose of relief and recovery; aid should be given and used to progressively reduce the need for aid.[33]

3. Although some aid could come from states, substantial federal aid will be required in the transition because the cities in greatest need are concentrated in states disproportionately affected by the major changes in the nation's industrial structure.

4. Flexibility will be essential in developing the most useful patterns of transitional aid. Where existing patterns or adaptations of them will be serviceable, they should be preferred to methods that appear abruptly new.

5. A mutual understanding and confidence must be established between the givers and recipients that each accepts and will maintain its responsibility during the transition. While the understanding may be expressed partly in legislation, its greatest strength will be derived from a recognition that all parties will benefit from the mutuality of interest.

Perhaps the best way to characterize this last principle is that it would be social compacts between cities and the rest of the nation—recovery compacts. Such compacts can come only from a national discussion—in conferences, conventions, and symposia, in newspapers, magazines, and television, in legislative chambers and Presidential addresses, perhaps even in a few books.

An experiment or two would help. Any city—or a metropolitan region—could take the initiative. It could formulate a multi-year program incorporating its own commitments, provisional commitments from other parties, and a statement of help needed from higher levels of government in the form of loan guarantees and grants. Except for grants, the above is a description of how the Chrysler corporation was saved. The program would be far less than required by the city for its recovery, but it would be an integrated package of undertakings benefitting all sections of the community and creative enough in its promise to make a just claim for the support of public opinion.

The Chrysler example is suggested as a basic model because it is a demonstration of a multi-party partnership succeeding because all interested parties agreed to interdependent obligations and performed them. With appropriate adaptation, the model could be applied by a city intent to free itself from permanent dependency and could thereby become the first step in the development of a recovery compact.

Success Story Presenters

Akron

The Honorable Roy Ray, Mayor
Paul Poorman, Editor, *The Akron Beacon Journal*
Robert Edwards, Deputy Mayor, Economic Development
Ted Curtis, Partner, Curtis and Rasmussen, Inc.

Baltimore

James W. Rouse, Chairman, The Rouse Company

Cincinnati

Nelson Schwab, Jr., Managing Partner, Graydon, Head & Ritchey
The Honorable David Mann, Mayor
Carol Davidow, Coordinator for Schools, Cincinnati Business Committee
Mary Gladden, Career Coordinator and Counselor, Cincinnati Academy of Mathematics and Science
Cameron Shafer II, District Staff Manager, AT&T Long Lines

Cleveland

The Honorable George V. Voinovich, Mayor
William R. Reidy, Partner, Coopers and Lybrand
Thomas E. Wagner, Partner, Calfee, Halter & Griswold

Columbus

Barry K. Humphries, President, Renaissance Group
Ralph W. Smithers, Director, Department of Development
Patrick N. Grady, Coordinator of Neighborhood and Commercial Revitalization, City of Columbus

Fort Wayne

Harlan Holly, President, Lincoln Life Improved Housing

Dr. Abraham Farkas, Director of Community Development and Planning, City of Fort Wayne

Indianapolis

A. L. Taggart, President, Near North Development Corporation
John Kraus, Deputy Mayor

Milwaukee

David G. Meissner, Executive Director, Greater Milwaukee Committee for Community Development
Stephen F. Dragos, Executive Vice President, Milwaukee Redevelopment Corporation

New Haven

F. Aldrich Edwards, Executive Director, New Haven Downtown Council
Ralph W. Halsey, 3rd, Director of Office of Community and State Relations, Yale University

New York City

Michael J. Teatum, Jr., Director of Area Development, Brooklyn Union Gas Company

Oakland

The Honorable Lionel Wilson, Mayor
Robert Shetterly, Chairman of the Board, The Clorox Company
George Williams, Director, The Office of Economic Development and Employment, City of Oakland
David Self, Executive Director, Economic Development Corporation of Oakland

Pittsburgh

David Bergholz, Deputy Director, Allegheny Conference on Community Development

St. Louis

Eugene R. Kilgen, Executive Director, Washington University Medical Center Redevelopment Corporation
Charles Kindleberger, Planning Director, Community Development Agency, City of St. Louis
James O'Flynn, President, Regional Commerce and Growth Association

Richard C. Ward, Principal, Team Four
Samuel B. Guze, M.D., President, Washington University Medical Center
John G. Roach, Vice President, Pantheon Corporation
John J. Wuest, Senior Vice President, Mercantile Bank

St. Paul
Delano Erickson, Principal and Vice President, BWBR Architects

Salt Lake City
Sydney Fonnesbeck, Chairperson, Salt Lake City Council
Vernon Jorgensen, Director of Planning & Zoning, Salt Lake City
Wendell J. Ashton, Publisher, *Deseret News*
Michael Chitwood, Executive Director, Salt Lake City Redevelopment Agency
Peter Cooke, Executive Director, Price/Prowswood Partnership
Richard Nordlund, Vice President, Triad Utah
Wesley B. Thompson, Assistant Administrator, LSD Hospital

Springfield, Massachusetts
The Honorable Theodore Dimauro, Mayor
Carlo A. Marchetti, Executive Director, Springfield Central, Inc.
David Starr, Publisher, Springfield Newspapers

Tampa
Jeffrey D. Thaxter, Assistant Director, Downtown Development Authority

Washington, D.C.
Robert O. Boulter, Vice President, Jubilee Housing, Inc.

Notes

Preface

1. Paul R. Porter, *The Recovery of American Cities* (New York, N.Y.: Sun River Press, Two Continents Publishing Group, Ltd., 1976).
2. Federal subsidies have also aided some suburbs at the expense of central cities, as noted by Mark J. Kasoff in the November, 1977, issue of *Nation's Cities*. The principal subsidies were contained in highway programs that by providing convenient access helped to stimulate the building of new suburbs. It is doubtful, however, that this will generate significant political support for a permanent dependency of cities.

Chapter 1

1. John Whybrow and Rachel Waterhouse, *How Birmingham Became a Great City* (Birmingham: John Whybrow, Ltd., 1976). Also Asa Briggs, *Victorian Cities* (London: Oldhams Press, Ltd., 1963).
2. Will Durant, *Caesar and Christ* (New York: Simon and Schuster, 1944).
3. Laura Wood Roper, *FLO: A Biography of Frederick Law Olmsted* (Baltimore: Johns Hopkins University Press, 1973). Except as otherwise noted, information about Olmsted in this chapter was obtained from the Roper book.
4. Elizabeth Barlow, *Frederick Law Olmsted's New York* (New York: Praeger Publishers, 1972).
5. Ibid.
6. Roper.
7. Barlow.
8. Roper.
9. Barlow, p. 38.
10. Ibid., p. 40.
11. Ibid.
12. Thomas S. Hines, *Burnham of Chicago* (Chicago, Ill.: University of Chicago, 1979).
13. The full-length biography besides Roper's is Elizabeth Stevenson's *Park Maker*.
14. Hines. Except as otherwise noted the information in this book concerning Burnham was obtained from Hines's book.
15. Ibid.
16. Ibid.
17. Ibid.
18. Jack Finscher, *Smithsonian* (July, 1983).
19. Roper, p. 375.
20. Hines.
21. Ibid.

22. Ibid.

23. Ibid.

24. Louis Henri Sullivan, *The Autobiography of an Idea* (New York: Doves Publishing Company, 1956).

25. Hines.

26. Spencer Crump, *Henry Huntington and the Pacific Electric* (Los Angeles: Trans-Anglo Books, 1970).

27. *Encyclopedia Britannica*, Vol. 11, p. 111.

28. Spencer Crump, *Ride the Big Red Cars: How Trolleys Helped Build Southern California* (Los Angeles: Trans-Anglo Books, 1965).

29. Crump, *Henry Huntington and the Pacific Electric.*

30. James Thorpe, "The Founder and His Library," *Huntington Library Quarterly*, August 1969.

31. Crump, *Henry Huntington and the Pacific Electric.*

32. Ibid.

33. Robert O. Schad, *The Founder and the Library* (San Marino, Cal.: Henry E. Huntington Library and Art Gallery, 1931).

34. Another early suburb, perhaps preceding any dependent upon railroads, was Williamsburg, adjacent to Brooklyn on the East River opposite New York. (The consolidation of Manhattan Island and four other boroughs did not occur until 1898). *Curry's Guidebook* in 1853 said of Williamsburg that its residents were "of the sterling middle class" who commuted to New York by ferry. Quoted in John A. Kouwenhoven, *The Columbia Historical Portrait of New York* (New York: Harper and Row, 1972).

35. Roper.

36. A minor bit of esoterica: Frank Nixon, father of a future President, was a Pacific Electric motorman in its early years.

37. *The Plaza: An American Original.* A publication of the J. C. Nichols Company, Kansas City, Mo. Except when otherwise noted, information about Nichols in this chapter was obtained from this booklet and three other company publications: *J. C. Nichols Company*; *The Story of the Country Club Plaza*; and *J. C. Nichols Company: 75 Years.*

38. *J. C. Nichols: 75 Years.*

39. A remembrance of the author, who lived in Kansas City during the 1920s.

40. *Cowtown 1890 Becomes City Beautiful 1962.* A publication of the Kansas City Board of Park Commissioners, 1962.

41. Hines.

42. George Koppe, *The Kansas City Star*, October 18, 1981.

43. Robert A. Caro, *The Power Broker: Robert Moses and The Fall of New York* (New York: Alfred A. Knopf, 1974), pp. 10; 147–171.

44. Caro. p. 360.

45. Ibid., p. 372.

46. Ibid., pp. 455–467.

47. Ibid., p. 12. Money spent on urban renewal in New York City to 1957 was $267 million; in the rest of the nation, $133 million.

48. Ibid., pp. 1005–1025.

49. The Rouse Company Report of Annual Meeting of Shareholders, May 25, 1979.

50. Boyd Gibbons, *Wye Island* (Baltimore: Johns Hopkins University Press, 1979), p. 14.

51. Ibid., p. 17.

52. Virginia Benson, research in progress at College of Urban Affairs, Cleveland State University.

53. Report to the Commissioners of the District of Columbia, 1955. Copy available at the Library of Congress.

54. Gibbons, p. 18.

55. *Fortune*, April 10, 1978, p. 85.

56. Rory Miller, *Progressive Architecture*. Quoted in *Time*, August 24, 1981.

57. The Enterprise Development Company Annual Report, 1982.

58. Page Laws, *The Wall Street Journal*, August 12, 1983; Guy Friddell, *The Virginian Pilot*, June 20, 1983. Mark Potts, *The Washington Post*, July 25, 1983.

59. Barlow, p. 31.

60. Caro, p. 177.

61. Rouse Company Report, May 29, 1979.

Chapter 4

1. Rolf Goetze, *Understanding Neighborhood Change* (Cambridge, Mass.: Ballinger, 1979).

2. Rolf Goetze, *Rescuing the American Dream* (New York: Holmes and Meier, 1983).

3. Jane Peterson, "Anguish and Joy in a Changing Neighborhood," *Historic Preservation*, July/August, 1983.

Chapter 5

1. The technical distinction between non-profit and not-for-profit does not affect the discussion in this chapter.

2. Private conversation with Battelle Memorial Institute officers, including Drs. Sherwood Fawcette and Ron Paul.

3. Department of Development, City of Columbus, *Columbus Innovative Grants Program*, (unpublished case study), 1981.

4. Much of the legal action surrounding Gordon Battelle's will establishing the institute is not central to the Renaissance program. Briefly, however, the Attorney General of Ohio charged that, contrary to the provisions of the will, Battelle had not distributed profits to local charities and that it had engaged in activities not anticipated in the will. The protracted negotiations over the will and settlement did generate negative community attitudes. It also helped to motivate institute management and directors to engage in some kinds of community projects it had formerly shunned. Renaissance is only one of these projects. Battelle in recent years, through the Battelle Memorial Institute Foundation, has been a major fundor of the city convention center and community facilities throughout the city.

5. Wendy Adler Jordan, "Uplift for a Downtown Neighborhood," *Builder*, February, 1982, p. 59.

6. S. Jerome Pratter and William Conway, *Dollars from Design*, National League of Cities, 1981, pp. 35–40.

7. Denise Melilli, "St. Lewis Success Story," (unpublished), 1981.

8. *Development Summary*, Washington University Medical Center, 1982.

9. *Project Reference File*, Urban Land Institute, Vol. 20, No. 20.

10. Op. cit.

11. F. Aldrich Edwards, Address to the College of Urban Affairs, Cleveland State University, Urban Scholars Program, June 1981.

12. Halsey, op. cit.

Chapter 7

1. Ken Auletta, *The Underclass* (New York: Random House, 1982).

2. Prentice Bowsher, *People Who Care: Making Housing Work for the Poor* (Washington, D.C.: Prentice Bowsher Associates, 1980), p. 238.

3. Ibid.

4. Elizabeth O'Connor, *Call to Commitment* (New York: Harper and Row, 1963), p. 23.

5. Elizabeth O'Connor, *The New Community* (New York: Harper and Row, 1976).

6. Bowsher, *People Who Care*, p. 242.

7. Robert Mullen, *The Latter-Day Saints* (New York: Doubleday, 1966).

8. Raymond D. Gastil, *Cultural Regions of the United States* (Seattle: University of Washington Press, 1975), p. 237.

9. Thomas F. O'Dea, *The Mormons* (Chicago: University of Chicago Press, 1957), p. 81.

10. Ibid.

11. Gastil, *Cultural Regions of the United States*, p. 237.

12. Joel Lieske, *The Quality of Life in U.S. Metropolitan Areas* (Cleveland: Cleveland State University College of Urban Affairs, 1983).

13. William James, *The Varieties of Religious Experience* (New York: The Modern Library, 1929).

14. Neal A. Maxwell, *The Smallest Part* (Salt Lake City: Deseret Book Company, 1973), p. 4.

15. O'Dea, *The Mormons*.

16. "Welfare Services" (Salt Lake City: The Church of Jesus Christ of Latter-Day Saints, 1979).

17. O'Connor, *The New Community*, p. 48.

18. Ibid., p. 38.

19. Ibid., p. 52.

20. Ibid.

21. "Welfare Services."

22. Lieske, *The Quality of Life in U.S. Metropolitan Areas*, Table 3.

23. O'Connor, *Call to Commitment*, p. 23.

24. O'Connor, *The New Community*, p. 64.

25 "Welfare Services."

26. Ibid.

27. Carl Everett Ladd, "Traditional Values Regnant," *Public Opinion*, Vol. 1, 1978; pp. 45–9; Robert A. Dahl, *Who Governs?* (New Haven, Connecticut: Yale University Press, 1961); Dorothy Buckton James, *Outside, Looking In* (New York: Harper and Row, 1972).

28. Ferdinand Tonnies, *Community and Society*, Edited by Charles P. Loomis (East Lansing, Michigan: Michigan State University Press, 1957).

29. John J. Harrigan, *Political Change in the Metropolis*, Second Edition (Boston: Little Brown, 1981), p. 30.

30. Robert L. Lineberry and Ira Sharkansky, *Urban Politics and Public Policy*, Third Edition (New York: Harper and Row, 1978).

31. Gastil, *Cultural Regions of the United States*, pp. 48–52; Edmund Burke, *Reflections on the Revolution in France and on the Proceedings in Certain Societies in London Relative to That Event*, Edited by William B. Todd (New York: Rinehart, 1959).

Chapter 8

1. Bernard Mehl, *The High School at the Turn of the Century* (Champaign, Ill.: University of Illinois, 1954).

2. Lawrence A. Cremin, *The Transformation of the School, Progressivism in American Education 1876–1957* (New York: Alfred A. Knopf, 1961).

3. "The Metropolitan Experience," *Traditions of American Education* (New York: Basic Books, Inc., 1976), pp. 91–128.

4. Thomas James and David Tyack, "Learning from Past Efforts to Reform the High School," *Phi Delta Kappan* (February, 1983), pp. 400–406.

5. Charles William Eliot, "The Unity of Educational Reform," in *American Education, Its*

Men, Ideas, and Institutions (New York: Arno Press and The New York Times, reprinted 1969), pp. 315-339.

6. *Cardinal Principles of Secondary Education*, Bulletin #35, 1981, Department of Interior, Bureau of Education. Reprinted 1937, 1956, 1962. Distribution to date: over 150,000 copies.

7. Richard Gross, "Seven New Cardinal Principles," *Phi Delta Kappan*, Vol. 60 (September, December 1978), p. 291.

8. "Quality, Not Just Quantity," *Time*, September 6, 1982, p. 59.

9. "Five Ways to Wisdom," *Time*, September 27, 1982, pp. 66-72.

10. Richard Mitchell, *The Graves of Academe* (New York: Little Brown, 1981), p. 85.

11. Ibid., p. 69.

12. Chester E. Finn, Jr., "American Education Revives," *Wall Street Journal*, July 7, 1982, p. 1.

13. Peter Arasian, George Madaris, Joseph Pedulla, *Harvard Education Review*, 1978, pp. 49-4, 462-484. Reprinted in *Minimal Competency Testing* (N.J.: Educational Technology Publications, 1979), p. 49.

14. "Taking Business to School," *Cincinnati Post*, December 15, 1982.

15. John Chaffee, Jr., *Business School Partnerships: A Plus for Kids* (Arlington, Va.: Special Report, Education USA), p. 9.

16. Ibid., p. 9.

17. Excerpts from speech by W. W. Abbott, National Assembly of State Superintendents of Education, Columbus, Ohio, August 4, 1982.

18. *A Guide: The Way to Middle School*, The Reizenstein Consortium in cooperation with the Pittsburgh Public Schools, 1980, Allegheny Conference on Community Development.

19. *Small Grants for Teachers: A Handbook*, Allegheny Conference on Community Development, One Oliver Plaza, Pittsburgh, Pa. 15222.

20. Jobs for America's Graduates, Inc., descriptive materials, Suite 305, 1750 Pennsylvania Avenue, NW, Washington, D.C. 20006.

21. Roland Barth, *Run School Run* (Cambridge, Mass.: Harvard University Press, 1980). See also, Willard Duckett, et al. *Why Do Some Urban Schools Succeed?* (Bloomington, Ind.: Phi Delta Kappan Press, 1980).

Chapter 9

1. Interview with Carl Moore, Professor Communications, Kent State University, August 2, 1982.

2. Interview with Jon Kinghorn, Senior Project Officer, Charles F. Kettering Foundation, August 5, 1982.

3. Evaluation reports from participants (per David Garrison, Cleveland State University staff), August 5, 1982.

4. Wallace Wolking and Hannah Weiner, "Structured and Spontaneous Role Playing," *Training and Development Journal* (June 1981), p. 111.

5. Ibid., p. 111.

6. Norman R. F. Maier, Allen R. Solem and Ayeska A. Maier, *The Role Play Technique: A Handbook for Management and Leadership Practice* (San Diego, Calif.: University Associates, Inc., 1975).

7. Op. cit., Wolking and Weiner, p. 112.

8. Interviews with Carl Moore, August 2, 1982; Jon Kinghorn, August 5, 1982; and William Eddy, August 10, 1982.

9. Interview with Alan Beals, Executive Director, The National League of Cities, August 20, 1982.

Chapter 10

1. *Cities' Congress: Roads to Recovery*, Report on Proceedings, College of Urban Affairs, Cleveland State University, 1982.

2. Daniel Yankelovich, *New Rules* (New York: Bantum Books, Inc., 1981), p. 248.

3. John Dewey, "Democracy and Educational Administration," *School and Society*, (April 3, 1937).

4. John Friedmann, *The Good Society* (Cambridge, Mass.: MIT Press, 1979), p. 53.

5. James A. Christenson, and Jerry W. Robinson, Jr., *Community Development in America* (Ames, Iowa: Iowa State University Press, 1980), p. 12.

6. Arthur Morgan, "The Community: The Seed Bed of Society," *The Atlantic Monthly*, (February 1942), pp. 222-225.

7. Andrew M. Greeley, *A Future to Hope In*, particularly his chapter "A Community to Belong to" (Garden City, N.Y.: Image Books, 1970), pp. 67-69.

8. Ibid., p. 64.

9. Donald I. Warren, *Helping Networks, How People Cope With Problems in the Urban Community* (Notre Dame, Ind.: University of Notre Dame Press, 1981), p. 166. Greeley, p. 64.

10. D. I. Warren, p. 166.

11. Yankelovich, p. 244.

12. D. I. Warren, pp. 175-177.

13. Ibid., p. 169.

14. Roland L. Warren, *The Community in America* (Chicago, Ill.: Rand McNally & Co., 1963), pp. 15-17.

15. Friedmann, p. 3.

16. Ibid., pp. 10-11.

17. Leonard S. Cottrell, Jr., "The Competent Community," in *Further Explorations in Social Psychiatry*, edited by Bartren H. Kaplan, Robert N. Wilson, and Alexander H. Leighton (New York: Basic Books, Inc., 1976). Roland L. Warren, "The Good Community— What Would It Be?" *Journal of the Community Development Society*, Vol. I., (Spring 1970), pp. 14-23.

18. Ibid., This entire section is condensed from the two articles.

19. Ward Goodenough, *Cooperation in Change* (New York: Russell Sage Foundation, 1963), pp. 88-89.

20. R. L. Warren, 1963, Chapter 10.

21. Cottrell, p. 557.

22. Friedmann, pp. 3-4.

23. Greeley, p. 72.

24. Cottrell, p. 555, and Morgan, p. 225.

25. Cottrell, p. 557.

26. Thomas R. Dye, and Harmon L. Zeigler, *The Irony of Democracy* (Belmont, Calif.: Wadsworth Publishing Co., Inc., 1970), p. 6.

27. R. L. Warren, 1963, p. 320.

28. Bernie Jones, "Evolution of Community Development Systems for the Western Slope: Second Round Evaluation of the Western Colorado Rural Communities Program," (Denver: Community Research Center, University of Colorado at Denver, 1981).

29. R. L. Warren, 1970, Cottrell, op. cit.

30. R. L. Warren, 1963, pp. 303-339.

31. Cottrell, pp. 550-555.

32. Unpublished transcripts of *Cities' Congress: Roads to Recovery*, City of Akron presentation, 1982.

33. Unpublished transcripts of *Cities' Congress: Roads to Recovery*, City of New Haven presentation, 1982.

34. Unpublished transcripts of *Cities' Congress: Roads to Recovery*, City of Akron presentation, 1982.

35. James Rouse, keynote Speech at *Cities' Congress: Roads to Recovery*, June 9, 1982. It should be noted that Mr. Rouse is personally involved with Jubilee Housing. It seems he has learned something about doing work in very poor communities and applied it to other related inner-city development efforts.

36. Friedmann, p. 4.

37. Alexis De Tocqueville, *Democracy in America, 1935. A New Translation*, by George Lawrence, edited by J. P. Moyes and Max Lerner (New York: Harper and Row, 1966), p. 485.

38. Warren says, "The 'great change' in community living includes the increasing orientation of local community units toward extracommunity systems of which they are a part, with a corresponding decline in community cohesion and autonomy." R. L. Warren, 1963, p. 53.

39. R. L. Warren, 1963, p. 89.

40. Dye and Ziegler, p. 7.

41. D. I. Warren, p. 159.

42. Greeley, p. 77.

Chapter 11

1. Mark I. Gelfand, *A Nation of Cities: The Federal Government and Urban America, 1933-1965* (New York: Oxford University Press, 1975), pp. 205-216. See also Chester Hartman, *Yerba Buena: Land Grab and Community Resistance in San Francisco* (San Francisco, Calif.: Glide Publications, 1974).

2. June Thomas, "Urban Displacement: Fruits of a History of Collusion," *Black Scholar* II (Nov./Dec., 1979).

3. George Sternlieb, "The City as Sandbox," *City Scenes: Problems and Prospects*, ed. by J. John Palen (Boston: Little, Brown, and Co., 1981), p. 14.

4. *Report of the National Advisory Commission on Civil Disorders* (New York: Bantam Books, 1968).

5. U.S. Department of Commerce, Bureau of the Census, *Money, Income, and Poverty Status, 1980* and *Characteristics of Population Below Poverty Level, 1979, 1981*. Recently the Reagan administration has considered changing the definition of income to include non-cash benefits such as food stamps and subsidized rental housing. Such a move would reduce the number of people officially defined as poor.

6. U.S. Department of Commerce, Bureau of the Census, *Household and Family Characteristics: March, 1981*.

7. Daphne Spain, "A Gentrification Scorecard," *American Demographics* (November, 1981), p. 14.

8. Thomas, "Urban Displacement."

9. Spain, "Gentrification Scorecard," p. 18. Note also the figure for Philadelphia.

10. See Karl Taeuber, "Racial Segregation: The Persisting Dilemma" and U.S. Department of H.U.D., "Measuring Racial Discrimination in American Housing Markets," both in Palen, *City Scenes*, pp. 159-177.

11. Census data in table in Thomas A. Clark, *Blacks in Suburbs: A National Perspective* (New Brunswick, N.J.: Center for Urban Policy Research, 1979), p. 55.

12. In 1981 the mean family income for suburban black families was $20,362; for central city black families, $16,415. For whites, the mean family income in suburbs was $30,655; in central cities, $26,612. U.S. Bureau of the Census, *Characteristics of the Population Below Poverty Level, 1981*.

13. John H. Mollenkopf, "The Crisis of the Public Sector in American Cities," *The Fiscal Crisis of American Cities: Essays on the Political Economy of Urban America with Special Reference to New York*, ed. by Roger Alcaly and David Mermelstein, Vintage Books (New York: Random House, 1977), p. 118.

14. Ibid., p. 118. See also Hartman, *Yerba Buena*, for a case study of this process. One primary reason for opposition to Yerba Buena was the loss of blue-collar jobs; between 1960 and 1970 manufacturing employment in San Francisco fell by 19 percent, employment in finance-insurance-real estate rose 37 percent, and service employment rose 41 percent; pp. 65, 79.

15. Jacqueline Mazza and Bill Hogan, *The State of the Region, 1981: Economic Trends in the Northeast and Midwest* (Washington, D.C.: Northeast-Midwest Institute, 1981), pp. 74–79. The Institute's definition of regions is unique: with the Midwest they include the states of Illinois, Indiana, Iowa, Michigan, Minnesota, Ohio, and Wisconsin. Their Northeast includes Connecticut, Delaware, Maine, Maryland, Massachusetts, New Hampshire, New Jersey, New York, Pennsylvania, Rhode Island, and Vermont. All other states fall within their definition of the South or the West.

16. U.S. Bureau of Labor Statistics, *Employment and Earnings*, (January, 1982).

17. Revised 1975 estimates of the differences in these rates can be found in David M. Gordon, "Counting the Underemployed," in *Problems in Political Economy: An Urban Perspective*, ed. by David Gordon, 2nd ed., (Lexington, Mass.: D.C. Heath and Co., 1977), pp. 70–75.

18. U.S. Bureau of Labor Statistics, *Employment and Earnings* (January, 1982).

19. U.S. Bureau of the Census, *Characteristics of Population Below Poverty Level*.

20. Conference notes. Also telephone interview with David Meissner, Executive Director, Greater Milwaukee Committee for Community Development, August, 1982.

21. Hartman, *Yerba Buena*, pp. 178–180. See also Edward C. Koziara and Karen S. Koziara, *The Negro in the Hotel Industry*, Report No. 4 of *The Racial Policies of American Industry* (Philadelphia: University of Pennsylvania Press, 1968).

22. See *Civil Rights and the Housing and Community Development Act of 1974, Vol. II: A Comparison with Model Cities*, A report prepared by the Michigan Advisory Committee to the U.S. Commission on Civil Rights (June, 1976). Also Bernard J. Frieden and Marshall Kaplan, *The Politics of Neglect: Urban Aid from Model Cities to Revenue Sharing* (Cambridge: The MIT Press, 1977).

23. David Bergholz, "Marshalling Support for Public Education," *Place* (May, 1982), pp. 6–7.

24. Brian Berry and John Kasarda, "The Pattern and Timing of Suburbanization," *Contemporary Urban Ecology* (New York: Macmillan, 1977), pp. 179–194.

25. *The New York Times*, January 31, 1982, February 21, 1982; Rochelle Stanfield, "Reagan's Policies. . . ," *National Journal*, December 19, 1981.

Chapter 12

1. In fact, in a widely cited populist statement about public policy, Berger and Neuhaus argue that the concept of dependency is internally contradictory because of a continuing, strong public desire for public goods and services counterposed against an equally "strong animus against government." Peter L. Berger and Richard John Neuhaus, *To Empower People*, Washington, American Enterprise Institute from Public Policy Research, 1977, p. 1.

2. "Welfare" includes providing direct aid to the needy, similar aid delivered through state and local governments, and state and local programs for the needy supported by federal grants. It does *not* include social insurance programs (social security, unemployment compensation, etc.). John W. Ellwood, et. al., *Background Material on Fiscal Year 1982 Federal Budget Reductions* (Princeton University, Princeton Urban and Regional Research Center, 1982), pp. 35–37.

3. Bennett Harrison and Barry Bluestone, *The Deindustrialization of America* (New York: Basic Books, 1973); Robert Reich, *America's Next Frontier* (New York: N.Y. Times Books, 1973).

4. See, for example, Pat Choate, "American Workers at the Rubicon," *Economic Develop-*

ment Commentary 6:2 (Summer, 1982), pp. 2-10; Otto Eckstein and Robert Tannenwald, "Productivity and Capital Formation," *Toward a New U.S. Industrial Policy*, ed. Michael L. Wachter and Susan M. Wachter (Philadelphia, Penna.: University of Pennsylvania Press, 1981), pp. 127-142; Eli Ginzberg, "The Mechanization of Work," *Scientific American*, 247:3 (September, 1982), pp. 67-75; Ira C. Magaziner and Robert B. Reich, *Minding America's Business* (New York: Harcourt Brace Jovanovich, Inc., 1982), esp. pp. 41-64.

5. This is clearly the case in Chicago as reported by Michael Young of Shlaes and Company and verified by the author. Other than in the high growth cities of the Sunbelt, I find no evidence to suggest that the Chicago situation is not a more general one.

6. A major difficulty with evaluating the success stories shared at the Cities' Congress is that each city had considerable latitude in choosing what to report. The meanings of a non-report range from arbitrary or accidental omission to a lack of value attached to the event. Furthermore, the case of union involvement is thoroughly compounded by the often disinterested attitude of union leadership. It should be noted only five union representatives were present among the more than three hundred Congress conferees.

7. "High-tech" is a colloquial expression covering all efforts to employ new technology to mechanize work processes. As such, it can and does permeate all sectors of the economy. Examples include the combine in agriculture, the continuous longwall miner, computer-assisted design in manufacturing, telecommunications in commerce, and information-age office technology. Whole firms or even sub-sectors of the economy often are organized around the new technology and have become the primary object of economic development efforts. For a comprehensive introduction to the mechanization of work, see *Scientific American*, op. cit.

8. Walter Corson and Walter Nicholson, *Trade Adjustment Assistance for Workers: The Results of a Survey of Recipients under the Trade Act of 1974*, Princeton, Mathematics Policy Research, 1980, reported in D. Quinn Mills, "The Human Resources Consequences of Industrial Revitalization," Wachter and Wachter, op. cit., pp. 257-280.

9. See also, Choate.

10. "University Officials Get Advice on Developing Research Parks," *Economic and Industrial Development News*, 1:8 (September 27, 1982), pp. 1-3.

11. Roger W. Schemmer *Business Location Decisions* (Englewood Cliffs, N.J.: Prentice-Hall, Inc., 1982).

12. Bennett Harrison, *Rationalization, Restructuring, and Industrial Re-organization in Older Regions: The Economic Transformation of New England since World War II* (Boston, Mass.: Joint Center for Urban Studies of MIT and Harvard, 1982).

13. For further elaboration, see Robert Mier, "High Technology-based Development: A Review of Recent Literature," *Journal of the American Planning Association* (Summer, 1983).

14. These and other questions have been raised locally about the city's partnership with WUMC. Interview with Yvonne Ryan, the Director of the Missouri Public Interest Research Group on August 15, 1982.

15. More and more cities are recognizing this. "Cities Seek Greater Return on Real Estate Investments," *Urban Economic Developments*: VI, 4 (April 30, 1982), pp. 1, 7. Nevertheless, Oakland's robust real estate market is probably atypical in its strength because of two major events: the opening of the line to San Francisco, and the flight of capital from Hong Kong which Oakland has particularly skillfully exploited. As Paul Porter so aptly says, "luck and skill make any policy look better." Personal correspondence from Porter, May 27, 1983.

16. Because Oakland perceives downtown development so atypically—as intimately connected to neighborhood and job development—I have chosen not to review it under the earlier topic of "Service Sector Emphasis."

17. For further information on Jubilee Housing and a number of similar organizations in other cities, see Prentice Bowsher, *Making Housing Work for the Poor* (Washington: Prentice Bowsher Associates, 1980).

18. John M. Goering, "The National Neighborhood Movement: A Preliminary Analysis and Critique," *Journal of the American Planning Association* 45:4 (October, 1979), pp. 506-514; Paul Levy, "Unloading the Neighborhood Bandwagon", *Social Policy* 10:2 (September-October, 1979) pp. 28-32; Charles Hampden-Turner, *From Poverty to Human Dignity*, (Garden City: Anchor Press, 1975).

19. The ultimate success of these efforts to catalyze the local economy are an object of sore debate.

20. Harry C. Boyte, *The Backyard Revolution: Understanding the New Citizen Movement* (Philadelphia: Temple U. Press, 1980).

21. Berger and Neuhaus, pp. 8-18; Harry C. Boyte, "Reagan vs. the Neighborhoods," *Social Policy* 12:4, (Spring, 1982), pp. 3-8. "Historical Perspective on the Practice and Purpose of Self-Help Housing," *Self-Help Housing: A Critique*, ed. Peter M. Ward, (London: Mansell Publishing Ltd., 1982).

22. Peter F. Drucker, "Demographics and American Economic Policy," Wachter and Wachter, pp. 237-256.

23. It has also been shaped by the author's efforts to evaluate the potential effectiveness of Enterprise Zone legislation. Robert Mier and Scott E. Gelzer, "State Enterprise Zones: The New Frontier?" *Urban Affairs Quarterly*, 18:1 (September, 1982), pp. 39-52.

24. For an example involving insurance companies, see "Older Industrial Cities Seek New Support for Neighborhood Self-Help Public, Private, Community Partnerships," *Building Blocks* (Summer, 1982), p. 1.

25. Such bargaining is the essence of the negotiated and tri-partite agreements experiments of the last few years. "The Negotiated Investment Strategy: Review of Concepts and Implications for Revitalizing Cities," A Report by the Subcommittee on Revitalizing American Cities of the Committee on Economic Development, Kettering Foundation, Dayton, Ohio, November 17, 1980; Douglas C. Hinton, "Rethinking Urban Governance: An Assessment of the Negotiated Investment Strategy," S.R.I. International Center for Public Policy Analysis, Menlo Park, Ca., July, 1981.

26. Mier, "High Technology-Based Development."

27. "Jobs," *The Washington Papers*, Chicago, The Harold Washington for Mayor Committee, March, 1983, pp. 3-9.

28. Bill Barnhart, "New development chief stresses jobs: Mayor's choice marks change in Chicago's hunt for industry," *Chicago Tribune*, August 7, 1983, Sec. 6, p. 8.

Chapter 13

1. Paul R. Porter, *The Recovery of American Cities* (New York: Two Continents Publishing Group Limited, 1976), pp. 14-15.

2. "Hardship" is a composite index including population decline, age of housing, and economic conditions. See Richard P. Nathan and Paula R. Dommel, "The Cities," in *Setting National Priorities: The 1978 Budget*, ed. by Joseph A. Pechman (Washington, D.C.: The Brookings Institution, 1977), Table 9.2, pp. 290-291.

3. Scott Greer, *Urban Renewal in American Cities* (New York: Bobbs-Merrill, 1965), p. 3.

4. James San Jule, "Housing Comes Into its Own," Transcript from meeting on *Guidelines to Success in Multifamily Housing*, April 9-11, 1969, Associated Home Builders of Greater East Bay, San Francisco.

5. Robert E. Olson, *URC: Renewal Gone Astray*, Ph.D. Dissertation, Washington University, St. Louis, 1975, p. 11.

6. Quoted in Mandelker, Feder & Collins, *Reviving Cities with Tax Abatement* (New Brunswick, N.J.: Center for Urban Policy Research, 1980), p. 40.

7. Professor Louis A. Ferman, quoted in *The Cleveland Press*, November 29, 1981, p. A-8.

8. For earlier examples of this propensity, see Peter H. Rossi and Robert A. Dentler, *The Politics of Urban Renewal*, (New York: Free Press of Glencoe, 1961); Scott Greer, *Urban Renewal and American Cities* (New York: Bobbs-Merrill, 1965); Martin Anderson, *The Federal Bulldozer* (Cambridge: MIT Press, 1964).

9. David L. Birch, "Who Creates Jobs," *The Public Interest*, (Fall, 1981), p. 7.

10. Katherine L. Bradbury, Anthony Downs, and Kenneth A. Small, *Futures for a Declining Area: Simulations for the Cleveland Area* (New York: Academic Press, 1981).

11. For what appears to be a more realistic look at the prospects for revival of older industrial cities, see James W. Fossett and Richard P. Nathan, "The Prospects for Urban Revival," in *Urban Government Finance*, ed. by Roy Bahl, (Beverly Hills, Calif.: Sage Publications, 1981); and George Sternlieb and Kristina Ford, "The Future of the Return-to-City Movement," in *Revitalizing Cities*, ed. by Herrington J. Bryce, (Lexington, Mass.: Lexington Books, 1979).

12. For a more complete discussion see Robert C. Holland, President, Committee for Economic Development, speech transcript at the Roads to Recovery Congress, June 9, 1982, p. 4.

13. "U.S. Steel Move Unsettles Steel City," *The Wall Street Journal*, December 7, 1981, p. 26.

14. Alexander Hamilton, *The Works of Alexander Hamilton*, Volume 3, ed. by John C. Hamilton, (New York: J. F. Trow, 1950), p. 246.

15. Emmett S. Redford, *Administration of National Economic Control*, New York, New York, 1952, p. 229–230.

16. For an existing conflict in St. Louis, see "Plans for Park-Like Mall Stir Battle in Downtown St. Louis," *The Wall Street Journal*, July 21, 1982, p. 25.

17. Anthony Downs, *Opening Up the Suburbs: An Urban Strategy for America*, (New Haven, Conn.: Yale University Press, 1973), p. 1.

18. These comments draw on William J. Baumol's article, "Macroeconomics of Unbalanced Growth: The Anatomy of Urban Crisis," in *The Modern City*, ed. by David W. Rasmussen and Charles T. Harworth (New York: Harper & Row, 1973).

19. Budget of the U.S. Government, Fiscal Year 1979.

20. Nathan and Dommel; also, The President's Urban and Regional Policy Group, *A New Partnership to Conserve America's Communities: A National Urban Policy*, (Washington, D.C.: U.S. Government Printing Office, March 1978).

21. "Forgotten Triangle is a Faded Promise," *Cleveland Plain Dealer*, July 13, 1980, p. 32A.

Chapter 14

1. Since roughly 1965, the U.S. has been experiencing a decline in the rate of growth of industrial productivity. Between 1973 and 1978 the rate of private sector productivity growth is estimated to have decreased approximately 66 percent from the comparable rates in the benchmark period of 1948–1973. See J. R. Norsworthy, et al., "The Slowdown in Productivity Growth, An Analysis of Some Contributing Factors," in *Brookings Papers on Economic Activity*, Vol. 2 (Washington, D.C.: The Brookings Institution, 1979), pp. 387–421.

For a discussion of the regional, state, and metropolitan dimensions of the productivity slowdown, see Larry C. Ledebur and Ron Moomaw, "The Productivity Paradox," Urban Institute Report, 1981.

2. After years of relative price stability, inflation became a dominant issue in the 1970s. From the end of the Korean War until 1965, prices rose less than 1.5 percent per year and between 1965 and 1970 an average of 4.2 percent. In the following decade, inflation averaged 6.7 percent with a high of 11 percent in 1974. Accompanying this erosion of purchasing power was the growth in state and local taxes and the effects of the progressivity of the income tax, the notorious "bracket creep," relentlessly pushing taxpayers into higher tax brackets. The protest of taxpayers/voters to inflation and rising taxes was vented in the "tax revolt" initiated by California's Proposition 13 slashing property tax rates by 57 percent, followed by similar taxing and expenditure limitations in a dozen other states. The tax limitation movement is discussed in Alvin Rabushka and Pauline Ryan, *The Tax Revolt* (Stanford: The Hoover Institute, 1982).

3. *The Economist*, 1980, p. 14.

4. Ezra Solomon, *Beyond the Turning Point: The U.S. Economy in the 1980s* (San Francisco: W. H. Freeman and Company, 1982), p. 1. In addressing the problem of government,

Solomon argues: "Washington in 1973 was unusually ill-prepared for the challenge it faced. The Congress had become an undisciplined collection of conflicting fiefdoms, each with its own set of special interests—a body which had accumulated so many parochial priorities that it behaved as if it were unable to pursue any genuine national priority. Presidential leadership— the ability to see clearly what the one or two critical national priorities are and to mobilize the people and Congress to act on them—simply did not exist. . . ."

5. Bernard L. Weinstein and John Rees, "Reagonomics, Reindustrialization, and Regionalism," *Society*, Volume 19, No. 5, (July/August 1982).

6. Limitations of space preclude extensive review of the dimensions of the Reagan "revolution." Readers wishing greater detail are referred to *The Reagan Experiment*, John L. Palmer and Isabel V. Sawhill, eds., (Washington, D.C.: The Urban Institute Press, 1982) and Robert H. Freilich, Gregory D. Cox, and Elizabeth Hall, "1980–81 Annual Review of Local Government Law," *The Urban Lawyer*, Volume 13, No. 4 (Fall 1981).

7. "The President's Federalism Initiative: Basic Framework," White House release, January 1982, p. 17.

8. Ibid.

9. The Advisory Commission on Intergovernmental Relations has proposed a somewhat different reordering of the intergovernmental system. Under their recommendations the following programs would be federalized: income security, housing and energy assistance, Medicaid, food stamps, job training/rehabilitation, job placement, child care, occupational health and safety, and meat and poultry inspection. Further, the following programs would be retained and consolidated: education (mandates), public housing merged with community development block grants, medical research, state and area agencies on the aging, community action agencies, general revenue sharing, water pollution control, environmental protection, community and rural development, transportation, criminal justice research and training, economic development districts, regional action commissions, and civil preparedness.

10. "Block Grants and the Intergovernmental System," Hearings before the Subcommittee on Economic Goals and Intergovernmental Policy of the Joint Economic Committee, July 15 and 18, 1981, p. 53.

11. Ibid., p. 18.

12. For a review and assessment of the Commission Report see Larry C. Ledebur, "Fluctuating Fortunes," *Transaction/Society* (March/April), pp. 20–21.

13. President's Commission on a National Agenda for the Eighties, Final Report.

14. Draft 1982 Urban Policy Report, U.S. Department of Housing and Urban Development, undated, p. 3 of Overview.

15. Committee for Economic Development, *Public-Private Partnership: An Opportunity for Urban Communities* (New York: CED, 1982), p. 6.

16. This section draws from an unpublished paper by Larry C. Ledebur, "Economic Development Corporations: Catalysts for Public-Private Partnerships," prepared for the Council on Urban Economic Development, March 1983.

17. National Council for Urban Economic Development, *Coordinated Economic Development* (Washington, D.C.: NCUED, 1978), p. 167.

18. CED, p. 29.

19. U.S. Department of Housing and Urban Development, unpublished survey, 1981.

20. CED, p. 3.

Chapter 16

1. For present, generally accepted estimates of ages of the sub-species, agriculture, and cities as an historic form, see Richard Klein, Chapter 13; Andrew Sherratt, Chapter 15; and Joan Oates, Chapter 16, *The Cambridge Encyclopedia of Archeology* (New York: Crown Publishers, Inc. 1980).

2. United Kingdom Census of Population, 1981, H. M. Stationery Office, London.

3. Except when otherwise identified, British data referred to in this chapter was collected by Porter while a visiting scholar at the University of Aston, Birmingham, England, in 1982.

4. Interview by Porter with John Zetter, director OECD Urban Affairs Department, Paris, Dec. 20, 1982.

5. Jacob A. Riis, *How the Other Half Lives* (New York: Scribner, 1890). A selection of Riis photographs is contained in the *Columbia Historical Portrait of New York* by John A. Kouwenhoven, (New York: Doubleday and Co., Inc. 1953).

6. U.S. Bureau of the Census, decennial housing census reports. Data compiled by Porter.

7. Gary Gappert, *Post Affluent America* (New York: Franklin Watts, 1973). See also Gappert, *Cities in the 21st Century* (Beverly Hills: Sage Publications, Inc. 1983).

8. *Reader's Digest*, Sept. 1983, p. 90.

9. *Wall Street Journal*, Sept. 30, 1983, p. 1.

10. James Madison, "Doubts About Democracy," Paper 49 in *The Federalist Papers*, selected and with an introduction by Andrew Hacker (New York: Washington Square Press, Inc. 1964).

11. Dively Award judges are Lawrence A. Appley, chairman emeritus, the American Management Association; John J. Gilligan, professor of law, University of Notre Dame, former governor of Ohio; Karen N. Horn, president, the Federal Reserve Bank of Cleveland; James T. Lynn, managing partner, Washington office of Jones, Day, Reavis and Pogue, former secretary, U.S. Department of Housing and Urban Development; and David C. Sweet. Details on the Dively Awards Program can be found in "The Role of Corporate Leadership in Urban Development," by Janet Bennet Eadie presented to the 1984 Annual Conference of the Urban Affairs Association in Portland, Oregon, March 22, 1984.

12. U.S. Census, 1980.

13. James W. Rouse and Nathaniel S. Keith, *No Slums in Ten Years: A Workable Program for Urban Renewal* (Washington, D.C.: Commissioners of the District of Columbia, 1955).

14. Howard J. Sumka, "Neighborhood Revitalization and Displacement," *Journal of the American Planning Association* (Oct., 1979).

15. The event is often described as a "trickle down of housing." For the people who do the moving, however, the change is a move-up to something better. It seems appropriate to describe the process from the point of view of the occupants.

16. Quoted by Thomas S. Hines, *Burnham of Chicago* (Chicago: The University of Chicago Press, 1979), p. 333.

17. See note 13.

18. Porter, *The Recovery of American Cities* (New York: Two Continents Publishing Co., 1976), pp. 133–138.

19. Robert A. Caro, *The Power Broker: Robert Moses and the Fall of New York* (New York: Alfred A. Knopf, 1974), p. 7.

20. *The Affordable Community* (Washington, D.C.: The Urban Land Institute, 1982).

21. *GEAR: Glasgow Eastern Area Renewal* (Glasgow: Scottish Development Agency), 1982.

22. Robert L. Asher, *The Anglo-American Colloquium on American and British Innovations in Urban Policy* (Cleveland: College of Urban Affairs Publications Dept., 1984).

23. *The City of Birmingham Envelope Scheme: Monitoring Report*, City of Birmingham Environmental Health Department, City of Birmingham, 1982.

24. *Contact: Issue 1*, City Council Urban Renewal Section, City of Birmingham, 1982.

25. Critics are quoted in Krumholz chapter.

26. David Reed, "Detroit Faces the Rising Sun: A New Day Dawns for the Motor City," *Reader's Digest*, Sept. 1983.

27. Much of the construction of Central Park in New York City was performed as a municipal unemployment relief program in the recession of 1857.

28. During World War II, a high degree of labor-management cooperation in improving efficiency was obtained in defense production. See Porter, *Labor in the Shipbuilding Industry, War Labor Policies* (New York: Philosophical Library, 1945).

29. Bayard Rustin, "Civil Rights 20 Years Later," *Newsweek*, Aug. 29, 1983.

30. William Raspberry, "Time to Wake Up," *The Washington Post*, Sept. 28, 1983.

31. See Lewis Mumford, "Mother Jacobs' Home Remedies," *The New Yorker*, Dec. 1, 1962—a rebuttal to Jane Jacobs, *The Death and Life of Great American Cities* (New York, 1961).

32. *Goals for Dallas—The Possible Dreams*, Dallas, Goals for Dallas, Inc.

33. The use of aid to remove the need for aid was the principle of the European Recovery Program, popularly known as the Marshall Plan. Apart from this principle, a Marshall Plan for cities, as has often been proposed, would not be practical because the conditions are not comparable.

Index

population, 34–35, 47, 82, 93, 219–20, 221, 228
Porter, Paul, 111–112, 161, 173, 241
Potter's House, 74, 75
poverty/poor, 87, 89, Chapter 11 *passim* (143–59), 161, 178, 186–87, 192, 214, 225–26. *See also* race
power, 152–55, 156–57, 181–83, 207–208
prenatal assistance, 87–88
President's Commission for a National Agenda for the Eighties, 196–200
private sector. *See* partnerships, public-private
Private-Sector Initiatives, Task Force on, 203
problem solving, 122, 126, 131, 137–38
Procter and Gamble, 105, 106, 107
productivity, 243n1
Progressive Movement, 8
Proposition 13 (California), 31, 243n2
Pruitt-Igoe (St. Louis, Missouri), 221
public labor costs, 184–85
Public-Private Partnership: An Opportunity for Urban Communities, 204, 210
public sector. *See* partnerships, public-private

quality of life, 170–71, 206

race, 26–27, 75, 178, 187–88, 189, 213; employment and, 148–51; income and, 144–48. *See also* desegregation; poverty
Ralston Purina Company, 217
Raspberry, William, 226
Ray, Roy, 134, 218
Reader's Digest, 224
Reagan (Ronald) administration, 111, 158–59, Chapter 14 *passim* (191–208), 239n5; cutbacks by the, 180–81, 185, 228; economic recovery program of, 53, 192, 194–97, 200–204; New Federalism of, 195–200, 244n9; urban policies of the, 166, 196–200. *See also* dependency/self-sufficiency
real estate market, 166–67, 241n15
recovery. *See* redevelopment
recovery compacts, 228–29
redevelopment, 24–25, 26, 27, 31–32, 85, 154, 166–67, 173, 175, 179, 180; bargaining process and, 167–68, 171; beautification and, 7, 8, 13, 153–54, 175; business and, Chapter 4 *passim* (42–51), 152, 154, 156–57, 201; central business district and, 24, 25, 26, 27, 163; citizens groups and, 154–55; city gov-

ernment and, 188–90; conditions for, 43–44; failures of, Chapter 13 *passim* (173–90); federal government and, 31–32, 41, 43–44, 53, 62–63, 173–74, 202, 203, 215, 243n4; financial aspects of, 153–54; guidelines for, 228–29; leadership and, 152–55, 207–208; ownership and, 168, 169, 170; physical (visual) aspects of, 151, 153–54, 174, 183. *See also* education; employment; partnerships, public-private; poverty; Rouse, James Wilson
redlining, 43, 45
region: definition of, 240n15
religion/churches, Chapter 7 *passim* (71–92), 226
relocation. *See* displacement
Renaissance Center (Detroit, Michigan), 154, 178, 179
Renaissance Project (Columbus, Ohio), 52, 54–57, 61–64, 133–34, 135, 136, 137, 138, 139, 177, 217
Reorganization of Secondary Education, Commission of the, 95–96
Reston, Virginia, 19
revitalization. *See* redevelopment
Riis, Jacob, 214
risk, investment/political, 204, 211
Riverside, Illinois, 6
Roach, John G., 165–66
Rockefeller, Nelson, 16
role playing, 112, 113, 114–19
Ronis, Leonard, 117
Root, John W., 3, 7–8
Roper, Laura Wood, 6
Rouse, James Wilson, 1, 17–20, 21, Chapter 2 *passim* (22–32), 138, 151, 152, 161, 164–65, 166, 170–71, 172, 178, 210, 221, 226; Jubilee Housing and, 75, 76, 219, 235n39
Rustin, Bayard, 226
Ryan, Yvonne, 241n14

Saarinen, Eero, 41
Saint-Gaudens, Augustus, 7
Salt Lake City, Utah, 73, 77–91, 133, 135, 136
San Antonio, Texas, 189
San Francisco, California, 8, 152–53, 240n14
Santa Monica, California, 189
Savas, E. S., 166
Schiering, G. David, 108